"Just like life itself,
knowledge is never complete, nor valuable,
unless is shared".

CLOSE CALLS
This book is a collection of the contributors' mem-
oirs and presents their current recollections of
past diving experiences—ones they lived to tell
about. Some events have been compressed and
some dialogue has been recreated. The opinions
expressed throughout this book are the opinions of
the individual contributor and do not necessarily
reflect the opinions of any other contributor, or the
publisher.

For permissions contact:
BECAUSE I CAN Ltd
1 Charterhouse Mews
London EC1 6BB, UK
www.stratiskas.com

Printed by Printing.gr
Second printing, 2021
ISBN 978-1-5272-6679-7

Edited by Paul Fisher
Copyediting by Pat Jablonski and the inDepth
copyedit Team: Allison Brunner, Catherine
Taber-olensky and Kelli Thomerson
Cover photo by Laurent Miroult

Proceeds from the book will be donated to DAN's
DAN (Divers Alert Network - Europe) Claudius Ober-
maier Fund. A significant contribution to help divers and their families who find themselves in need.

CLOSE CALLS

BY STRATIS KAS

A COLLECTION OF
LIFE-CHANGING STORIES
FROM THE INDUSTRY'S
GREATEST.
IF THEY MADE MISTAKES,
YOU WILL TOO.

A REALLY CLOSE CALL

BY STRATIS KAS.

TRIMIX & CAVE INSTRUCTOR
PUBLIC SPEAKER / AUTHOR
AWARD WINNING PHOTOGRAPHER AND FILMMAKER

LOCATION OF INCIDENT
AMPHITRITE CAVE, GREECE

This cannot be happening!

My thoughts went to, "How stupid could I be?" For at that particular moment in time, in that particular cave, I knew that I would be leaving everyone I cared for. Knowing that no one would know what actually happened, knowing there would be a formal inquiry, knowing blame would be assigned, if only to justify the loss and ease the pain for those who were left behind, I felt immense sadness.

The end was near, and I was at fault.

My brush with death began on one idyllic late spring day in Greece after a week or so of strong north winds. Finally the sea lay calm, just what I had been waiting for. My chance to go cave diving again. Full disclosure: I was a man not trained in the specifics of cave diving practice. How had I managed to avoid such a crucial necessity?

With procrastination—never quite finding the perfect time. I suffer from claustrophobia, and caves frighten me. Yet they fascinate me at the same time, and over a number of years,

I had managed to accumulate many hours in caves and caverns as an uncertified diver, if a conservative one. I wrongly believed that what I lacked in training, I could make up for with common sense. I'm lucky to be alive.

So there I was, on a fast-approaching dive boat, feeling and looking like some kind of superhero. Dive plan properly checked and ready, rule of thirds calculated. All was good.

My buddy and I entered the water. Last checks.

As expected, all ok. My excitement was higher than usual, but I knew it to be both normal and under control. Slowly descending I made use of the technical skills I had long since integrated into my standard routine and tried to recall cave protocols and procedures that I had seen in diving videos or read in manuals. I reached the cave's entrance, buzzing with confidence, a great day was about to get even better, at least so I thought.

Open water, cavern, cave. Primary and secondary tie-offs, check. Proper marking, check. Communication, check.

Photos by Laurent Miroult

This cave had been on my list for a while. Sure, I had flirted with it many times, peeking into it, even reaching as far as the permanent mainline, but I had always stopped there. Today felt different. I was focused, I was calm, and I was ready.

Camera in hand, I started filming; although, in my amazement, I almost dropped it as soon as I reached the first big open room that now confronted me. Perhaps 150, maybe even 200 m/656 ft of open space, completely covered with white sand and stalagmites rising up like mountains covered with snow. This was better than I could have imagined.

Depth check, gas check, camera check, battery 80%. All good, proceed.

A primary mainline was already laid through the cave which ran through large open cavern rooms with many smaller and extremely decorated side passages. It was incredible; actually it was better than incredible—it was stunning.

My buddy was right beside me, and visibility was impressive to say the least—so much so, it gave us confidence to leave that main line, that lifeline to the outside world. We would quickly sneak over and check out a series of formations we could see that took on the appearance of a medieval prison door. Thin columns were very close to each other, but could we pass through and progress further? Yes we could.

The deeper we penetrated into the cave, the more decorated it became, but as we knew, much more fragile also. Perfectly placed stalagmites within another progressing-but-short passage gave the appearance this time of a crocodile's open mouth—perhaps an appearance that should have been a sign to not enter?

This passage became so small that contact with the floor was unavoidable, and its beautiful white powder coating did not like us one bit, for the moment we touched it, we instantly turned thirty or more meters of gin-clear water into a cappuccino-like, zero-visibility passage.

Now it was definitely our time to return, and it quickly became apparent that both of us had unknowingly been touching the floor for the entire length of the passage we had swam through and stupidly hadn't realised it.

With no flow of water through the cave, we decided to avoid returning down the passage now with that hanging white cloud, and instead continued along another side passage where we could see a previous diver's line.

All seemed fine, perhaps, as we thought we were doing the right thing. Then, sure enough, we soon saw the end of that line. At this point, I won't deny I began feeling the first signs of stress with my mind repeatedly questioning if this was right, and what should I do? As I arrived at the end of the line, I suddenly saw another line, a yellow one, which I thought to be the main line, the one we had come in on.

The stress eased, and I felt okay again, gas check OK, camera battery, 0%, OK, I could live with that, since I had shot lots of footage, I thought.

As there were no line markers indicating our exit, I began looking for anything that was familiar from our journey in, but from the formations that now presented themselves, I didn't seem to recognize anything. It must be the other way, I thought—it has to be—so I chose what my instinct said and went with it.

After following what I thought to be the main line for possibly five minutes or so, we reached a point where the bottom of the cave was no longer visible, perhaps a depth in excess of maybe 40 m/130 ft.

My mind said, keep going this way, stay on the line, all will be good, but then soon after we saw something that I knew almost certainly did not look right!

At that time, and still to this day, it was one of the most impressive formations I have ever seen towering high, right in front of us. What should have given me a feeling of awe, instead made me almost sick as a perfect formation,

millions of years old, that looked more like a column from the Parthenon, standing perhaps 25 m/82 ft in height indicated that this was definitely not the way we had come into this cave!

We were lost!

Even if we had swum at a different depth, I was sure that I would have noticed and filmed this impressive and massive column of sheer calcite beauty.

In a fraction of a second, my somewhat calm mind turned instantly into one of utter fear not to mention one of absolute stress. In a frantic moment of panic, I could do nothing other than look to my buddy in hope of an answer.

As I moved around to look at him I remember how calm he was—holding a camera in his hands like nothing had happened.

Quickly, I turned to my wet notepad and in a barely legible phrase scribbled the words, "where is the exit?"

Reading my words, he now understood the situation, and no longer was he calm, his eyes so wide I felt I could see inside them.

With a gesture that could only mean, "how should I know?" he grabbed my wet notes so violently that they almost dropped into the bottomless darkness beneath us. In a somewhat calmer manner he wrote, "YOU were supposed to lead, YOU know the cave, how should I know?".

That was it. I thought surely this cannot be happening; how stupid can a person be?

Now was NOT the right time, none of those thoughts mattered. What did matter was breathing natural air and looking into the sunshine outside of this cave.

What was now happening to us now I had read only in stories, seen in the movies, or heard from other divers, but I never believed it could happen to me. I began thinking about imminent death and thoughts of life were immediately thrown at me. It felt like I had to remind myself of all the good and important moments that meant a lot to me. Or, as I felt right there, to punish me by showing me how stupid I was.

But still, I thought, how was this even possible? I had done everything right? Hadn't I?

Our only chance of survival in what was now a seriously deteriorating situation was trying to mentally retrace our steps.

At that point, I also thought to avoid monitoring my air supply because the now-bad situation I knew would only become worse by knowing how little breathing time I had left to find the way out of this alien environment and situation I had got us both into. With stress levels almost through the roof, I did not want to risk a full-blown panic attack, and I knew my air reserve was what it was. If there was enough, I would find out in due course; likewise, if there wasn't, there was nothing I could do about it.

So what should I do?

Try reversing the imaginary tape, try to figure out what went wrong and how to rectify it. Find our way back to the correct main yellow line—back to the place where we had jumped to this line we were now on what I thought to be the main yellow line—from that secondary line that led into that zero visibility. Hopefully from there on, I could find the correct line and make the connection we desperately needed to the world outside.

My mind still told me it felt safer on this primary yellow line and didn't want to go back to that secondary line, but I had to. I decided to focus on visualizing our way back. If I could get us to that point where the prison door columns were, surely I would be able to "see" the main line again.

Suddenly it hit me: I hadn't recognised anything looking to the left when we first got to the main line, because as we went to the secondary line, we were moving parallel to it. Therefore, we bypassed a big part of the primary line. This would mean that none of the landmarks in that section would have looked familiar. Without hesitation, I signaled my buddy to follow and rapidly started to swim back.

Acutely aware that that my gas consumption was probably greater than normal, I desperately tried to calm my breathing and instead look for clues. One turn, two turns, nothing? could we be going even further in?

Stratis, stay calm.

One thing that I am not is religious, but right there in my head I prayed, and as I did, momentarily the formations began to feel much more familiar and also the water seemed warmer, which meant we were within a thermocline, something we had experienced on our way in.

However, nothing gave me positive confidence until I saw our reel. In an amazing moment of euphoria, our regulators almost fell out of our mouths, the combination of screaming amongst laughing was almost uncontrollable. There was hope still.

Gas check, situation ok. Although well within thirds of our safety margin, I knew the exit to be near, so near in fact that within a short distance of swimming, I could actually see the beautiful rays of light from the outside world penetrating through the water.

The feeling was something I will never forget, a feeling of such relief, but also a feeling that this ridiculous lesson of life would hopefully never allow me to ever experience it again.

So, what had gone wrong?

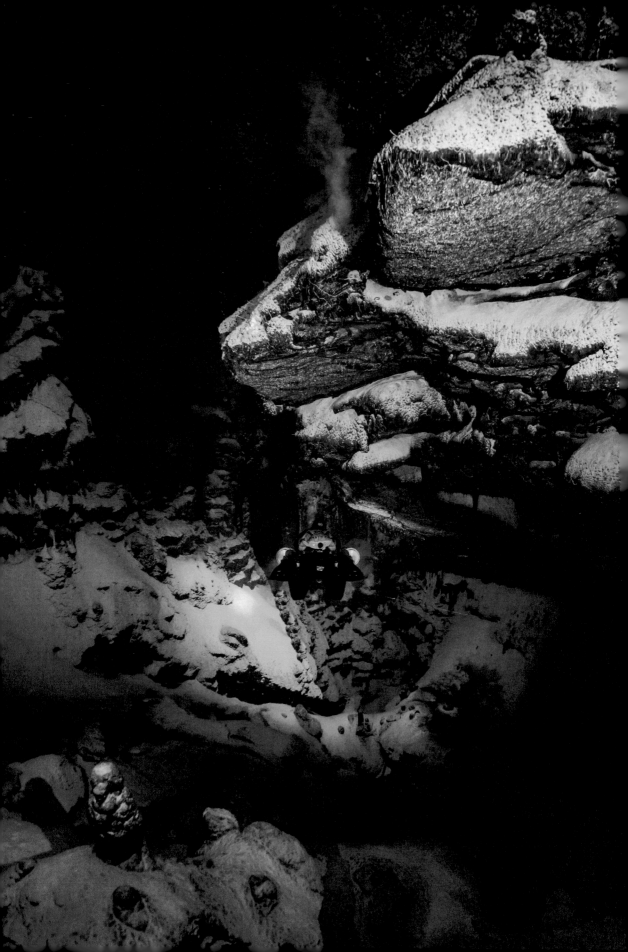

In a nutshell, ignorance of the risks and confidence that the mainline provided total safety. But above all, maybe man's reliance on technology? Of course, we wanted to film and show the world our exploration into the realms of planet earth and the beauty she so often secretly hides away. With that said, both of us had viewed the cave, mainly through the viewfinder, and thus the lenses of our cameras, rather than our eyes. We filmed as we swam.

We had learned a hard lesson: despite the camera's wide angle technology, it could never be equal to the human eye. We had missed valuable visual reference points our own eyes would have given us. As cave divers, we absorb and act as we penetrate through the journey into the cave. No man-made creation could EVER replace the situational awareness a human brain could have on such a journey into such an environment.

The boat ride back home on that particular day felt longer than usual. Silence fell upon all, as thoughts were deep. In the days and years after that day, especially that particular dive, I became very good at creating excuses or finding reasons in order to skirt around talking about it.

My buddy on that dive was known to be a notoriously private person, which gave me a degree of comfort that our "secret" was safe from all.

Many years have passed since that day, and I have since become a cave diving instructor.

That incident is well and truly embedded into my memory, and that alone helps me teach others in a way no other instructor could who had never experienced a lost line in a cave. I have also since participated in many dedicated filming expeditions, and collectively with that and during my teaching, I have never personally talked about that particular day and that very specific incident.

But many a time have I thought to myself, why is that? Why shouldn't I ?

In 2018, I was invited to a conference as a guest speaker to deliver a presentation on the subject of how to conduct filming safely on cave diving expeditions.

A fellow speaker, and good friend whom I consider to be one of the most daring and successful explorers I have ever known, opened my eyes to what I had hidden from myself for so long. When I asked him what his dream subject for a really good presentation would be, he replied "I would like to present to divers my own mistakes".

Humbled by the fact that this legendary diver, this superstar of the world I lived for, was comfortable enough to challenge his own status, admit his life mistakes, and thus shake his own reputable foundation of teaching, I had little if any excuses to now keep my own secrets locked away in a box.

That was the moment that the idea was born for this entire collection of close calls, of near death experiences, from legends, superstars, and idols from within this passion.

A volume of published stories where the stars of scuba diving open up to all and confess their own true close calls. That was of course if I could twist their arms into doing so!

For me, I got lost in a cave, underwater and in a place where man was never meant to be, let alone live and survive like a fish. Luck played its part, and so did fate, in meeting my superstar and listening to what he told me. In doing so, I myself have opened up.

"Close Calls" is a gift for all divers from all walks of life, stories and confessions for us all to look up to the legends, for the inspiration, for the lessons, but most of all for what makes us all equal humans in the quest for our own survival and life.

By making a celebration of those bad days, this book is their tribute to honesty. Only by accepting and acknowledging our own mistakes, do we learn from one another and thus hand our truths down to those who will follow in our footsteps.

Photo by Laurent Miroult

FOREWORD

BY
MICHAEL MENDUNO

The Quest To Improve Diving Safety

"Being able to share and discuss mistakes—the foundation of Just Culture—is the first step to improving diving safety. It requires a community effort."
—Gareth Lock, The Human Diver

Improving diving safety i.e., reducing risk, was one of the main factors that drove the emerging technical diving community to adopt mixed gas technology and later rebreathers as we sought to expand our collective underwater envelope—that is, to dive deeper and stay longer. At the same time, safety has arguably remained a continuing challenge—call it a work in progress—for the tech community since its emergence more than 30 years ago.

Viewed from a historical viewpoint, increases in fatalities have occurred in waves paralleling the introduction of new diving technologies. In each of these periods, the community came together to address the safety issues at hand.

Empowered by the advent of primary lights, reels, backplates, and larger cylinders, early cave divers—tech's predecessors—suffered a spate of fatalities in the 1970s. In response, famed cave explorer Sheck Exley turned to "accident analysis" to understand what was killing cave divers. His book, Basic Cave Diving—A Blueprint for Survival, set out ten recommendations for safe cave diving based on his findings. Over time, these were largely adopted by the cave community. The result was a gradual decrease in fatalities.

Similarly, the emergence of tech diving in the late 1980s through the mid 1990s, saw diving accidents and fatalities on the rise. Unlike the military and commercial diving communities, which had deep pockets, extensive infrastructure, tightly controlled diving operations, and were subject to government regulation, the sport diving community's transition to mixed gas technology was largely a seat-of-the-pants venture. Unfortunately, this resulted in a disproportionate number of early tech divers losing their lives as the community sought to develop standards and protocols for mixed gas diving and to train practitioners accordingly.

Accordingly, in the Fall of 1992, we began to report on individual tech diving fatalities through my magazine, aquaCORPS: The Journal for Technical Diving, and its sister publication, technicalDIVER, using Exley's accident analysis format.

Over the period from the Fall of 1992 to the Winter of 1995, we reported on 44 incidents that resulted in 39 fatalities and 12 injuries in aquaCORPS Incidents Reports,[1] which quickly became the best-read section of the magazine. In addition, a group of us worked to extend Exley's original ten recommendations to mixed gas diving. The result, "Blueprint for Survival 2.0: 21 Operational Guidelines for Technical Diving," first published in aquaCORPS #6 June 1993, represented a community-consensus standard of best practices.

One of my favorite quotes at the time was brought to my attention as the community struggled to cope with an alarming number of fatalities that threatened to shut tech diving down. It read, "Safety is the key consideration in diving; it entirely controls depth capacity," from a paper titled, "Safe Deep Sea Diving Using Hydrogen," published in the Marine Technology Journal in 1989.[2]

I imagine few people would consider dives to 500 m/1632 ft plus breathing hydreliox (oxygen, helium, hydrogen) mixes would be considered "safe." However, the quote resonated with us at Key West Diver, where I had the aquaCORPS office. We understood, if you can't do it safely—that is within acceptable risk—you can't do it!

The number of annual tech diving fatalities gradually decreased as the community established gas analysis and labeling standards, as well as reliable gas switching protocols—two of the biggest causes of fatalities at the time outside of "deep air" diving—and as the newly created technical training agencies improved the quality of their technical training. However, considerable shame and blame was still involved in acknowledging mistakes and incidents, including decompression sickness (DCS).

The fear of and stigma surrounding DCS led us to pointedly characterize it as the "sexually transmitted disease (STD) of diving" in the aquaCORPS BENT issue circa January 1993; our focus was to remove the stigma. For good reason!

As explained by safety advocate Nancy Leveson, a Professor of Aeronautics and Astronautics at MIT, "Blame is the enemy of safety."

The third wave of tech diving fatalities began in the early 2000s as mixed gas rebreathers began to gain traction. More than 200 sport divers died on rebreathers between 1998-2010. Not surprising, improving rebreather diving safety was the number one priority of the Rebreather Forum 3.0, which was held May 2012 in Orlando, Florida.

In his talk at the Forum, "Killing Them Softly," Dr. Andrew Fock, head of hyperbaric medicine at Albert Hospital in Melbourne, Australia, and a rebreather diver himself, estimated that the fatality rate for rebreather diving was as much as 10x greater than diving open circuit scuba. His results were later published in a 2013 paper "Analysis of recreational closed-circuit rebreather deaths 1998-2010."[3] It was clear from the presentations and discussions at the Forum that it was non-technical factors, for example, not using a checklist or getting distracted when assembling the rebreather and missing a step, that were killing divers, not the equipment.

It was around this time that retired British Royal Air Force senior officer and navigator turned technical diver Gareth Lock burst onto the tech diving scene. His self-defined mission: to bring aviation's rich body of knowledge of "human factors" and their impact on safety and performance to the sport diving industry. Having begun his PhD thesis in 2012, which examined the role of human factors in scuba diving incidents, Lock, who contributed his own close call story to this book, began publishing articles and papers as well as speaking at numerous diving conferences on the subject.

In its simplest form, his message might be summarized as follows: 1) We recognize that we are all fallible and are prone to mistakes and errors. 2) Most divers don't plan or intend to get hurt or die on a dive, and 3) We need to create systems, protocols, and a culture to protect ourselves so we don't get injured or lose our lives as a result of being human. According to Lock, one of the first steps, as highlighted in the opening quote, is to foster a Just Culture, an environment where divers can share their experience and stories without fear of recrimination or shame.

With the increased community awareness and communications surrounding rebreather safety, including a renewed focus on checklists and human factors, the fatality rate for rebreather diving has arguably decreased over the intervening years since Rebreather Forum 3.0.[4] As anesthesiologist Dr. Simon Mitchell noted at the sixth International Rebreather Meeting held in Ponza, Italy, last year, "Human factors are the most important, but also the most difficult, path to improving rebreather diving safety." His point applies equally to open circuit diving as well, which is one of the reasons this book is so important and valuable.

Cave diving instructor and filmmaker Stratis Kas was inspired to organize "Close Calls" a few years ago while attending a diving conference where he learned that one of his friends and heroes planned to give a presentation and share the mistakes he had made as a diver. His friend's willingness to be vulnerable helped Kas to come to grips with and acknowledge his own early mistakes learning to cave dive. It also provided the idea for the book.

Kas' concept was simple: If high profile divers and dive industry leaders were willing to share their own mistakes and lapses of judgement, many of which nearly cost them their lives, it would help rank-and-file divers realize that they are fallible and subject to making similar errors. Kas then approached renowned Italian shipwreck explorer Edoardo Pavia, who agreed to be a co-author.

Close Calls comes at a time when individual diving fatality reporting is largely nonexistent as a result of our litigious legal systems, and all of us are the losers. These days it is rare to learn what happened when an accident occurs, as the parties involved are not willing or are advised not to talk for fear of legal reprisal.

In fact, it may be months or years, if then, that the details of the accident are ever revealed. As a result, we are deprived of learning from others' experience.

Fortunately for us, detailed stories about divers' close calls are even more important and valuable for the community than what can be gleaned from fatality reports after the fact. In the first place, it is generally acknowledged that close calls happen with much greater frequency than fatalities, making them more representative of the types of problems divers experience.

Second, they provide us with a window into our fellow divers' minds to help us understand why their actions made sense to them at the time. As a result, they not only help us appreciate our own mortality, but they also enable us to appreciate and learn from others' experience in a deep way.

I want to applaud and support my fellow contributors. It takes courage to be vulnerable and admit to one's mistakes, especially in an industry where shame and blame still persist. And you have to be willing to accept a bit of embarrassment. What was I thinking?!? In fact, on a scale of one to ten, ten being fully achieved, Lock, now the principal of The Human Diver Ltd., told me he estimates that we are only at four to five in terms of realizing a Just Culture. Hopefully Kas' and Pavia's book will serve to give our community another needed push forward.

Michael Menduno, editor-in-chief of InDepth and contributing editor at Alert Diver.eu

[1] The reports have been republished in their entirety in "Examining Early Technical Diving Deaths: The aquaCORPS Incident Reports (1992-1996)", in InDepth V 2.2, March 2020

[2] Imbert G, Ciesielski T, Fructus X, Safe deep sea diving using hydrogen. Marine Tech Soc J. 1989; 23(4): 26-33. Fock AW.

[3] Analysis of recreational closed-circuit rebreather deaths 1998-2010. Diving and Hyperbaric medicine. 2013 June; 43(2);78-85.

[4] The number of annual rebreather diving fatalities have remained roughly constant at about 20/year, while the use of rebreathers is believed to have grown considerably over the intervening eight years.

ALDO FERRUCCI

CAVE & CCR INSTRUCTOR
TEC & TRIMIX TRAINER ITALY, FRANCE & EUROPE

LOCATION OF INCIDENT
LOCATION GREAT BARRIER REEF MARINE PARK
RAINE ISLAND

My story begins on Raine Island, on the edge of Australia's Great Barrier Reef, where the largest colony of green turtles in the world can be found. I was there as safety officer and backstage cameraman during the shooting of Jacques Perrin's film, *Oceans*.

Turtles were not our target, but rather green humphead parrotfish (Bolbometopon muricatum), a species that we had tried to film on several previous occasions without success. Finally it seemed the right time, several schools of the parrotfish were present on the reef, and at last we were making the images requested by the producer.

We had two separate dinghies—on one side were the freedivers who took care of finding the fish and following them so that the videographers with rebreathers could get to the target with ease and start filming.

When the fish swam away, the faster and lighter freedivers resumed following the school, so that the videographers could get back on the raft and return to the school without having to look for it again.

It was a system that required operators and their assistants to make various descents and ascents from the dinghy, with the removal of diving equipment, due to the lack of a suitable climbing ladder for the weight. But aside from some physical work, the system was paying off.

Then there was the moment when the motor of the freedivers' dinghy began to malfunction, forcing the divers to return to the boat which was in a sheltered position on the other side of the island, since the sea conditions had worsened.

Photo by Thierry Rolland

For us, therefore, it was a matter of making the last descent, and then we too would return to the base. We began to go up, passing the large video cameras first, then the operator's equipment, the operators, the other assistants, and, as usual, I was last.

I had removed the rebreather and was raising it up when I heard a scream and then was hit by the dinghy, which had been thrown into the air as if it were a mere leaf by a considerably larger wave.

Rolling in the waves, unable to tell which way was up, luckily brushing the reef without bumping into it, I had the reflex to take the mouthpiece of the rebreather that was still in my arms and to breathe into it, until finally I returned to the surface. And here I have to thank the fact that I had not only developed the habit myself, but I also taught students to never close the cylinders and to set a surface set point until the rebreather is safely stored in the boat.

Once afloat, I looked around and, apart from the overturned dinghy, I could not see any

of the other seven passengers, and I began to worry. Bubbles rose from the bottom, so I somehow strapped the rebreather on and descended as fast as possible to see who it was. I luckily discovered that the bubbles were coming from only the mouthpiece of one of the rebreathers that had opened during the accident.

I closed it and inflated the BC to send it to the surface. Floating on the surface again, I finally began to see the other castaways, and one by one I placed them safely on the floating wrecks and brought them ashore. Once secured near the beach, I decided to go back and try to recover the video equipment, which would, in the following weeks, be necessary to continue filming. I returned to the reef, and by taking advantage of the waves, I managed to pass over it and make it into the open sea.

I was beginning to see debris at the sea floor, so I knew I was at the right spot. I collected various pieces of gear a little at a time until I realized that the conditions of the sea had further deteriorated and I would be unable to get close to the coral points without risking crashing into and damaging them. I decided to go back into the lagoon, but my attempts were in vain. I bumped into the rocks but without hurting myself too much, and I understood that in addition to the increasing size of the waves I had to deal with the reality that the tide had retreated, making my attempts impossible. I decided then to look for a better spot by swimming along the reef.

Up until that point, the succession of events had caused me to ignore what had been happening around me.

In addition to the massive presence of green turtles, this reef is also very popular with sharks, especially tigers, since the turtles are their favorite prey.

In fact, I realized that my fidgeting and moving about had attracted their attention, and I had a few circling around me. I immediately realized the danger, but at the same time I acknowledged the fact that at that moment, I could not avoid it. I decided not to fin on the surface, where I would be easy prey for them, but to dive, finning as calmly as possible, and staying as close as possible to the reef, in order to control any attacks and try to somehow see clearly.

My system seemed to work, and for the moment I was no longer the center of their attention. The minutes passed quickly without me finding a passage and entering the lagoon, and my oxygen supply began to run low. I decided to lower the set point to the minimum possible, and after a while I deactivated the solenoid to manually put the minimum amount of oxygen needed in order not to go into hypoxia.

I absolutely didn't want to ascend to the surface, where I couldn't see what was going on below me. The oxygen ran out, and I still hadn't been able to find a passage, so I started doing SCR with the diluent, which is air. In the meantime, a slight current had risen, and it took me away from the island, causing me to struggle to not let myself be carried away,

knowing full well that the closest island was Tonga, several thousand kilometers away.

I breathed and moved as slowly as possible, without panicking, and consumed as little oxygen as possible. In this way I was able to gain enough time to finally find a passage and enter the lagoon. There the water was shallow and there were no sharks, so I could finally re-surface and swim to shore.

Several hours had passed since the shipwreck, and I was grateful for having clear ideas about what to do with my rebreather to make it last as long as possible, and for not having succumbed to panic. Otherwise I would not be here today to tell my story. My biggest mistake, however, was putting myself in danger for equipment that, although very expensive and necessary, would never be worth a life.

Aldo Ferrucci *decided to make diving his main activity 25 years ago. Whilst he was travelling in the US, he first heard about nitrox, trimix, and rebreathers.*

He was fascinated by these new diving technologies and he started using gas mixes like nitrox, then trimix, before taking his first course in semi-closed Drager Dolphin rebreathers in 1995.

Aldo started his career as a Lawyer, but soon gave everything up to become a professional diver and trainer. He was also a diving supervisor for various television projects and movies, including Oceans, Thalassa, and Ushuaïa.

ALESSANDRA FIGARI

CAVE & CCR INSTRUCTOR
TEC & TRIMIX TRAINER @ CAVE TRAINING MEXICO
ASSOCIATE MEMBER OF THE EXPLORERS CLUB

LOCATION OF INCIDENT
TORTUGA WALL, QUINTANA ROO, MEXICO

After my buddy and I got certified as trimix divers, we decided to do some dives at our new certification limit in order to get used to the fact that no instructor was supervising us.

Once we felt comfortable with those dives, we decided to go progressively deeper, adding 6 m/20 ft each time. I soon found that the extra travel- and bottom-gas cylinders were making me heavy, causing me to descend too fast. To counteract this I decided to reduce my lead weights and thermal protection.

This was my first mistake—you should never change more than one element at the same time in your configuration so that you can get used to it and decide if it works. I changed my back plate from steel to aluminum and chose to use a semi-dry suit instead of my usual 7 mm wet one; my reasoning was that by using a more buoyant suit I would not sink so fast.

It was a beautiful day and the ocean was calm.

Gear, gas, dive and emergency plans: all checked. Nothing could spoil our dive. The hyperbaric chamber was informed about our trimix deco dive, just in case. Our boat captain was the one we always used, so we felt comfortable that he knew when to meet us at the end of our drift dive.

We jumped into the water and descended to 6 m/20 ft for a bubble check. Everything was okay, so we gave the descend signal. As I released all the gas from my wing, my descent speed was a lot slower than usual. I started thinking that it was maybe too slow and that I should call the dive. The descent was less than half of my usual speed.

We continued our way down. This was my second mistake.

What I should have done is added some extra weight if it was available on the boat, or just rescheduled our dive for another day.

I didn't. "It will be fine, I can deal with it," I thought. But, I did not. I didn't consider that during our ascent my cylinders, with little or no gas in them, would be lighter as well, and that of course would affect further my already incorrect buoyancy. The dive was great as usual: large sponges, turtles swimming with us, bull sharks cruising.

Then we started our ascent.

Everything seemed fine to begin with, but when we reached our 25 m/82 ft stop I started feeling that something was not quite right. I was feeling a bit too buoyant even with very little gas in my wing. I immediately wrote on my slate a message and showed it to my buddy: "not enough weight, stops from 12 m/40 ft up will be hard."

He acknowledged, and we continued our ascent with me still controlling the speed and stops acceptably well. By the time we reached 12 m/40 ft, I felt a much stronger lift, as anticipated.

On the way up I had been trying to think of possible solutions to get through these next stops without jeopardizing the safety of my buddy; my idea was to find a big, stable rock, tie a lift bag to it, inflate the bag and complete the dive using its line to avoid an uncontrolled ascent. I explained the plan to my buddy and pointed to the perfect place to execute it. I was using double aluminum 80 cf cylinders, and my buddy was using double 15 L steels. We each had an aluminum 80 cf cylinder plus two aluminum 40 cfs. My buddy then told me to stop.

He completely deflated his wing and asked me to hold on under his cylinders, bracing against them as a sort of 'ceiling' in order to see if we could control my buoyancy like that.

It worked, but I was not happy putting him at risk because of my mistake. As tech divers, we should never risk the safety of others, even when we face a serious problem. When our 12 m/40 ft stop was completed, we ascended to our next deco stop. At that point, I saw another rock that I thought that my lift bag could be attached to. I pointed it out to my buddy, saying that I was going to follow my plan.

He insisted that we should continue with me holding on below him as, with his heavier cylinders and full weight-load, his idea seemed to be working (so far). I was only about a 1 m/3.3 ft deeper than him, so my deco was not affected.

We switched from tables to our computers and communicated using touch contact. Ultimately we managed to complete our ascent including the 6 m/20 ft deco stop and surface safely.

What I learned from this experience: don't mess around with your buoyancy too much by changing more than one element of your configuration at the same time. More changes mean less control. Vary one thing at a time and judge what effect it has had before you think about changing something else.

If you see that something is unexpectedly different during your descent (too slow in my case), always call the dive. Things will only get worse, and you may not be as lucky as I was. There is nothing wrong with calling the dive if you feel there is an added risk factor you have not planned for. Don't waste time when you do encounter a problem on a dive; respond to it as soon as possible and work to find a solution. In a real emergency, even a minute without knowing what to do could be long enough to put your life at risk.

Try to depend only on yourself during the problem solving so that you don't put your buddy at risk. One dead diver is already too many—two is even more stupid. Don't underestimate the importance of a problem encountered during the start of a dive; ignoring it and just assuming that you will handle it when the time comes is not a correct dive plan.

In the end, everything turned out okay because we were a good team, we trusted each other, we worked efficiently and we communicated well.

However it could easily have gone the other way, and we certainly risked getting hurt.

I often discuss this early mistake of mine with my tech or cave students. Mistakes will happen. We have to be able to tell others about them, recognize where we went wrong, and learn from them. Safe diving.

Alessandra Figari *has been in love with the ocean since she was a kid. She used to read books about the ocean, in particular about dolphins.*

Her dream was to study oceanography or marine biology to enable her to work (not in a park) with dolphins and study their communication. She ended up studying languages and working as a Project Manager for medical researchers. In 1999, she got certified as an open water diver. Alessandra moved to Mexico and in 2004, when she became a PADI Course Director.

She became a tech full cave instructor in 2007 and a CCR trainer in 2015 for the Poseidon MKVII. In later years, she became an instructor in other CCR units, which she believes represent the future of technical diving. In 2013, she was nominated as Associate Member of the Explorer Club in New York for her work teaching environment conservation (cave, ocean, and land) and the importance of exploration.

In 2020, she still enjoys teaching people how to dive, respect the ocean, cenotes, and caves, how to contribute to conservation, and how to be safe. Her love for the ocean is now shared with a love for caves.

Caves are, to Alessandra, the perfect habitat, where all her senses are active and alert and her soul is enriched each minute she spends in them. Her most challenging cave trimix dive was Eagle's Nest, Florida, which is considered as the "Himalaya of Cave Diving".

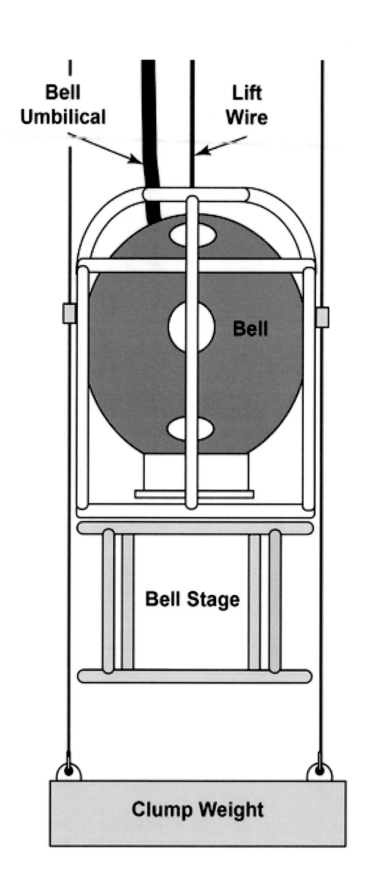

ALESSANDRO MARRONI

PRESIDENT, CEO & CHIEF MEDICAL OFFICER
@DAN EUROPE FOUNDATION

LOCATION OF INCIDENTS
FORTIES FIELD, NORTH SEA

I believe that like any diver I did stupid things in my more than 60 years of diving and happened to come close to situations that might have evolved into real emergencies, were it not for luck and perhaps a little nerve and know-how. But, you know, that's the way it is with the sea and water in general. It's not the element we were born for, even though we start our existence in it with energy supplied by our own personal gas and food bank (mom), through a nice and very functional umbilical cord.

See, it's almost like we were all born commercial-diving techies!

As it happens, the two episodes I like to remember as "close calls" are related to my past experience in the commercial diving realm, as a young Field Diving Medical Officer on offshore pipe laying or drilling vessels, and a more expert diving doctor ten years later.

Having been a diver since childhood and a diving instructor since the age of twenty, it was natural that when I finished my medical studies I wanted to be a doctor specialising in diving medicine; I went for a resident program in occupational medicine at the University of Genova. That's where my mentor, Professor Damiano Zannini, was working on developing deep trimix and saturation diving protocols and tables for the Italian National Oil Company (ENI)—so diving occupational medicine, specifically saturation diving medicine, was the topic of my specialty dissertation.

As a resident, it was also very natural that I would be sent out to the field, to do 'practical placement' and complete my training. In consequence, I spent almost three years wandering around barges and drilling rigs from the North Sea to the Red Sea and the Persian Gulf, learning things that have never abandoned me.

The two close calls I like to remember happened in the North Sea, about 16 km/10 m east of Aberdeen, in the area called "Forties Field," where Saipem, a company of the Italian ENI Group, was contracted to lay a sea line or pipe from the field to Peterhead, Scotland, a nice town north of Aberdeen.

Close Call #1: The Facts
1975 - At that time, after completing my residency, I was Saipem's Diving Medical Officer. We were working on Forties Field with a very large sea line laying barge, the Castoro 2, proudly strutting its eight hundred ton mega-crane, which at that time was one of the biggest barge-mounted cranes in the world.

Castoro 2 also hosted a very advanced (for the time) saturation diving system, able to host up to six divers, who would work shifts around the clock in saturation for periods of up to a maximum of twenty one days, at a depth of 130-140 m/426-459 ft. From there, they would check the oil-well heads and valves, and scrutinise the correct connection and function of the massive sea line that was laid down from the barge to the bottom, using a kind of sled, called "The Stinger."

The Story
I was not diving, as my job was to check and control the saturation habitat, the health and safety of the divers, and oversee the correct timing and depth differential of the "Saturation Excursion Dives" from the "Storage Depth." As much as I loved the job, it was not "wet" enough for me, and I was missing the water.

One day, together with the project manager (and friend of mine), Franco Lo Savio, we decided to go down for a "One ATM Bell Dive" to see what was going on down there and check the valves, the sea line etc. It was supposed to be a very short touch-and-go dive, so we did not arrange to have any umbilical for air circulation connected to the bell, but simply had the bell lowered down with its normal clump weight and lift cable system.

Instinctively, before entering the bell, I decided to fill a shopping bag with a couple of kilos of soda lime from the sat-diving life support system to bring with us. One never knows.

So down we went. It was great to see what the divers had done and the environment they were exposed to, as well as observe the many large cod swimming around. After about ten minutes at a depth of 130 m/426 ft we told the control room guys to lift us up. We started leaving the bottom, but it was then that Murphy's Law struck!

A strand of one of the steel cables from the clump weight system broke and stopped the bell's bracket from freely sliding along the cable. So there we were, stuck close to the bottom and without any fresh air supply from the surface.

"No panic guys, the boys at the surface know best,and they will bring us out soon," we said to each other. We started applying the low oxygen consumption protocol—no chatting, no useless movement, stay calm, and wait. Meanwhile, the attitude of the cod changed. They suddenly appeared curious about us and were peeping through the bell's portholes with what I interpreted as a curious face. I now understood what it felt like to be behind the bars in a zoo with visitors looking at you!

Time went by, and the boys above still had not figured out a way to rescue us. The bell was too deep for a bounce dive, and the surface diving team was only equipped for checking the Stinger, using compressed air scuba to a maximum depth of 50 m/164 ft. The Sat Divers were all in their habitat, and the bell with us inside was at more than 100 m/328 ft down.

The ambient air was getting thicker, and we were starting to feel the CO_2 buildup—that's when I remembered the soda-lime shopping bag that I had instinctively picked up.

I grabbed it and started slowly mixing it with my hands, lifting handfuls and letting them sprinkle down back in the bag. Definitely not the best scrubber, but it was all I had! Can't say if and how it really worked, but it gave us a sort of peace of mind.

Meanwhile, the surface boys had devised a way to pick us up, using the Castoro 2's mega-crane and lifting hook to grab the two cables of the Clump Weight System together and gradually lift the entire apparatus approximately 10 m/33 ft at a time until we eventually reached the surface!

Something I will not forget!

Close Call #2: The Facts
November 28th, 1985, offshore Ancona, Italy - A commercial diver operating an excursion dive from a saturation storage depth of 64 m/209 ft to the working depth of 70 m/229 ft, had his arms sucked into a 25 cm/10 in venting valve of the sea-line flooding head. The four brackets protecting the valve stopped the further penetration of the arms into the pipe, but the diver was pressed against them by both shoulders and upper sternum, with a pressure gradient of 8 ATA to 1.

The diver came from a saturation habitat with PPO_2 of 346 mbar, PPN_2 of 1303 mbar and helium for the balance. The diver had a bottom mix of heliox 88/12 (88% helium, 12% oxygen), which was breathed through a Kirby Morgan Helmet. The diver was conscious, although in deep pain, fear, and distress.

The flooding and compression of the pipe was started from land, 64km/40 mi away, as it was impossible to cut the pipe immediately by explosive. However, the compression of the pipe was slow, and the pressure gradient sucking the diver in could not be quickly overcome.

At 08:00 of the morning after, a buddy diver, who had spent the night close to his friend, although at risk of being sucked in himself, unbolted the flange connecting the valve to the pipe. The pipe pressure at that time was 4.5 ATA, with a remaining gradient of 8 to 4.5.

The valve was tied to a steel cable connected to a winch on the barge, and the diver was pulled away at 09:00 with a force of four tons on the 1.5 m/5 ft cable excursion on the winch.

The tenders reported that the diver's hands were protruding out through the valve and were balloon-shaped for a moment, but immediately shrank as the valve slid out and fell down. At 09:45 the diver was back into the saturation habitat.

At that time, I had left Saipem and was working with the University of Chieti School on underwater and hyperbaric medicine as the Director of the Hyperbaric Medicine and Saturation Diving Simulation System in Teramo, Italy, but was still connected with Saipem and its Underwater Operations Manager, Franco Lo Savio, (the same as Close Call #1—funny isn't it?).

Franco had called me during the night describing the situation. Suspecting a severe crush injury and compartment syndrome, I summoned a vascular surgeon colleague to accompany me.

While reaching the barge, having identified the possible need for increased injured tissue oxygenation at depth, I suggested modifications to the saturation protocol to ensure higher than usual oxygen pressures while waiting for the medical team to reach the diver.

When we reached him in the saturation habitat, though he was conscious and alert, the situation was more serious than we expected.

The diagnosis was of a severe crushing trauma of both hands and arms, with compartment syndrome of upper arms and shoulders. Urine output was low, with risk of renal failure, and the diver was in pre-shock conditions.

We began an aggressive surgical and medical treatment at depth, while the saturation decompression was started. Both

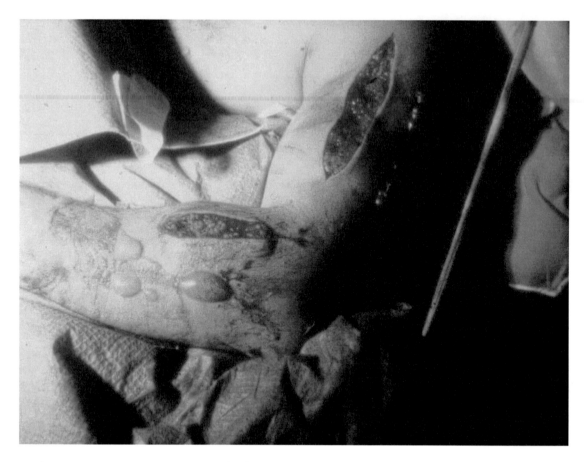

saphenous veins were incannulated for fluid and drug therapy and multiple fasciotomies were done to decompress the compartment syndrome. Blood and urine tests showed massive signs of muscular damage.

In addition to the fluid and drug treatment, a hyperbaric oxygen (HBO) treatment protocol at depth was started, by preparing a varying PO_2 mixture to assure a treatment pressure of 2.5 ATA for ninety minutes, every eight hours for the first twenty four hours, and every twelve hours for the following twenty four.

The saturation decompression lasted until December 1, during which period the medical team visited the diver at depth for a second time since November 29.

The diver was then transported to a specialized surgical and hyperbaric facility in order to continue treatment.

Multiple surgeries and continuing HBO were ultimately required. The diver eventually made an acceptable recovery, with functional arms, but his hands were mutilated and he suffered significant disability.

The Story
So far, it may seem a rather exceptional case of a commercial diving accident requiring a kind of medical intervention which is both expected of a diving doctor and is part of the emergency procedures manual for any saturation diving operation.

So what is strange, and why do I remember this as a "close call?" Not because of the HBO treatment protocol applied at pressure, although that was at the time an unprecedented, or at least an unpublished, procedure. We had to vary the oxygen percentages in the breathing mix provided to the diver to assure a constant 2.5 ATA O_2, while at the same time the ambient pressure was being decreased as per saturation decompression procedure! This was quite unique but it was part of my skills, knowledge, and duty.

No, not that! Here once again Murphy's Law visited! The Emergency Operations Procedures had foreseen the possibility of a so-called 'doctor dive' to visit the saturation divers in the habitat, but only assumed bottom time for the deep trimix habitat dives of up to thirty minutes.

The clinical situation we encountered was such that it required almost ninety minutes of bottom time for my colleague, although a vascular surgeon, to find, expose, and incannulate suitable peripheral veins to supply the diver with the necessary fluid and drug therapy. As a consequence, we didn't start our return to the surface until more than ninety minutes at the bottom at an average depth of 55 m/180 ft in a trimix atmosphere. And my colleague wasn't even a diver!

The close call was that I had to recalculate our deco profile after a doctor dive that was three times longer than expected, and for which there were no prepared tables! I still remember sitting in that bell and my colleague asking me what I was doing and if everything would be okay.

Meanwhile, I was calculating our estimated inert gas uptake and planning the safest possible ascent profile, using a mnemonic proportion-based method, with the help of a pencil and some toilet paper!

Finally, I was able to communicate the new profile to the support team on deck, together with the instruction to increase the PPO_2 in the bell, to further help wash out the inert gas.

We finally emerged without event, and I kept reassuring (and lying to) my brave colleague who kept asking me if everything was okay, until the morning after.

When twelve hours had passed I could finally tell him, "My friend, NOW we're okay!"

He was so professional, and brave, that later on he accompanied me for the second doctor dive, although definitely shallower and more relaxed.

Prof. Alessandro Marroni, MD, MSc, FUHM, FECB (aka "Doc") *is the founder and President of DAN Europe. He is a Diving and Hyperbaric Physician and Researcher, specialised in Occupational Medicine, Anaesthesiology, and Intensive Care.*

A passionate diver since his early years, he learnt SCUBA at the age of 13 and has been an active Instructor since 1966.

Author of over 250 scientific papers and publications, he is particularly active in underwater medicine research, with special interest in the prevention of barotrauma and dysbaric illnesses in diving, and in the development of advanced techniques for remote diver's physiological monitoring and of bidirectional diving telemedicine.

He serves as Vice President of the European Committee for Hyperbaric Medicine (ECHM), President of the European Foundation for the Education in Baromedicine, Secretary General of the European College of Baromedicine, and President of the International Academy of Underwater Sciences and Techniques.

He is also a Past-President of the International Congress on Hyperbaric Medicine and of the European Underwater and Baromedical Society.

ALEX SANTOS

OWNER @ PHILTECH DIVERS
& UNDERWATER CONTRACTORS

LOCATION OF INCIDENT
NE HYDROPOWER TUNNEL, PHILIPPINES

Battling out an argument regarding which way to exit an underwater tunnel at a depth of 90 m/295 ft is one of the most nerve-racking pickles I have dealt with in my diving career. In November of 2008, a dive buddy and I did exactly that, and it could have ended either one, or both of us. Since then, I have continued diving the same tunnel over the past twelve years but have learned to accord it every respect for its latent but unpredictable temperament.

The story behind this "Close Call" is known only to the handful of divers who have worked with me inside this deceptively easy burrow. We often hear that experience is the best teacher, and I assure you this phrase is no cliché. With both gratification and embarrassment, I invite you to relive this experience vicariously through the following anecdote.

Perhaps you might find value in this experience and make good use of it when planning similar dives. If not, then I hope it brings some thrill at least, as a result of my own errant folly and blunders.

Setting the stage for my close call requires some understanding of my experiences as a commercial diver. For reasons that escape me, my company attracts some of the oddest underwater jobs, the majority of them taking place in some very unwelcoming environments. It is also the case that working repetitively under adverse conditions can anesthetise your sensation of fear. For example: imagine yourself diving in a 20 m/65 ft vertical pit filled with a mixture of water and bentonite (a viscous grey sludge used to prevent the walls of the pit from collapsing). Your objective: to recover the very drill bucket that bore the pit, now stuck at the bottom.

Photos by Ram Yoro

The instant your mask sinks into bentonite, your world turns black. Full-face masks are mandatory unless you want to risk a craggy facial. I like repeatedly sticking a thousand Lumen torch against my mask–just for kicks I guess–knowing full well I will see nothing.

The drill bucket is no more than 3 m/10 ft in diameter by about 1.30 m/4.2 ft in height. You must enter the bucket through a triangular opening on top, just big enough for a convoluted squeeze forcing you to kneel. And while you are doing so, a prayer or two won't hurt. This miniscule space cannot accommodate cylinders; even if it could, you wouldn't see your pressure gauge. So, except for a four-litre bailout, your gas is all surface-supplied. Recovering the bucket may necessitate employing several techniques, one of which requires wiggling the bucket using the drilling rig above to help you yank-off an enormous retaining pin. All this work must be performed whilst being shaken inside this tin can and are as blind as an olm.

While this may sound frightening, our jobs are carefully reviewed for potential risks and "what ifs". Careful planning and evaluation that must satisfy our safety standards is our only green light. In less frightening jobs, disaster hides in silence, waiting for just one imprecise move. Every action is therefore deliberate and must be perfectly executed. My point being that frequent exposure to stressful and brutal conditions can toughen the nerves. And while this may develop positive reactions to extreme diving emergencies, it can also make you fearless to a fault. I could have summed this all up in one word: overconfidence.

Among the more regular types of job we do is working in underwater tunnels to perform repairs or undertake routine safety inspections, and this is where the drama took place.

By 2008, I had done many dives in various tunnels with differing arrangements and had done so enough times to intuit every possible scenario.

Or so I thought.

Up in the northern mountains of the Philippines, there is a lake that hides a water tunnel used for generating power. Of all the tunnels I have worked in, this one was the simplest—being straight and without branches. I have done many dives here at varying times of the year. To gain access to the tunnel, we must first enter a cylindrical tower that juts above the lake bottom.

Once inside the tower, a gaping hole can be seen that continues down a vertical shaft. Nearing the bottom, the shaft starts to curve, forming a sloping elbow. When the elbow bottoms out, the tunnel begins. The tunnel spans a total of 640 m/2100 ft. That night, our dive window being from 1 am to 6 am, we only needed to inspect a gate 300 m/984 ft from the elbow.

Being 'very' familiar with the construction features of this tunnel, I had memorised two parallel concrete joints that run the entire length of the tunnel floor. I had accustomed myself to using these as my guidelines instead of laying a nylon line, which takes up more time. My buddy then was Jamie (not his real name), and I trained him in technical wreck and trimix. He is also a veteran of body recovery inside deep wrecks.

This night was his second dive in the tunnel. The visibility at the shaft was less than 2 m/6.5 ft as expected, and our bottom depth was 90 m/295 ft. Our plan, as usual, was to drop our travel gas at the end of the elbow and proceed with three cylinders of trimix to inspect and document the gate. Descending the vertical shaft was without surprise and accompanied by hubris as I pictured exactly how the dive would transpire. Deeper into the shaft however, the visibility dropped until only our lights were visible to each other. This was new, I thought, but carried on.

Unable to see bottom, we hit the elbow like skidding hamsters desperately trying to break our slide.

Mindful not to use our fins, we plowed through a layer of silt, stirring up what must have been a mushroom cloud. Never have I encountered this much silt in this tunnel, and it made a huge mess. Being too late to hit the inflator, we surrendered ourselves to slither to the bottom and stop. By this time, I no longer could see Jaime, nor he me.

Expecting he was nearby, I groped in the silt cloud on all fours until I managed to grab a part of him. In hindsight, I still wonder what part of him that was. He never did say, but I gripped him like a vise. We eventually managed to get close enough for our lights to be of some worth. With what little visibility we could use, we both gave the thumbs-up to ascend back up the shaft, and as we rose above the silt cloud, the visibility improved a little.

Expecting to go through the shaft, we continued our ascent. Then jarringly and without warning – boink! Our heads hit the tunnel ceiling hard. While massaging my head, I looked at Jaime. His body was upright but his head was pressed sideways on the ceiling.

Our faces were instantly painted with disbelief. "How the devil did we get inside the tunnel?" we asked ourselves. Fortunately, the visibility at the ceiling was just enough for us to see our bubbles rolling along a slight incline. With Jaime's head now straight, common sense hinted that our bubbles were moving up towards the vertical shaft.

Though we couldn't see past a metre, we agreed to follow our bubbles. The vertical shaft could be no more than a minute away. Mysteriously however, we kept on following our bubbles unmindful of the time. Evidently fear began impairing logic as we kept on swimming, unaware that we were in fact going into the tunnel. Since the tunnel has no distinct features, everything looked the same, and we couldn't tell exactly how far we swam. We had tunnel vision, literally and figuratively. The ludicrously long swim finally jogged me back to sanity and I realised our direction couldn't be right.

Fortuitously, swimming the wrong way brought me close to a familiar sound, one that I have heard many times deep inside this tunnel–the sound of clanking tools,

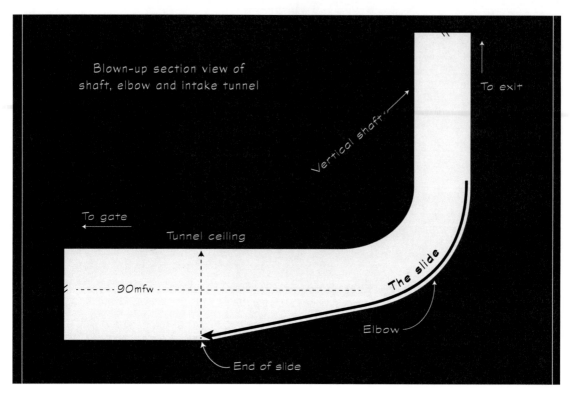

Blown-up section view of
shaft, elbow and intake tunnel

To exit

Vertical shaft

To gate

Tunnel ceiling

90mfw

The slide

Elbow

End of slide

which meant we were approaching the gate. It was faint at first but got louder the farther in we went. The clanking was from workers hammering on the machinery above.

I was now certain we had gone the wrong way and was immediately relieved. I stopped us both and with convincing eyes, pointed to go back to where we started. Jaime's immediate acknowledgement was reassuring. Wasting no time and hugging the ceiling, we began swimming back.

Because of our initial swim in the long and wrong direction, I knew it would take some time to return to the vertical shaft. Neither of us checked our computers so we had no clue how long that would take. But since I was now convinced of the way out, I was prepared for the long swim back. I checked my gas and I had plenty. So, I finally relaxed. But that was just me.

Unfortunately for Jaime his state of mind was quite the opposite. He was utterly confused and terrified. To him our direction was unclear, and the poor vis messed up his orientation.

The growing fear in him began disquieting his mind. He had no clue what the clanking sounds meant. Although he was following me, he was doing so thoughtlessly. His mind weighed heavily with doubt, and his fear began to swell. I guess he was starting to lose it. Being in front of him, however, I was oblivious to his plight.

For anyone lost in an overhead setting, a few seconds of searching for the line or exit is quite an eternity. Having reached his threshold for patience combined with heavy breathing and thoughts of losing gas, Jaime grabbed and tugged my fin forcefully and repeatedly. I turned to check on him, fearful he was empty. Luckily, he was not, but was running low. Saucer-eyes are never good to see but they were staring right at me as he pointed towards the clanking–the wrong way!

Oh man, I knew this moment could go all kinds of wrong and that very thought triggered my own fear. But as calmly as I could, I said "no, this is the way out" and with comforting eyes I tried. But again, and this time with vigorous body language, he insisted we go back!

"Ok, now what?" I thought.

At 90 m/295 ft of depth, not knowing exactly where we were, and with Jaime's gas running low, I decided this was no place to argue nor let this crisis escalate to a struggle.

So, I gave him an emphatic "this way is out" and quickly turned towards the exit. I swam a bit faster, just enough to keep him from grabbing my fin again. Jaime being low on gas, I knew he would swim towards where there was more–me. I dared not look back but made sure I could see his light in case it swiped for an emergency. Mercifully, it was steady. After a hefty chase, we came upon a slight dip in the ceiling and as we swam past it...presto! The vertical shaft!

Like flipping a switch, our fears turned to relief as we shook each others' hands and our heads. Our thoughts were awash with the prospect of seeing our loved ones again, a common phenomenon I believe among those who have gazed at death and survived. It took a few minutes to quiet our beating hearts, and the idea of breakfast was a good sign of restored coherence. We still had our ascent to deal with and managed that while sharing gas towards our deco station. Once we got there, we had copious amounts of oxygen, and plenty of stop time to thank God and all the saints, and to mull over the serious realities of life, like insurance policies, my daughter's trust fund, and educational plan. She was only a few months old.

Upon returning to our rooms, I quickly rolled out the section plan of the tunnel, and it was only then that I understood why we missed the vertical shaft. The drawing clearly showed that the elbow begins at a much higher elevation than the tunnel and ends a few meters inside it. What was I thinking?

There are many take-away lessons from this story, but the true culprit that began the chain of chilling events was utter arrogance. I could make a longer list of specific blunders but am quite sure you get the gist. Safe dives!

*At age nine, **Alex Santos** got his first few scuba lessons in his uncle's swimming pool. During his teens, he played hooky to dive in nearby reefs without agency training. Years later, he was compelled to get certified so he could join his girlfriend who was a certified diver. Henceforth armed with a license, he finally could travel and legitimately extend his fins. His appetite for discovering the marine world inevitably led him to technical diving—his ticket to encountering life beyond conventional depths. He introduced tech diving to the Philippines in 1993, the same year he founded Philippine Technical Divers. In 1995, he became the Philippine licensee for IANTD, spreading technical diving to the rest of Asia from where many students came to be trained.*

These days Alex is primarily involved in commercial diving. He and his PHILTECH team are known to perform the most peculiar underwater jobs and in harsh conditions. Being at the cutting edge of diving allows him to observe early manifestations of DCS due to their unconventional diving activities and behavior. To keep his team DCS free, Alex has studied and developed procedures for in-water recompression using oxygen. His recompression techniques have been successful in reversing early symptoms of DCS. It has also been used successfully in delayed treatment of DCS. He is also certified in hyperbaric oxygen therapy.

Cave exploration, however, is his true passion. Alex is a member of the Filipino Cave Divers, an active group of select individuals who apply their various expertise in the study, exploration, and preservation of underwater caves. With a background in Geology, he is better able to study, understand, and appreciate the speleogenesis and properties of underwater caves. For many years, Alex has been involved in deep recovery work, both for valuable objects and victims of drowning. His experience in body recovery inside sunken ships has been called upon many times during disasters at sea. Besides his PHILTECH team, he has trained recovery teams both locally and from abroad. Alex still loves teaching wreck and cave diving. Due to his work in predominantly overhead environments, he shares this gained knowledge and experience with his students.

ANDY TORBET

PROFESSIONAL DIVER & FREEDIVER
UNDERWATER EXPLORER FOR SCIENCE, TV, AND FILM
TV PRESENTER AND STUNTMAN
FELLOW OF THE ROYAL GEOGRAPHICAL SOCIETY
FELLOW OF THE EXPLORERS CLUB

LOCATION OF INCIDENT
LOCH LINNHE, SCOTLAND

Have you had a close call? Have I?

To answer this question, we first must define the term. This will be different for all of us. We all have different priorities in our lives, different motivations, and different levels of acceptable risk and consequence.

Even the characters within this book, woven together with the common thread of a passion for the underwater world, will give divergent answers. But this is my chapter, so this is my definition.

A close call is the time you almost died. And, underwater at least, I can think of only one. Things have gone wrong in the past—and will continue to go wrong despite my best efforts—but this was when I, a self-confessed control freak, had no control. It was only luck that saved me.

And I do not believe in luck.

Many years ago, while serving as an Army Diver and Bomb Disposal Officer, I found myself conducting some training at the bottom of a sea loch in Scotland. We were using surface-supplied diving helmets.

This gear provided both limitless amounts of gas—in this case air—being pumped down to me, and communications with the Dive Supervisor on the surface.

We were doing some underwater demolitions training and I was at the end of a work-line, which was reeled out about 10 m/33 ft along the seabed from the shot. This would enable me to locate the work area regardless of the visibility. As I toiled away at my task, giving progress reports to the surface, my helmet began to flood.

And, as I tilted my head back in a vain attempt to raise my gaping mouth and flaring nostrils above the water, I began to feel the talons of fear clawing into my gut.

We are often told in diving not to panic, don't be scared: sage advice, but ultimately worthless. Anyone who tells you they never panic underwater has never almost drowned. I do not mean that they had to bailout, had to find a lost reg, had to swim to their buddy to share gas. I mean they had one crushing breath left in their body and no obvious option for another.

To labor under the delusion that you are somehow impervious to fear and panic is not only naïve, it could ultimately prove to be fatal. I have had people approach me and remark how they can hold their breath, even under stressful conditions for one, two, three minutes.

My record is just over four and a half minutes. And yet, during the times I've had things go wrong, I think I had less than ten seconds to sort the problem out. I also lose IQ points when things are going horribly wrong.

So, if your solution to a potentially lethal problem involves long, complicated reactions, involving dextrous manipulation of your kit in the correct sequence, which takes time to accomplish, you're going to die. What you really want is a big, magic, red button in the center of your chest with "Take Me Home" printed on it. Or, to use the much quoted but still very pertinent phrase, "Keep It Simple, Stupid."

Back in those days, the military and commercial equipment I was using provided no means of self-rescue.

We wore waistcoats full of lead, a weighted helmet, and boots with lead soles. None of which a diver could remove quickly. We were equipped with a 1 L/1 qt bottle containing enough gas to compensate for dry suit squeeze at these depths, but we had no means of controlling buoyancy.

I could still hear the Dive Supervisor's voice asking, "Diver Torbet, are you well?" but, with the microphone underwater, I could not reply. I did try purging the helmet with air, but it made no discernible difference. It may have temporarily dropped the water level but critically not below my nose. So, I did the only thing I could do. I ran.

Doing nothing is never the solution. Ever. If you, having considered the situation, have chosen to do nothing, to wait, to pause any engagement, that is not inaction; it is actively making a decision, albeit a decision to hold any action for the time being.

By "do nothing" I mean to take no action at all, including thinking: to remain a passive observer of the situation directly affecting you and make no choice or decision.

Choose and act. You may choose wrong. You may choose left when you should've chosen right.

But I guarantee this: Standing in the middle of the road with your thumb up your arse is always a bad move. My first course of action should have been to signal the surface with tugs on my air-hose and comms cable, but the weight and length of hose paid out meant they were not detecting my pulls.

So I ran. Not very quickly I admit, considering the situation I faced, but in a panicked slow-motion I pumped my arms and legs across the seabed, hauling on the work-line for purchase and guidance, as I was now effectively blind.

My plan was simple. I would get to the shot line and then haul myself up the 50 m/164 ft of thick rope, bypassing the hour or more of decompression I was due, get to the surface where the lads would rescue me back onto the pontoon, remove the helmet, and I'd be alive.

Bent, but alive.

We never actually found out what went wrong with the equipment, or what would've happened if I had continued with my plan, as the problem self-rectified.

As I reached the shot line, having been "running" in a near-horizontal position, I grabbed the shot line and sharply stood up. Something must have dislodged from the place-where-it-should-never-have-been, because as I thrust that first hand up towards the surface, my helmet cleared.

I heard the Dive Supervisor screaming down through the speaker, "Diver Torbet, are you well?" "Diver well," I replied, before turning around and going back to work. In the calm light of day, sitting down safe and relaxed, and going over this incident, it is clear I wouldn't have made it to the surface in time.

But I got lucky. I shouldn't have needed to.

To what? Get lucky?

This incident highlights a lack of personal control; we have to take responsibility for our own safety. In this example, I had no control over most of the factors keeping me alive, nor had I any mechanism for self-rescue. I was no longer the master of my own destiny, which meant that I was forced to either take no action or take the only action available to me, which was ultimately pointless.

So, over the years, what I've learned during high-risk search and bomb disposal operations—and what I practice now—is how to take something which is innately dangerous, like diving, and make it acceptably safe by attempting to predict and control the risks.

I sit down and think about all the things that can go wrong. Then I work out ways to remove the chance of that risk occurring, or to bring the chances down to acceptable levels, or, if

Photo by Martin Hartley

that is not possible, to have a simple and fast back-up plan ready to go.

An example: my rebreather keeps me alive. If it fails, I die. I can neither eliminate the risk of this occurring completely nor reduce it to such a degree that I will gamble my life on those odds. Although my current CCR has never failed me in all the years I've dived it, I assume it will fail every time I submerge. So I take, as I'm sure we all do, a bailout option to make sure I can get home from the most remote part of the dive. I am scared, I am paranoid.

But I am scared and paranoid before the dive, so when I hit the water I can relax.

We do not save our lives in the moment disaster strikes, but in the hours, days, weeks, months, and years leading up to it. And in that paranoid preparation and planning, I include mitigation against myself. A common thread amongst these diverse chapters will be the humility of these highly competent and experienced divers; I never underestimate my own potential to be a bloody idiot. And don't be fooled into thinking because you've been lucky so far this will continue.

Taking a stroll across a minefield and not getting blown up is not proof it was a clever thing to do. Sometimes people get lucky, sometimes they get unlucky. The trick is to make sure it's irrelevant which hand you're dealt.

Have I had a close call? I have had rebreathers fail, regs fail, lost the line in a cave, suffered silt outs, had to improvise my deco schedule to adjust for lost gases, got stuck, got entangled, got lost, and the list will continue to grow. But I've always had the tools in place to enact at least an imperfect alternative plan and keep myself alive.

I do not consider, for example, having to bail off your rebreather onto your alternative gas source, a situation you have predicted, planned for, and practiced, a close call.

Photos by Martin Hartley

You were never in any danger, and that was down to you.

To summarise all of this in one sentence, I will quote 1513 by Niccolò Machiavelli: "All courses of action are risky, so prudence is not in avoiding danger, it is impossible, but calculating risk and acting decisively"

Put the effort in, over the many years, to arm yourself through training, experience, and planning, injected with a healthy degree of paranoia and humility, rather than putting blind faith in luck.
I dive. I don't roll dice.

Andy Torbet *is a professional cave diver, freediver, climber, skydiver, and outdoorsman. He combines these into an actual job as an explorer, TV presenter, filmmaker, writer, and stuntman.*

After ten years in the British Forces as a Bomb Disposal Officer, diver, and Paratrooper, Andy left to pursue a career in exploration and adventure media.

This has seen him on underwater adventures around the world, including freediving beneath the Alaskan ice, shipwreck diving on Britannic, and global cave diving projects including ice-cave diving in the Arctic.

Out of the water, he stood inside a 700-degree fireball, climbed a 12-story glass building, and jumped out of a plane at 8,500 m/28,000 ft. He is a Fellow of the Royal Geographical Society, The Explorers Club, and represents Team GB at Speed Skydiving.

He has written over 250 articles, one book, and is an amateur father to two young boys.

AUDREY CUDEL

DIRECTOR @ AUDREY CUDEL TECHNICAL LTD
TECHNICAL DIVING INSTRUCTOR / CAVE EXPLORER
UNDERWATER PHOTOGRAPHER

LOCATION OF INCIDENT
YUCATAN PENINSULA, MEXICO

My first visit to the Yucatan Peninsula, Mexico, dated back to 1989 during a winter family holiday dedicated mainly to fulfilling our anthropological curiosity for the ancient Mayan world.

I remember staring at the tranquil, green, opaque surface of Chichén Itzá's "Sacred Cenote" as our guide told stories of the human sacrifices that happened there as a form of worship to the Mayan gods and those mortals who lay beyond this murky surface.

Thirty-one years later, as I was spending yet another winter in Quintana Roo State, Mexico, I received a late-night call from my friend Sabine Sidi-Ali.

A few days earlier she had told me about her current project: she was planning to return to an unexplored cave spotted in Yucatan two months before, and now she was inviting me to join her to see if there was potential for further exploration.

As I hung up the phone, I felt a growing exhilarating sensation, an overwhelming feeling of excitement. I started packing straight away and hardly slept that night. We left early the next morning. The car was packed with enough sidemount cylinders to be self-sufficient for three days at least, since we knew that we would be far from any filling station.

Also packed were various gas mixes that might be required depending on the depths we would find, rebreathers, survey slates and compasses, a line knotting piece of wood, reels, two solid rucksacks to pack all our dive gear, and two transport racks to carry our cylinders to the entrance.

Photos by Audrey Cudel

The location was just three driving hours away, which gave us time to discuss our respective (limited) exploration experience. We would do a dive that same afternoon to decide whether our findings required for us to stay additional days.

Welcomed by the locals who gathered quietly in the town square on a bright sunny afternoon, it was not long before we got introduced to the deputy, who kindly offered to come along with a helper to carry our cylinders to the entrance whilst we transported the rest of our equipment.

The first ride to nowhere always feels too long; the first hike on the dry dusty grounds to reach the cave, even longer.

The entrance consisted of a small, collapsed well where two large hanging wasp nests added to the 'fun' of climbing up and down with all our equipment. We entered a massive section of dry cave and traded snacks and drinks with our carriers as thanks for their patience. About 60 m/198 ft in, heading southeast, a clear, inviting pool of water seemed to mark the start of the upstream part whilst another, larger, murky downstream pool lay thirty meters away on the opposite side.

The limited plan that day was to check whether the upstream access led anywhere at all. Sabine would lay the line while I would check for more leads and document the dive. We would both survey the line on the way out.

Technical dive planning usually involves backup plans and "what if" scenarios. Feeling in a bit of a rush, we skipped this part. So far, the adventure felt similar to any other experience I had experienced in the Mexican jungle.

We tied the first arrow underwater at the beginning of the line and entered an unspoiled environment where all was as pristine and unknown as it was fragile.

A few meters after our descent, we spotted a bunch of round, brown objects, which to my naïve mind looked like coconuts that had rolled down the slope. I began to wonder "how could coconuts roll down that far from above, in a land with no palm trees nearby?"

We moved closer.

To my shock we found ourselves facing nine well-preserved human skulls of different shapes surrounded by other bones: spine, femurs and fibulas. I felt speechless and, briefly, lost all desire to explore any further. Exchanging looks of excitement, we nevertheless decided to move on.

The close call came about thirty meters in. A seemingly promising passage led to a far more restricted silty area. The deeper it went, the narrower it became. As part of the ceiling started breaking down, visibility eventually went down to zero, and Sabine was nowhere to be seen! Even though we were connected through the line, the collapse made it hard to follow.

My brain opened a whole Pandora's box of questions: "What are we doing here?" "Shall I move on or let go and head back?" "To what extent is exploration team or solo work and what should come first: safety or exploration?" "What are the options if she is stuck on the other side of the collapse, unable now to back off?" "Maybe, after all, the skulls were warning signs!"

Remembering that beyond any risk, panic is a cave diver's worst enemy, I decided to move on and push more. After what seemed like an eternity but was actually only a few minutes, I spotted a weak light beam coming towards me. Sabine had managed to find her way back, pushing through what had fallen down. I felt a bit shaken by what had happened and how poorly we had planned; as an instructor and safety diver, proper planning is usually my priority.

Exploration is different. It had affected my focus.

I messed up collecting the first data of our survey. Despite this, we surveyed more inviting passages, laying an additional 135 m/442 ft of line.

Later that night, while knotting line for the next days, we discussed our "Close Call" and how to respond if it were to happen again.

We were no longer exploring solo. We were a team.

We decided to dive more independently, allowing for a more efficient search for new leads and also to avoid the impact of two divers following each other in a potentially collapsing environment.

We agreed to stick to the same range in order to mitigate risk, to rely on separate lines, to keep more distance, and if we did end up facing hazardous situations, to try to deal with them as much as possible on our own.

As the next days went by uneventfully, we felt confident of being able to individually deal with potential dangers. Our exploration progressed more efficiently as well, as we were able to cover more area.

On day two, we collected measurements of the skulls and bones and extended the search for leads which resulted in an additional 177 m/580 ft of new line being laid before we ran out of any apparent passages to move further.

Day three was dedicated to the exploration of the murky downstream part, far too narrow to lay more than 30 m/100 ft of line. Only one skull, some ribs and a few collarbones arose from the thick silty layer. The cave location and data have been communicated to the Archeological authorities.

Beyond fulfilling a childhood dream of seeing the human remains that lay under the Sacred Cenote's murky surface, of going where no one has been before, both the actual and inner-self exploration experience was even more rewarding.

Audrey Cudel *started diving in the south of France in 1994 and became passionate about deep technical diving in 2006. She changed career ten years ago as she got more involved in sidemount, Cave diving training and exploration projects.*

She is also a renowned underwater photographer whose style is known within the technical diving community.

In 2012, she founded one of Malta/Gozo's most famous technical diving facilities, which she ran for seven years before establishing her own company, Audrey Cudel Technical.

After 28 years of diving, she now operates in Egypt, Malta/Gozo, Mexico, Hungary, France, and Spain. Audrey specialises in sidemount essentials, technical sidemount, cave diving training, and related equipment development and trading. She has worked as a safety diver and camera assistant on many technical diving events, including deep diving world record attempts and cave diving documentaries.

She is a brand ambassador and has been actively contributing to various magazines, agencies, and website publications with articles and photography. Her spare time is dedicated to cave exploration, photography/video, and development of diving equipment.

BEATRICE RIVOIRA

PARTNER @ ZERO EMISSIONS
MARINE BIOLOGIST & CCR INSTRUCTOR

LOCATION OF INCIDENT
CAVE COUNTRY, FLORIDA, USA

How do you define a close call?

Is it a situation where you almost died?

A scary moment? Or a situation that could have been fatal had you not reacted in a certain way? Maybe a mix of all these.

When I was asked to write about a close call, I felt uncertain about which one of the different situations I have encountered could be the one to use. Like any diver who has dived for a while in different environments and with different equipment, I have had troubles from time to time. Up to now I have been able to face them, sometimes alone, sometimes with a little help, but all of them made me grow.

So, how to pick up one? In the end, I chose one of my first cave-diving emergencies—one that could have ended up very differently had I lacked the proper training.

I was in Florida for some diving in the cave country. This time, my buddy Nadir and I decided to focus on only one cave to visit some passages that we had not seen yet in our previous trips.

We started the week easily, checking our units, getting confident again with the current and the environment. We did a couple of dives a day, completing different circuits, and progressively moving further into the cave.

The caves were quite crowded during those days, so we tended to move away from the main tunnels; we added one more jump every day or swapped our roles when laying lines to keep practicing.

Photo by Silvano Barboni

On the day in question, we put our bailouts into the water and did our pre-dive checks on the units; everything was working properly. We went through the map once again and discussed our roles, signals, and emergency plans.

I would be the one laying the jumps today. We got into the water, did our last checks together, and started the dive. We swam towards the entrance and waited for another group to exit the cave before going in.

The current was strong, and making our way in was an effort. We left the oxygen and kept swimming until the first junction. We confirmed it to each other, and I laid the jump. In the side tunnel, the current was a little weaker, finally allowing us to catch our breath after the effort of swimming against it for the whole of the way in. The tunnel was big, with rocky walls and a silty bottom; we left one of our bailouts and kept going.

Everything was fine. We swam until we reached the next turning point, and I laid a second jump, always paying attention to the line that someone had already put in place before; evidently another team was ahead of us, probably with the same destination.

We kept going and placed the third jump. The tunnels were getting lower, with more sand and mud on the bottom as, by now, the current had vanished. We could see some silt still suspended, probably due to the team ahead of us swimming by.

We reached the point where we were supposed to attach our reel to keep going and saw another reel not too far away. Obviously going in the same direction we wanted to take as well. The passage was low and the visibility was getting worse.

As we were laying our reel, we saw the team ahead of us coming back and we stopped to let them pass.

Visibility was now quite bad.

After the second jump, we had not had many changes in depth, but I kept manually adding some diluent in order to breathe comfortably, like a second nature. All the values on the unit were fine, and I was so focused on doing a good job with the lines and not lifting the silt that I failed to notice how frequently I was adding it.

We had just gotten through a very narrow passage under a boulder when Nadir asked me if we wanted to keep going or not, as the visibility was now bad.

The feeling that something was not quite right started to tickle my mind, and I called it. My buddy was ahead of me, fingers around the line, he passed under the boulder once again, and I followed.

Suddenly came a breath that was definitely too wet and I knew what was soon going to happen. Unfortunately I was in a bad position to be able to work on the loop properly without stirring up everything even more, so I checked the handset, took another short breath, held it and quickly moved towards the wall where I knew I would have a bit more open space. I could clearly feel the water in the loop now. My side on the wall, I clipped the reel, took my bailout, emptied the loop and made a diluent flush on the unit.

Everything seemed fine again.

The loop was dry, I could breathe, and values were stable. I caught up with my buddy who was waiting for me on the line, and we kept moving towards the exit. I had not even reached the start of our reel when the loop started flooding again and, this time it was much faster.

As we were close, I called Nadir; he took the reel whilst I quickly moved to the front and felt water with the distinctive acidic taste in my mouth. This time the loop simply sank as soon as I took it out of my mouth. Values were not good anymore, and my breath had definitely gotten shorter and quicker.

The whole unit was completely flooded and was not an option anymore.

At this point, we were almost at our furthermost point inside the cave, with bad visibility, silty bottom, and one reel. Three jumps ahead of us at the maximum depth till the gold line, my deco was getting longer every minute, and my SAC (Surface Air Consumption) rate was now higher than usual. And I was definitely aware of all that.

Nadir kept watching me closely until I was on my proper bailout, then he said: "Are you ok? Let's exit".

No need for extra communication.

All bailout and emergency procedures kicked into place like a well-oiled machine, our exchange in roles was smooth, and we started exiting in a quick but controlled manner.

I focused on keeping my breathing under control, and it took several long minutes to slow it down, as I had probably built up quite a lot of CO2.

We finally reached the main tunnel where the current was now helping us to exit, but it was also annoying, as every time that we had to do a deco stop, it was pushing us further up.

After a couple of hours of deco, done in every crevice we could find, and several bailout switches later, we finally exited the water. Me, with a massive headache and a bunch of well-used bailouts.

Later, when we examined my gear, we found a cut, about the width of a fingertip, in the counterlung. The cause was a metal bar that had become uncovered and slowly abraded the plastic every time I exhaled.

When the unit failed, every fibre of my body was focused on getting us out safely and not leaving space for any more mistakes. Units do fail, and we do as well, but our training, along with clear communication and proper bailout

planning, made the situation almost easy to handle—but not less stressful.

If you are prepared, then an incident like this will probably end as something to chat about while drinking a beer.

If you are not, it may become worse than just a close call.

Beatrice Rivoira *is an Italian professional scuba diver with a Master's Degree in Marine Biology and Oceanography.*

She started diving at 14 following in her brother and father's footsteps and is now an OC & CCR technical instructor.

She keeps on travelling around the world to dive in different environments and always keeps an eye on the natural features and inhabitants of these wonderful places. She then shares her experiences on environmental education projects, hoping to inspire more and more young people to protect and discover the natural beauties of our world.

She has co-authored a book about Mediterranean Sea biology,Biodiving: Environments and Organisms of the Mediterranean with Francesca Notari, contributed to several other texts, and translated different diving texts into Italian to help spread the knowledge in her country.

In 2013, she joined ZeroEmissions, with which she continues to teach and educate. In 2014, she became a member of the Fourth Element Dive Team.

BECKY KAGAN SCHOTT

PROFESSIONAL PHOTOGRAPHER & VIDEOGRAPHER
TECHNICAL DIVING INSTRUCTOR

LOCATION OF INCIDENT
LAKE SUPERIOR, MI, USA

I've been actively diving in the Great Lakes for ten years, trying to capture powerful imagery of its many shipwrecks. Back in 2017, I had planned a fun trip with my dive buddy up to Isle Royale National Park, a 65 km/40 mi long island in Lake Superior.

It's not an easy location to get to, and there was only one charter to take us there.

It was 25 hours of driving from where I live to get to the location where the boat was docked.

My buddy and I spent all summer doing work-up dives in 3° C/37.4° F water and diving deeper wrecks to prepare. We chose to do this trip in September because it takes a long time for Northern Lake Superior to get thermoclines, which are more comfortable to do decompression in after a deep dive.

The wreck I most wanted to see was that of the S.S. Kamloops, a ship with a tragic story that I was very drawn to.

In late November 1927, the S.S Kamloops was dispatched up the lakes carrying a mixed cargo from Montreal to Thunder Bay, and the last time she was seen was at dusk on December 6, coated in ice and steaming north in a heavy storm.

A search had begun on December 12, but neither the ship nor the 22 men and women aboard were seen alive again.

It wasn't until June the following year that some of the bodies were found on a nearby island, meaning they had survived the shipwreck only to die horribly from exposure in a harsh winter on land.

Photos by Becky Kagan Schott

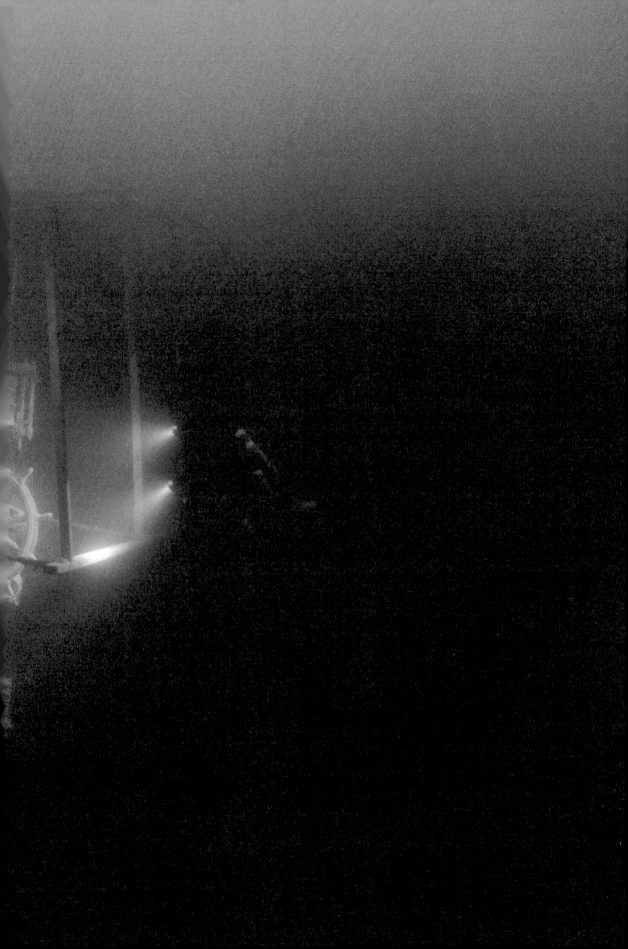

A tragic message in a bottle was also found from Alice Bettridge, the last survivor. The location of the S.S. Kamloops remained a mystery until 1977, when the vessel was discovered northwest of Isle Royale, lying at an angle on her starboard side in 83 m/272 ft of dark water.

She still had her mixed cargo of fencing, toothpaste, shoes, and life savers in the holds! A body was also discovered inside the engine room and remains there respectfully today.

I pride myself on trying to photograph shipwrecks and bring their stories to life so that they are not forgotten, but I also endeavour to capture the mood and feeling of the place.

I expected the Kamloops to be dark with little to no ambient light, but I still wanted to get a wider perspective of the wreck, so I was diving with two other people to help me achieve this goal. I had planned these shots for years in my mind, and I was excited to finally get the chance to make them come true.

We pulled up to the site and prepared for our first dive of the trip. I could see the large rock wall near us and knew the wreck was at the bottom of it. We had to gear up one at a time on the transom of the boat due to space and then clip our bailouts in the water.

At the -6 m/-20 ft bubble check, my buddy and I looked at each other as the water should have been a toasty 21 C/70 F, but instead it was much colder, at 6° C/43° F. A storm had come through the previous days, and an upwelling must have brought colder water up to the surface.

We decided with a few signals to cut the dive time down so we would have a shorter deco obligation. It was a successful dive, but we didn't accomplish everything as a consequence of cutting it short.

Sunrise came and my buddy offered me the extra heated vest she had brought as backup.

It was a great idea due to the water temperature and the long two-hour dives. I had all of the right connectors for my drysuit, but it wasn't a vest I had used before. I wore the heated vest under my normal undergarments, zipped it up and put my drysuit on.

It was tight but I figured it would feel better once I got in the water. Normally I would never do a serious dive with a new piece of equipment without testing it on a shallower dive first. But this time, I did.

We geared up and did our pre-breathing while sitting on the back of the boat. The water was a bit more bouncy than the previous day. I jumped in and swam quickly towards my bailout bottles. Unfortunately, because of the current they were getting pushed under our boat.

I felt my breathing increase as I worked to get my bottles out from under the boat and clipped onto me, while trying to not get taken away by the current. I was breathing heavily but I assumed I would catch my breath during our bubble check.

As I descended down on the line, I felt a squeeze in my chest. I asked my buddies to hold on for a minute, but wasn't sure how to communicate what was going on. After a couple of minutes I told them I was okay, and we descended all the way to the stern of the Kamloops.

When we got there, the squeeze was unbearable. I felt like I couldn't breathe at all. The wreck was dark and spooky, adding to my anxiety.

I clipped my camera on, did a diluent flush and put a lot of extra air into my drysuit trying to relieve the overwhelming crushing sensation.

My buddies did what they were supposed to do and started to get ready for the shot I was planning to capture. I pushed myself and decided to stay close to the line for a few minutes just breathing.

I gently swam around gathering myself; when I passed by the open skylight to the engine room I could see the faint white part of the corpse still inside, sending haunting chills down my spine.

I looked at my computer.

I was ten minutes into the dive. I signaled to my buddies that I wasn't okay and gave them the thumbs up.

They knew me well enough after all of our diving together and understood that something wasn't right. I wasn't sure how to explain to them that I couldn't breathe well. I temporarily bailed out, trying to get some full breaths of gas and went back to my loop.

As we ascended, it didn't get better. It was the most agonizing decompression I've ever had to do. I just focused on my breathing and putting gas into my drysuit hoping it would relieve the crushing sensation, but it didn't. I never even turned on the vest!

I finished my deco, clipped my tanks on the line, and could barely get up the ladder and over the transom. I was so out of breath, my lungs hurt. I unzipped my suit and undergarment.

I never thought that adding just an extra layer would have resulted in such an awful surprise. There is nothing worse than feeling like you can't breathe with no way to solve that in the water. That was my last dive on the Kamloops that trip and my last dive using that particular borrowed heated vest. The wreck isn't going anywhere.

I ignored my own rule, which is to always try new gear on a shallow dive with no deco before taking it on a serious dive.

In this case, it was a cascade of issues from the current, the workload, and the extra layer with no stretch.

I am grateful I had dive buddies that supported

me the whole time and that I decided to call the dive when I did.

It could have been a lot worse. It's always okay to call a dive!

Becky Kagan Schott *is a five-time Emmy award winning underwater cameraman and photographer whose work appears on major networks including National Geographic, Discovery Channel, and Red Bull.*

She specializes in capturing images in extreme underwater environments including caves, under ice, and deep shipwrecks. Her projects have taken her all over the world from the Arctic to the Antarctic and many exciting locations in between.

She's filmed new wreck discoveries, cave exploration, and even cageless diving with great white sharks. She's earned a reputation for being able to bring back quality imagery from harsh conditions. Her biggest passion is shooting haunting images of deep shipwrecks in the Great Lakes. She combines her artistic style with powerful stories of tragedy, mystery, and survival to ignite the viewers' imagination. She's constantly pushing the limits and trying new techniques to capture the beauty of the underwater world. She's a frequent contributor to several dive magazines, and her photography has been used in books, museums, and advertising.

Becky has been actively diving for 26 years and technical diving for 22 of them. She has been an instructor for two decades and is currently an active TDI Mixed Gas CCR Instructor. She leads expeditions all over the world.

BRETT B. HEMPHILL

KARST UNDERWATER RESEARCH/KUR

LOCATION OF INCIDENT
EAGLES NEST, SPRING HILL, FLORIDA, USA

It was 1998, and Trimix certification had only been available in recreational diving for approximately two years. At that time, I had already been cave-certified for just over eight years.

Deep air-diving during this period was widely practiced and accepted. Many divers additionally believed that certain levels of nitrogen narcosis could be managed by repetitive dive tolerance training and concentration.

I had just purchased my first aluminium hull, ride-on DPV. After several scooter dives in shallow caves, I had contacted one of my cave diving partners named Bill. We both decided to take the DPV to a deep cave system known as Eagles Nest. We had accomplished dozens of what we considered "successful deep air-dives" in this cave.

We were both excited, knowing that this DPV was designed for deeper depths that would have easily crushed our shallow water recreational DPVs. Because we had swum to the first upstream super-room several times in the past, we decided scootering to this location was within our experience level.

We also decided it would be acceptable for me to tow Bill, as the DPV had more than enough power for this task. As we began to scooter across the pond our confidence started to rise. Beginning our descent, we reached the 2.5 m/8.2 ft diameter limestone solution tube. Exiting this chimney, we were at 24 m/79 ft, hovering on the ceiling of a massive cavern. With the top of the debris cone still nearly 30 m/98 ft below us, we made one final check of our logistical systems and began rocketing downward.

Photo by Matt Vinzant

Reaching a depth of 50 m/164 ft, we could clearly see the upstream cave guideline below us, sloping away into the darkness. As we struggled to clear our ears and maintain buoyancy during this rapid descent, I quickly glanced at my digital depth gauge—we were already passing 60 m/196 ft.

Unlike the gradually-elevating narcosis I had felt during our past swim dives, my senses were now being slammed by an unmanageable narcotic wave.

No amount of stamina or managing my mental focus could undo the chain of events that were unfolding.

People often say time slows down moments before a tragedy. I'm looking at my depth gauge for the last time, 80 m/262 ft.

Shut off DPV, I'm losing my peripheral vision!
Where's the guideline?
Tunnel vision now, unclipping DPV, which way is up?

Photo by Kirill Egorov

Where's Bill?
Lights disappearing, where's the guideline?
I can't see!
Oh my god, I can't see!
Holding light up to my eyes, still no vision.
I'm not unconscious, I'm blind!

I wish I could say I was able to keep myself from panicking, but that was not the case. As adrenaline shot through my body and mixed with the narcosis, my only thought was, "God, I don't want to die."

Seconds later, I collided into the upward slope of the cavern debris mound. The force of the impact knocked my second stage out of my mouth. A brief surge of water hit my lungs along with dirt and small pebbles. As I choked and gasped, some small still-cognizant part of my mind yelled, "There's a regulator around your neck on a lanyard!"

I found it, whether by muscle memory or just plain luck, but it did not reduce the fight-or-flight response that had me in its absolute control.

Then, suddenly, I became very still.

My pleas for God to save me stopped and my mind turned to thoughts of my wife and two children. An overwhelming sense of peace filled me, replacing the panic and fear.

A high-pitched ringing resonated in my ears, and I felt the sensation that I was rapidly ascending. The sound of gas rushing out of my over-inflated buoyancy compensator disrupted my brief moment of euphoria as a pinhole of light opened in my eyes.

Within seconds I broke the surface of the water. I remember there being some combination of yelling, crying, and brief laughter before the feelings of responsibility to my friend Bill had me submerging once again into the darkness.

I located Bill swimming to the top of the debris mound with my DPV in hand.

Following the dive, Bill explained that he too had suffered from the same momentary blindness but managed to let go of the DPV and grab the cave guideline at about 65 m/213 ft, as I kept scootering downwards.

Brett B Hemphill *is the current President of Karst Underwater Research. This non-profit group currently maintains multiple permits in the state of Florida for cave documentation and science.*

For over 30 years, with the support and companionship of family, friends, and team members, Brett Hemphill has assisted in exploring, mapping, and documenting many of the deepest, longest, and most unique, underwater cave systems in the United States.

In 2008, KUR team broke the United States deep underwater cave record at Weeki Wachee Springs in the state of Florida. Then, five years later, once again the U.S. record was set in Texas at Phantom Springs at just over 142 m/465 ft deep and nearly 2.5 km/1.5 mi back. Additional exploration and research locations include: Florida gulf coast, Missouri, Bahamas, Cay Sal Banks, Dominican Republic, and Yucatan Peninsula.

Brett speaks regularly on a variety of topics, chiefly: aquifer and cave conservation, exploration logistics, including application and safety for overhead environment equipment usage. He consults and designs underwater cave equipment for exploration use.

CHRIS JEWELL QGM

CAVE DIVER / BRISTOL EXPLORATION CLUB (BEC) / CAVE
DIVING GROUP (CDG) & BRITISH CAVE RESCUE COUNCIL
(BCRC)

LOCATION OF INCIDENT
WOOKEY HOLE – SOMERSET, UK

I've been cave diving since 2006, and I am what is normally referred to as a 'sump diver'; this means that I'm also a caver and that most of my cave diving starts a long way inside 'dry' caves.

I am equally at home underwater and above water, crawling and climbing through caves. Very often I use cave diving simply as a way to pass flooded sections of cave in order to visit dry passages beyond. It is also very common for UK sump divers to dive solo, as is the case in this story.

The closest cave to where I live in Somerset is Wookey Hole; this is a multi-sump cave, which means that to reach the final sump it is necessary to pass several other underwater sections of cave interspersed with dry passages. The current end of Wookey Hole is an 89 m/292 ft in the final sump, a point only

reached by Rick Stanton and John Volanthen in 2005.

In the early part of 2018, I began staging gear for several deep dives over the summer. However, the Thai cave rescue interrupted everything, and after we returned from Thailand, I then managed to hurt my back.

I spent several frustrating weeks waiting to recover until finally at the beginning of September, everything aligned. I had my equipment staged in the cave, I had a team of 'sherpas' to help me, and diving conditions were good.

We made the journey through the multiple underwater passages and dry chambers of Wookey until our team reached chamber 24, a dry and spacious section of cave where equipment had been staged.

Photo by Stu Gardiner

Due to the depth and dimensions of the underwater passage, I was using a custom, self-made, side mount rebreather.

I think side mount rebreathers always have compromises in their design and construction; I had used this rebreather on several previous deep dives at Wookey and elsewhere, and felt that I understood the unit's limitations.

After leaving surface in chamber 24, I made the short dive alone to chamber 25. The chamber itself is little more than a large air bell, but you are forced to surface here. From this point, the cave descends steeply down to its final limit at 89 m/292 ft.

Part of the reason that so few people have visited the absolute end of Wookey hole are the two deep restrictions underwater: the first is a gravel slope at 65 m/213 ft, which must be dug through before descending. Pushing the gravel out of the way in a low passage can take some time, and decompression penalties mount quickly at this depth.

Beyond the gravel slope, a boulder choke at 70 m/229 ft is then encountered.

When Rick Stanton and John Volanthen first found the choke, they had to use a lift bag to move rocks and engineer a route through. That was in 2006, and no one has been past this point since. When I arrived here, I inspected the hole and began inserting my legs into the gap. It was clear very quickly that to progress any further would require serious commitment and the removal of some cylinders. Deciding that this was enough for today and that I already had a very long decompression obligation, I started to head out of the cave.

After completing many stops on the way up, I finally reached the bottom of the shaft up to surface in chamber 25. After clearing my 9 m/30 ft stop, I settled in for a long, boring hang at 6 m/20 ft. One of the design compromises with my side mount rebreather is that there is only a very minimal water trap in the single counter lung.

This means that on long dives like this one, much of the condensation and saliva tends to end up in the scrubber. After approximately a two hour stop at 6 m/20 ft, both my computers gave me the all clear to ascend. I knew we needed to get the bailout cylinders out of the water today, so at this point I picked up a 10 ltr steel of 50% O2 and ascended slowly. I surfaced briefly in chamber 25 and stood up.

As I did so, I found it was, oddly, very difficult to breathe through the rebreather, which was now vertical. I was tired and cold and didn't think much of this, so I dived down again. Once horizontal in the water, the rebreather seemed fine, and so I continued out of the cave. Following the line downward, I ended up in a head-down position.

Then as I manoeuvred through the cave, I suddenly got what, at first, I thought was a mouthful of water. Then the burning started, and I realised it was a very nasty caustic cocktail. I grabbed the deep bailout regulator, which was clipped around my neck, but got a mouthful of water mixed with air, and I knew instantly that there was gravel under the diaphragm. Now my need to breathe was even greater, and the burning sensation was getting worse.

That steel 10 ltr tank of 50% was chest mounted with the regulator sitting right on top. Snatching this, I pushed the purge button hard before taking a deep breath. I had gas and plenty of it, but every breath was burning agony. I gulped several large deep breaths and tried to compose myself.

Fortunately, it was not very far to the surface in chamber 24 and my waiting team.

Taking a tight grip on the line, I swam quickly towards the surface whilst every breath continued to burn my mouth and throat. Once back on the surface, I rinsed my mouth over and over with cave water to try to remove the taste and burning sensation. Although it helped a little, the journey out from chamber 24 was still an uncomfortable one.

Photo by Richard Stevenson

Once at home, I inspected the rebreather for any leaks but found none, so I believe I simply got a mouthful of my own saliva, which was incredibly caustic as it had dwelt in the scrubber for several hours.

Standing upright in chamber 25 and then getting into a head-down position had allowed the liquid to move around the loop and into my mouth.

That is a mistake I won't be making again! Luckily, I had no permanent damage to my throat and mouth. Oh, and yes, I'll always ensure that I have two bailout regulators handy!

Chris Jewell *is an exploratory caver and cave diver who explores new cave passages in the UK and abroad. He's been leading successful cave diving expeditions since 2009, alongside his career in IT.*

Since then, his explorations have had him squeezing through tiny, muddy, underwater holes in Somerset, digging underwater in the Yorkshire Dales, and leading cave diving expeditions to Spain and Mexico.

In 2013, his international team of more than 40 cavers established the Huautla cave system as the deepest in the Western hemisphere.

The experience and knowledge gained through these expeditions led to his involvement in the dramatic rescue of 12 boys and their football coach from a flooded cave in Thailand in 2018.

CRAIG CHALLEN

CAVE EXPLORER

LOCATION OF INCIDENT
ROCKINGHAM, WESTERN AUSTRALIA

Amongst the general public, the image of technical diving in general, and cave diving in particular, seems to be that it is an extreme pursuit undertaken by a few, select, thrill-seeking individuals who take their lives in their hands every time they go into the water.

It is true that things can go wrong and that accidents do happen, sometimes with the worst possible outcome of a person dying, but these accidents are rarely the result of some uncontrollable, external factor coming to surprise the diver. Rather, they are almost without exception caused by fundamental, and usually fairly obvious, errors.

Worst of all, the risk of these errors does not necessarily reduce over time, as the extra safety that comes with experience is offset by the danger that comes with overconfidence, familiarity, and complacency.

I started technical diving in the late 1990s. It was a hugely exciting time, during the so-called 'technical diving revolution,' when it seemed that there was a new innovation, item of equipment, or ground-breaking dive almost every week. Front and centre of these innovations were rebreathers, which captured my attention as soon as I heard about them. After playing around with a semi-closed rebreather for six months, I bought a Prism Topaz rebreather and set about getting some experience on it.

One day I was going to do a routine practice dive in the ocean; I headed to the beach at Rockingham, south of Perth, and carried my gear down to the water. This beach has a wide shallow area of less than 1 m/3 ft deep that extends to about 50 m/164 ft from the shore, so you have a bit of a surface swim before you can dive.

After getting in the water and putting all my gear on, I discovered to my frustration that I had left my mask in the car back up at the carpark. So, off with all the gear, walk back up to collect my mask, and back down to the water again to repeat the gearing up process. About half an hour later I'm ready to go again.

The Prism rebreather is a fairly conventional electronic closed-circuit rebreather (CCR). Of importance to this story, it has an analogue secondary display and a head-up primary display that attaches to the top of the dive-surface valve.

The secondary meter runs directly off the voltage produced by the oxygen cells, which has the advantage that it will work even when the electronics are switched off or dysfunctional. The primary display uses LEDs to display the measured partial pressure of oxygen in the breathing loop.

It is powered by the electronics which are switched on by means of an external power switch that is usually located at the bottom of the over-the-shoulder counterlungs.

I checked the secondary display which was reading 0.7 atm, perfectly acceptable for a surface swim. Because I was on the surface in the bright sunlight, I was unable to see the LEDs on the primary display properly, but I was determined that I would watch the secondary instead for the five minutes or so before I expected to submerge.

Starting the swim, I found myself in choppy conditions due to a brisk wind and got distracted by trying to keep a constant heading to my destination. In what seemed like a very short space of time, my vision closed in and I felt suddenly light-headed.

Photo by Simon Mitchell

Looking at my secondary display I saw the oxygen PP was down below 0.1 atm, and I quickly hit the manual oxygen to restore.

At that level I must have been very close to unconsciousness; I was extremely lucky that I recognised the signs, which were quick and quite subtle. A few more seconds and I could easily have been unconscious and drowned in shallow water.

What went wrong?

When I had doffed my dive gear to return and get my mask, I had apparently switched the rebreather electronics off. Upon gearing up for the second time I had failed to follow the normal procedure, which included checking to be sure the electronics were switched on and working. Because the electronics were not operating, the oxygen injection solenoid, I was completely dependent on watching the secondary display and manually injecting oxygen–a process which was susceptible to the distractions of navigating whilst swimming on the surface.

This is an embarrassing and stupid series of events that could have ended in catastrophe, but also that could have been averted so easily by following proper procedure.

In another part of my life I am a pilot. When flying, I religiously use checklists and follow laid-down procedures; it is part of the culture of aviation. And yet curiously, when diving, I am far more lax about checklists. I cannot properly explain this; clearly I am the same person with the same risk tolerance and undertaking just as risky an activity, but if we want to avoid silly accidents, then this is a lesson we have to learn.

Other fields of endeavour have learnt the value of checklists from aviation, most notably medicine, with impressive results. It doesn't mean having to work through pages-long lists with dozens of items; on the contrary, well-designed checklists have only the minimum number of necessary items on

them. For example: my final pre-dive checklist that I quickly run through before submerging addresses only the things that will kill me on the dive. Are my oxygen and diluent turned on, is my bailout regulator working, are my primary and secondary displays working, is my wing inflator working?

This is what works for me, not necessarily what is going to be right for you, but I urge you to think about this and adopt the principle. If so, we will all live long lives with many more dives.

Craig Challen *is an Australian technical diver and cave explorer. After commencing cave diving in the 1990s, he was an early adopter of then rapidly-developing technologies such as closed-circuit mixed-gas rebreathers.*

He has explored caves throughout Australia and New Zealand, as well as in China, Thailand, Vanuatu, and the Cook Islands.

Craig also has an avid interest in shipwreck diving and has explored sites over the last 15 years in the South China Sea, Solomon Islands, Australia, New Zealand, the Mediterranean Sea, Thailand, Malaysia, and Indonesia. Craig is additionally an enthusiastic helicopter and aeroplane pilot.

In July 2018, Craig participated in the Tham Luang cave rescue of 13 people in Thailand. For his contribution he was awarded the Star of Courage and the Medal of the Order of Australia. He was named as the 2019 Australian of the Year jointly with his long-standing dive partner Richard Harris.

Photo by Heather Endall

CRISTINA ZENATO

CAVE EXPLORER / ADVANCED CAVE DIVING INSTRUCTOR
SIDEWINDER REBREATHER INSTRUCTOR
MEMBER OF THE WOMEN DIVERS HALL OF FAME
EXPLORERS CLUB FELLOW

LOCATION OF INCIDENT
THEO'S WRECK, SOUTH GRAND BAHAMA ISLAND

It was 1996, and I was a year and a half into becoming an open water instructor. Furthermore, I had already discovered the presence of caves on the island, fueling my dream to become a full cave diver and explore further. At the time, I was working for a company that didn't believe in the use of any gas mix but air; these were the years when EANx (Enriched Air Nitrox) made its way into the mainstream market, and that market rejected it as the most dangerous innovation ever introduced in the scuba industry.

My adventure buddy and I shared the desire to become technical divers and decided to experiment with EANx mixing on our own, after reading some literature on the subject. We created blends to allow us extended bottom time on some of the local recreational dives such as Theo's Wreck, at 30 m/100 ft of depth. We were also thinking about doing some dives off the ledge near Theo's Wreck to increase our tolerance of nitrogen narcosis.

On the day of the incident we were able to join a boat of divers heading out for a Theo's Wreck night dive, the pinnacle of night dives at the time. We had completed that dive many times and were always in awe of its beauty and colours. Finding ways to practice diving deeper was not easy; we had to join whichever boat was heading there without the complicating factor of guests onboard.

We decided we would use this opportunity to complete a deeper dive off the shelf. On our back, air was the gas of choice; for our additional tank we blended an eighty percent mix to use during our decompression. In the waning light we reached the wreck, secured our "decompression" and additional gas to it, and continued to a depth of 44 m/144 ft.

We didn't stay long, but we checked the shelf for nocturnal creatures and some unique finds. With twelve minutes bottom time and a screaming computer, we decided to start our ascent.

When we reached what should have been the wreck's location, we realised that we had not come back to the same place.

Darkness and narcosis had caused us to drift off our references. We ascended, but we could not find the wreck and more to the point, our additional tanks. We searched for a few minutes before realising the futility of the attempt; finally we decided that there was no option but to complete our ascent and decompression with just the remaining air in our tanks.

Photo by Curt Bowen

We didn't finish the required decompression stops; the lightness of our tanks and the lack of the planned-for enriched mix forced us to surface with more than ten minutes of required decompression remaining.

We surfaced about 50 m/164 ft from the boat, secured by mooring to the 63 m/206 ft long wreck and swam toward it.

We climbed back on the empty vessel, the rest of the divers still coming up on the line. We ditched our gear and sat on the deck in wide-eyed terror, thinking about the bubbles undoubtedly forming in our system, decompression illness (the bends) creeping through our blood to stop in as-yet-unknown places.

When the rest of the divers surfaced, we recounted our story; with frowns and disappointing looks, they gave us access to the oxygen kit.

When we got back, we decided to spend the night in the same place so that we could check on each other regularly. We drank water and orange juice through the night, and kept on monitoring for those signs that never came.

On that day, we learned many lessons. The fundamental one that guided me through the rest of my career to this current day was: training. Sure, we had read everything there was to read, but we had missed the fundamentals of hands-on experience. That incident launched my resolution to become a trained and competent cave diver—a modern Technical Diver.

Within a few months I had travelled from the island—where there were no available instructors—to Florida, there to embark on my training for full cave diver, advanced Nitrox and decompression procedures. I also learned something else that I always share with my instructors' candidates: it is human nature to venture beyond our limits, to test the extent of our capabilities.

Progress in our diving world has been made through the actions and attempts of those before us; we need to learn from them and from their mistakes.

If one day we become those who will pave the way for others, it is equally important to know that if we commit mistakes, we pause and learn from them.

Cristina Zenato *is an ocean and cave explorer, a shark expert, speaker, writer, and conservationist. She has been a professional diver since 1994.*

Among her qualifications are the following: she is a course director, an advanced cave diving instructor, and a mixed gas and rebreather instructor. She shares her time between teaching at professional and technical levels, working with sharks, exploring and mapping underwater cave systems, and her own continuing education.

Her current projects include interactive and 3D cave maps, photography, and videography of the uncharted areas in the Bahamas.

In 2019, she founded the non-profit organisation, People of the Water (www.pownonprofit.org), which she created to broaden the conduct and distribution of training, education, research, and studies relating to water, ocean, and environmental issues affecting the people and animals of those environments. After twenty-six years in this career, she is still diving and pushing the boundaries of our knowledge.

DANIELE PONTIS

FOUNDER OF BLUFORIA DIVE CENTER / KISS REBREATHER
ITALIAN DEALER / KISS CCR INSTRUCTOR
TRIMIX INSTRUCTOR/ CCR IT / CAVE INSTRUCTOR

LOCATION OF INCIDENT
SARDINIA CAVE, ITALY

I will not begin my story by telling you where I was, how old, and when. My priorities were different, I was different. Not unhappy, but hungry.

All I recall is this hunger.

I was ambitious, I wanted more and more every day. Every day one step closer to who I wanted to be and yet so far from the goals that I had set for myself, and that made me reckless.

I violently made my way in this world, thinking that I had to prove myself to others that never believed in me and never believed in my vision.

I was on my path, I knew it, and looking back I still think that I was—the only thing wrong was my mindset.

I rushed into things, blinded by my ambition to reach levels of experience that should take years to develop. The dives I made in those times were really risky, and I get goosebumps just thinking about it. I used to work solo, as I had no one that I could rely on as a dive buddy.

The only other person who sometimes took part in my dives was a skipper, a friend, that stayed on the boat while I was in the caves. My setup of choice was a rebreather on an open circuit side-mount arrangement, and I planned every dive thoroughly.

But not 'that' day. That day something went differently.

I was overly cocky, too confident in what I was doing, too confident in my abilities. I underestimated the exploration that I was about to undertake.

Photos by Mariona Yepes Daviu

Driven by boat to the chosen point by my pal, I jumped into this new cave that I desired to explore.

Two hours of complex and unfamiliar navigation passed, and I started having the sensation of something going wrong—dampness in my mouth that I supposed had something to do with the temperature in the cave, the intense use of the rebreather, or my breath.

Still, I kept going, completing five spools of navigation—even using the safety reel... it was madness, a mad man's choice.

I didn't adopt a correct dive plan—not that I had one that day—I just felt invincible. After a jump, I changed direction, diving deeper into a chimney. The downward-facing position poured a cocktail of sodium hydroxide into my mouth, and excruciating pain struck me.

My rebreather was flooded.

My first response was to take the breather out of my mouth and get to the open circuit tanks. It hurt like hell, and the chemical burns in my oral cavity didn't let me breathe properly.

Every sip of air was torture and my head began to spin. Where was I? I had to get out of there. My breathing increased, and the feelings intensified. I kept moving back and kept being confused. I couldn't find the right way out! I started to realise what I had done. How I could be so stupid, how I could have made such errors? I started to hate myself, and I began to hate the cave.

Why was I there? Why wasn't I with my daughter, why didn't I have the love I always desired, why was I so miserable?

In the rock labyrinths, where I had previously felt invincible. Suddenly, I was insignificant.

The perception of danger that I had, the small value of it, led me to that point.

I didn't love myself, I wasn't happy, and I started to understand that I had done something disastrous, something fucked up. I attempted again to find the route back, trying to remain calm, to reason a little. In the cave, the only sound was my gasping breath, every stingy breath of air reminding me that my time would be over at some point soon.

I only had two tanks, having left a stage a few meters from the exit of the cave.

Blinded by pain, my thoughts became heavy. Why was I crying? I wouldn't see my little girl grow up, and for what? It was the cave's fault, I was convinced. In despair, in madness, I began to blame the system that had welcomed me.

I was falling apart, I was insane, alienated. I could not find a solution, thinking that the cave was making me go round in circles. Only later, I realised that I was moving back and forth. I swam, I swam and I breathed. I didn't consult the instruments I had, I wasn't focusing. I took in a final breath from the first tank, passing to the second.

With that familiar gesture, my cold rationality took up space for a second, and I held on to that. I was lucid. I was calming down. I was driving away the negative thoughts, pushing away the image of my daughter, my love, and the things I could lose—things that I wouldn't accomplish.

Breathe.

Tenacious, I did not abandon myself to insanity anymore. I looked around, reconstructing a mental map, trying to distinguish the shapes of the cave.

With 50 bar/725 psi in the tank, the anguish rose again. I threw myself on a branch to the right, following what maybe was instinct, maybe survival force. Pointing the torch in front of me, I saw a white item. My spool, my number one spool.

I was on the mainline. How did I get there?

Where were all the others? I had come back through a place I had never seen, that I had not marked.

I rewound the jump line, getting back to the main, just to find the stage bottle that I left. I had 20 bar/290 psi left in the tank.

I managed to get out, reaching the dinghy where my friend, unaware of everything, had fallen asleep. When I touched land, I did not leave her for weeks. And I thought and I thought back over what had happened. From that day on, from that dive, I revolutionised myself, my way of getting into the water. I reworked my way of training.

Today, to my divers, I pass a different awareness, a responsibility that I have never abandoned again, just as I have never abandoned my caves.

Daniele Pontis *began diving in 1999. He subsequently abandoned his main career to commit himself completely to training other divers, developing innovative training procedures early-on.*

After some trips and training in places like Central America and Africa, he returned to Sardinia to found his own center, Bluforia. Since then, he has devoted himself to the underwater caves of the area, and to the training of technical diving using OC and CCR.

DAVID STRIKE

DIVING WRITER & RESEARCHER

LOCATION OF INCIDENT
NORTH SEA

In the early seventies, the heavy demand for divers to work on North Sea gas and oil platforms exceeded supply.

Wages were high. So was the diver mortality rate.

Confronted by a harsh environment and difficulties not previously encountered elsewhere in the world, many diving contractors found it more expedient to employ people with military diving experience. Their training would, it was believed, give the divers a survival edge.

As one of eight divers, I joined a team of other ex-military personnel with the contract to service all of one large oil company's offshore platforms and rigs. Based on a roster system of two weeks on the rig and one week ashore, there were always five divers on call.

On one occasion, we were employed in fitting anti-scouring devices to the legs of a drill platform almost midway between the UK and Holland, an area subject to strong tidal currents. Surface Demand Diving Equipment was not at that time mandatory, and it was standard practice to choose equipment based on the job in hand.

On this occasion, our equipment consisted of twin tanks; single-hose, up-stream regulators with an SPG, (no Alternate Air Sources.) No BCD's. In any event, our collective 'wisdom' suggested that they would only prove a bloody nuisance. And for thermal protection, we wore 6.5mm wetsuits. Normal practice was to dive in two separate sticks. The first three divers—standing in a purpose-built steel basket—would be lowered into the water by crane from the platform's deck.

Photos by David Strike

After decompressing on a buoyed line, the divers would return to this basket and be hauled back up to the platform deck. The remaining two divers were quickly briefed on the work status, and the process was then repeated.

On a Sunday morning, my buddy and I–already dressed in wetsuits–looked down from the platform's deck as the first three divers left the basket. A short while later one of the divers surfaced.

Struggling to reach the safety line that trailed from the basket, he appeared to be losing headway. Reacting to the situation, I grabbed a mask, weight belt, and fins, slid down the ladders to the lower catwalk—about three metres above the waves– donned the gear, and launched myself into the water.

After several minutes of furious swimming, I paused to check my position. My enthusiasm had carried me beyond the distressed diver–whose efforts to reach safety had finally been rewarded. It was now my turn to be swept away from the platform.

Finally giving up the attempt to fight against the current and breaking waves, I turned my back on the weather. I drifted, secure in the knowledge that my predicament was known to those onboard the platform, and that help—in the form of a stand-by vessel tasked among other things with picking up survivors in the event of a disaster—would soon arrive.

After thirty minutes with my weight-belt still in place to provide stability and offset the buoyancy provided by the thick neoprene, a trawler, the Margaret Christina, hove alongside. A scrambling net was lowered, and I was quickly on deck. Cold, rather than exhausted, I was asked how I took my tea. "Black without sugar" I replied. A crewmember handed me a large mug of thick, hot tea. I greedily drank it and was handed another.

My transfer back to the platform should have been a simple exercise.

Because of the rising sea state, it wasn't. The plan involved lowering a personnel transfer basket—rather like a large lifebuoy with a rope cage–from the platform down to the water's surface. With a lifeline secured about my waist, I was to leap from the trawler and swim towards it.

Wearing a weight belt, a mask, and fins, and trailing a lifeline paid out by one of the crewmembers, I leapt into the sea and swam towards the floating basket. As my fingertips touched its side, the line tautened.

To avoid collision with the rig, the Margaret Christina had quickly turned away from the structure. Conscientiously following instructions, the crewman tasked with holding the rope refused to release his hold. Dragged backwards through the water, I managed a piercing scream, "Let – gluuurg. - go – gluurg. - of the – glurg. - @.#$*&% rope.". He did. And I was hoisted back on to the platform with my dignity bruised. But with my weight-belt still firmly in place.

Several months later, we were tasked with surveying the seabed around a new, unmanned, production platform recently constructed next to a drilling-rig. The water depth was just in excess of 52,5 m/160 ft with an ascent/descent line running from the drilling rig's catwalk down to the base of the production platform.

It was a sunny day with the lightest of swells. A supply boat, with its stern moored to the drill rig, was preparing to offload stores and drill pipe when we entered the water. On this occasion, my buddy–new to the team–and I were the first to dive while the second group of three divers stood ready on the lower catwalk.

Despite the surface conditions, it was midnight-dark at depth, and we both carried lights. Our plan was to follow the horizontal struts connecting each of the legs while sketching 'mud maps' on slates as we went.

Because of the reduced visibility, we were no more than an arm length from each other.

Two or three minutes after arriving on the bottom—while traversing the first strut—my regulator went 'POP'. I gave a tentative suck on the mouthpiece. Instead of air, I received a trickle of water.

I immediately reached for my buddy, briefly shone the light on my face, spat out the regulator and indicated that I was in distress.

He stared at me.

I plucked his regulator from out of his mouth and took a healthy suck of air. He seized it back. In my mind's eye, I had a vision of us both buddy breathing and making our way back to the ascent line.

His view of the situation differed from mine. He disappeared.

Rather than ponder my predicament, I finned hard towards the surface. It would be nice to be able to say that I had calmly assessed the situation and was totally in control. Regrettably, I can't. All that I can say is that some prior training must have automatically kicked in. I ditched my weight belt and, keeping my airway open, "Aaaahhed" all the way to the surface.

At the surface, I registered the fact that the tidal flow had carried me some way from the platform. Despite the post-adrenaline exhaustion, my legs continued to pedal as I took in great gulps of air. Barely managing to keep my head above water, I became convinced that I would be swept away,

succumb to cold and fatigue, and become another statistic in the rising death toll.

Back on the platform, our predicament had gone unnoticed until the skipper of the supply boat who'd been standing on the bridge scanning the nearby ocean with binoculars spotted two figures on the surface. A radio call went out for the nearest stand-by boat to search the area.

Exhausted and lacking the good sense to ditch the twin-cylinders, my head was constantly dropping face down into the water as a stand-by boat pulled alongside. I was scooped out of the water and dumped onto the deck. My cylinders were removed and I rolled over into the scuppers where I lay face down being violently ill.

A short while later, I registered the fact that a voice was saying, "You could probably use a hot mug of tea. How do you take it?" I heard my buddy's reply and then the first voice saying, "What about your mate?" I rolled over. "Well, bless my soul. It's you, Strike. Black tea, no sugar, isn't it?" I was back aboard the Margaret Christina.

We were both quickly transferred to the drill rig.

Following a stint in the Deck Decompression Chamber for 'observation', the first thing that I did was to bitterly complain about the fact that the Chief Diver had presented me with an invoice for the dropped weight-belt. The second was to send a radio message "IOU" for drinks to the crew of the Margaret Christina.

Postscript.

With an eye on bottom-line profits—and not a little greed—what even then should have been regarded as obvious and common-sense safety procedures, went by the board. While we planned each underwater task in meticulous detail, we rarely if ever discussed or prepared ourselves for the "what if's" of diving.

The dive plan itself was virtually non-existent as far as emergency drills were concerned. In fact, a cynic might claim that our diving practices were appalling.

With the wisdom of years and the benefit of hindsight, I'm inclined to agree. Making mistakes, surviving them, and analysing what went wrong is, at times, part of the learning curve.

David Strike *has been diving since 1961. With a background that encompasses military, commercial, scientific, recreational and technical diving, he has dived and travelled extensively throughout the Asia Pacific region.*

Qualified on open circuit, as well as rebreathers, surface demand, and standard diving apparatus, Strike is a former recreational and technical diving instructor and instructor certifier whose diving credentials include certifications from ANDI, BSAC, IANTD, PADI and SSI, as well as the legendary diving company, Siebe-Gorman.

Establishing a successful, internationally-affiliated media organisation while simultaneously continuing to teach diving and study for an external university degree, he was one of the first divers in Australia to embrace technical diving. A prolific writer, Strike has authored a number of diving manuals as well as penning several hundred articles covering all aspects of diving that have appeared in publications and websites around the world.

Continuing to maintain a passionate interest in an activity that has dominated his life, David Strike has organised several world class technical diving events, is a regular speaker and presenter at regional and international diving events, a recipient of the ADEX Lifetime Achievement Award for contributions to technical diving, and a Fellow of the Explorers Club of New York.

DON SHIRLEY

CCR FULL CAVE / EXPEDITION TRIMIX / CCR
INSTRUCTOR TRAINER
LICENSEE FOR IANTD SOUTHERN AFRICA
OWNER @ KOMATI SPRINGS

LOCATION OF INCIDENT
BOESMANSGAT, SOUTH AFRICA

January 2005, Boesmansgat (Bushman's Hole).

One of my most public dives, but a very personal experience, was a close call, and I have spent a lot of time trying to tell people what happened before, during, and after that day. It is a very involved story and one that can be talked about for hours. Phillip Finch conducted in-depth interviews with me and all involved to write his book, Diving into Darkness, and although he told the story well, there is much more to it.

It was only when we were discussing the book when I realised that at no time during the dive had it crossed my mind that I would not exit alive. It was a near miss for me, though I had never really thought of it in those terms.

I had spent three months bringing the dive, the team, and all the logistics together, some 35 people on site with chambers, doctors, medics, and rope-trained rescue guys.

It ran like clockwork.

The dive was a body recovery with a team of divers working independently, offering support to each other and ready to assist if something went wrong and if it did not endanger their own safety. The plan meant Dave Shaw diving independently at 270 m/885 ft and me meeting him at 220 m/721 ft to take the recovered body from him.

As it happened, Dave was dead about the time I entered the water.

Photos by Roger Horrocks

I also had issues in the water which I will call events–of which I had eight in total.

All eight involved calling on learned muscle memory rather than active thought processes to get out alive. If something can go wrong, then one day it surely will, and on this dive just about everything that could go wrong did!

I will focus on one part of the picture and narrow it down to the events on my portion of the dive.

So, let me tell you about my dive.

Event #1

The leading issue on my dive didn't even begin in the water; it started the day before the dive when I changed a battery in the primary Hammerhead controller (version 2004). It didn't really need changing, but I wanted to have a fresh battery in to control the solenoid. Unfortunately, at some point during the battery change its soldered connection contact came loose. This meant that I had to open the handset, drain the oil and remake the connection. The oil's function was to fill the air spaces to prevent the controller from imploding. In a previous life I was an army Electronics Engineer and have fixed things in rough field conditions before, so it was not a daunting task. I swiftly got the handset working again, but in the process I lost some of the oil. This left a small bubble in the controller that I thought was acceptable. It turned out I was wrong; at 240 m/787 ft the primary controller imploded and was disabled.

Event #2

I stopped at 250 m/820 ft and dealt with the implosion. My PO₂ was a constant 1.1 bar from the rate of descent and the initial O₂ in the loop. I added O₂ manually to bring the PO₂ to 1.3. In doing so, I added too much O₂.

Event #3

I now had a PO₂ of 2.5 bar! Not healthy, especially with the upcoming deco issues where I knew my CNS clock was going to be wound several times past 100%. So, I flushed the loop. This took all my onboard diluent.

Event #4

I went open circuit. I had 2 x 80 Cf cylinders of 4/80 (~10L cylinders of 4% O₂ / 80% helium); OC at 250 m/820 ft makes the SPG move down with each breath. The only option was to exit, as my OC supply was dwindling quickly.

Event #5

I connected bailout gas to rebreather, flushed and maintained control of the machine, and continued with my ascent. I practice manual control often—again routine. Now what were my stops? As I was ascending, I looked for a schedule from the multiple plans on my slates. The only one that fit was Dave's 270 m/885 ft, five-minute profile. I used this, carrying on with my ascent while keeping one finger as a marker on the plan.

I still had the secondary display. This would monitor the O₂ levels but would not control the solenoid. Annoyingly, the screens scrolled, so every time I looked at the secondary, it had scrolled past the display I needed, and I had to wait for two menus to pass to see the monochrome display.

I got to the 150 m/492 ft cylinders clipped on the line. Two of those were mine, but I left them for Dave just in case he could follow me up. In my mind, I knew he was not coming back, but in my heart I hoped he could. I flushed the loop with the gas on the line to bring down the helium and left the cylinders.

I did this with each gas as I ascended, still on manual control. I met my support guys as I ascended. Around 100 m/328 ft, I started following the VR3 dive computer's plan, as all stops were matching the one-minute stops on the slate.

It just saved me keeping my finger on the slate.

At 45 m/147 ft, one of the support guys brought me a new VR3 (one of my two VR3s had flooded). I strapped this on, and I think this triggered another chain of events. The support diver left. I remember thinking several times on the dive that I was using very little O₂, and I kept having to remind myself to add O₂ (my metabolism is very slow). This was two hours into the dive. My recollection of this time is not very clear.

I ascended a few meters to the next gas. This time I picked up and clipped off the cylinder, turning it on as usual as the next available gas to breathe.

Event #6
Now I started to pass out.

I immediately bailed out to OC; this is my first action always. I made no conscious decisions

in this event; everything was muscle memory kicking in. I think breathing an OC "gulp of gas" gave me the counter diffusion event. I was spinning in a dream state and saw the black and white flashes as my light hit the roof and then the void. At some point I came into contact with the line and grabbed it.

I spanned around the line, then across the small roof section, and found myself at 36 m/118 ft. I came around enough to see that the VR3 was saying go back down to 46 m/150 ft. I went down and, as I knew I was going to need my OC gas now, I started collecting my cylinders.

Event #7
Every movement now made me physically sick. I would move and vomit and repeat. I followed the schedule on the VR3. Eventually I got back up to 36 m/118 ft and met Truwin

Laas–the next support diver. I wrote down exactly what was wrong, and he reported it to the surface. Then he came back down and clipped me to the line. From then on, there was someone with me all the time.

Event #8
I picked up the cylinder at 22 m/72 ft, clipped it off, and turned it on.

I distinctly remember thinking, "It's good that I can do everything by feel," but I took the wrong gas and started to breathe a 4/80—not the 50% as I thought.

I started to feel worse. Truwin quickly showed me my error and offered me the 50%. At this time, I could not move my head without spinning and I could only hang vertically. Try as I might, I could not stay horizontal.

Event #9
Eventually, I could no longer breathe from the demand valve and had to purge to force a breath in. This was due to the muscle power needed to draw down gas when I had been in a vertical position for so long. At 6 m/20 ft, my intention was to finish that stop on the VR3 but to miss the 3 m/10 ft stop, as I was already well over my planned time.

I was also going straight to the chamber at the top of the mountain. When I finally surfaced, I had dived for 12 hours 20 minutes. Looking back, if I had not dived with a damaged (though fixed) controller, I would not have needed the other skills to exit the water.

It's easy to say, "But avoid diving with impaired equipment and you prevent many problems!" I tell this to my students, but I still did it. In my defense, I did not think it was a problem at the time. The actions of bailing out, controlling PO_2 manually, and general muscle memory are important.

Without those I would not be here. Also, the sheer determination and confidence to deal with any problem in the water is absolutely essential.

Photo by Roger Horrocks

The in-water event at 250 m/820 ft was dealt with as any diver should at any depth.

Passing out and then spinning was actually the result of two related but different events. Passing out may have been a CO_2 problem or a low O_2 problem, or both. I do not know. Either will make you pass out without any warning. In the final analysis, most events happen on the surface. If you remember this, it may save you one day.

Normally accidents tend not to be due to one thing only, but a number of cascading events.

Don Shirley *is a world-renowned English cave diver and instructor trainer who currently resides in South Africa. He holds the license to International Association of Nitrox and Technical Divers (IANTD) Southern Africa Region.*

Shirley has been involved in diving since 1974, conducting recreational and technical training. Don started technical diving in the early 90s and has been teaching purely technical diving since 1996 when he moved to South Africa. He is an Instructor Trainer for IANTD and Divers Alert Network.

He was an electronics engineer in the British Army for 22 years. Aside from his extraordinary experience level, Shirley is most known for his relationship with David Shaw leading up to Shaw's death in 2005.

Don and his wife Andre Shirley currently own and operate Technical Diving Africa and the flooded mine system of Komati Springs in the Mpumalanga region of South Africa.

DOUGLAS EBERSOLE, MD

KISS CCR TRIMIX INSTRUCTOR TRAINER

LOCATION OF INCIDENT
MADISON BLUE SPRINGS, FLORIDA, USA

As a matter of introduction, unlike most of the authors in this book, I am truly a "warm water, pretty fish" diver at heart. I am definitely not an explorer. I have absolutely no interest in "going where no man has gone before".

I mainly enjoy warm water recreational and technical diving on closed circuit rebreathers, and I am an avid underwater photographer. While I enjoy cave diving for its technical aspects and the beauty of the geologic formations, I do not like small silty passages.

This will be important later in the story.

I consider myself to be a recreational cave diver who is very happy to follow the mapped passages of the popular caves in Florida and Mexico. This story began as a beautiful September day in north Florida.

I met a buddy of mine who was a cave diving instructor, along with two of her friends who were newly certified CCR cave divers. The plan was for a fun day of cave diving at Madison Blue Springs in Lee, Florida.

Madison Blue, on the west bank of the Withlacoochee River, is state-owned and managed as a county recreational park with picnic tables, a parking lot, and other facilities. More importantly, it is also a beautiful and very popular cave system in north Florida.

That morning, after assembling our rebreathers, the four of us looked at the map and planned our dive. We would go down the Rabbit Hole and take the gold line back past the Half Hitch restriction, for a total penetration of just over 500 m/1640 ft, to acquaint the newly-certified cave divers with this beautiful cave.

Photo by Laurent Miroult

My buddy would lead with me in position #2. The other two divers would be in positions #3 and #4. With this plan in mind, we geared up, walked down the wooden steps to the water and, after S-drills, entered the cave.

It was a beautiful and relaxing dive with a maximum depth of 23 m/75 ft and a run time of 122 minutes.

After a relaxing lunch, it was time for our second dive.

This plan would involve additional navigation to show the new cave divers more of this beautiful cave. We would jump to the Banana Room and then to the Godzilla Room before turning and exiting the cave. We all geared up and got in the water.

The diver order would be the same as for the first dive with my buddy in front, followed by me, and then by the other two divers. The dive started as planned; we entered the cave, jumped to the Banana Room and then moved on to the Godzilla Room.

Everything was going well and I was enjoying the relaxing dive. At the agreed point, we turned the dive and headed out. On the way out, my buddy signaled she wanted to change the plan and check out the Century Tunnel.

My first thought was "this was not part of our plan."

My second thought was that I had not been in the Century Tunnel, but I had heard it got pretty small and silty–not the type of cave diving I enjoy.

The other two divers were in favor of the change in plan, so I reluctantly agreed as well. We changed positions so that my buddy was in the lead, followed by me, and then by the other two divers. The farther we swam in, the narrower and narrower the passage became. I was comfortable with my diving skills in this small, silty tunnel, but I really wasn't enjoying it.

I would much rather have stayed with our original plan. Eventually, my buddy thumbed the dive and the four of us turned around.

This is when things went sideways.

As I turned and watched the two newly-certified cave divers—now in front of me—turn around, all I could see was a massive cloud of silt heading in my direction. I instinctively "OK'd" the line, and the four of us began our exit in no-visibility conditions.

Everything seemed to be going well when I suddenly ran into the diver in front of me. I stopped and waited for him to continue but he didn't. I felt him moving erratically and it was obvious that he was stuck in the narrow passage. I tried to use touch contact to get him to back up, but he continued to struggle.

I suddenly realized that if this diver panicked, I could die in this cave!

All of my training, skill, and experience were not going to help me if this guy was a cork in the bottle of my exit. Thankfully, my training kicked in and I just calmed my breathing and worked through the problem. At this point, I could only really take care of myself until the diver in front of me settled down. We were all on closed circuit rebreathers, so time was not really an issue. It was just a matter of relaxing, trying to get the diver in front of me to relax, and then help him get unstuck.

I was eventually able to get the diver in front of me to slowly back up and change his angle of exit. After what seemed like an eternity, he finally moved on ahead of me and out of my reach. I moved forward slowly and, as luck would have it, I got stuck in the same area where he had. I slowly backed up and changed my body position to try to navigate the restriction in no visibility.

As I was doing that, my buddy behind me then ran into my fins. Then I made it through, only to bump into the diver in front of me again.

He was now stuck in a different area of the tunnel. This time he was much calmer and slowly wiggled his way through. Eventually, we all made it out of the tunnel where visibility returned to normal. We picked up our jump reel and exited in the clear blue water. It was a true sigh of relief gliding back to the cave entrance with great visibility. We made our way to the exit, completed our deco, and then left the cave.

The group was very quiet for several minutes as we walked up the stairs, got out of our gear on the picnic tables, and stripped off our drysuits. Then one guy said, "Well, that sucked!" That was the ice-breaker we all needed to lighten up and debrief the event.

In thousands of dives, including hundreds of cave dives, this has thankfully been my only 'close call'. I'd like to think that has a lot to do with my training, my experience, and my skills, but I'm sure it also has a lot to do with luck.

What did I learn from this dive?

First and foremost: you should not bow to peer pressure. I knew that I did not like small, silty areas, and our agreed-upon plan did not involve going into one. I should have thumbed the dive instead of agreeing with the change in plan. With that, the whole situation would have been avoided. However, the other three members of the team wanted to change the plan, and I felt pressured into going along. Don't do that! Plan your dive and dive your plan.

Secondly, you should know the training, experience and, most importantly, the skill set of all of your team members. The two other divers in the group were friends of my buddy. I did not know them, and I certainly didn't know their skills or their comfort in an overhead environment. Yet, not only did I bow to peer pressure, I also put myself in a situation where, despite my knowing that this was going to be a tight and silty area, I allowed two newly-certified cave divers about whom I knew very little to be between me and a

safe exit. I should have had more situational awareness. As the tunnel began to narrow and I noticed the fine silt on the floor, I should have realized the potential silt-out with these two new cave divers trying to turn around in a very confined space. I also should have realized that the ceiling had areas where back mount rebreathers could easily get stuck on the way out. If these things had been in the front of my mind, I would have turned the dive earlier and not waited for my buddy to decide she couldn't go any farther.

We all make mistakes, whether through complacency, cutting corners on things we were taught in training or, as in this case, by bowing to peer pressure. The key is to survive your mistakes and learn from them so you don't make the same ones again.

Making mistakes, surviving them, and then not changing our habits is like playing Russian roulette.

Douglas Ebersole, MD *is an Interventional Cardiologist at the Watson Clinic LLP in Lakeland, Florida and is the Director of the Structural Heart Program at Lakeland Regional Health, an 850-bed tertiary referral hospital in Lakeland.*

He has been diving since 1974 and is an avid recreational diver, technical diver, rebreather diver, and cave diver. He is also a recreational, technical, and rebreather instructor for several training agencies, is a cardiology consultant to Divers Alert Network, and is the Florida Sales agent for KISS Rebreathers.

EDD SORENSON

CAVE EXPLORER

LOCATION OF INCIDENT
JACKSON BLUE, MARIANNA, FLORIDA, USA

I had been exploring a new section of Jackson Blue in Mariana, Florida, and had laid several thousand m/ft of line. The current end of my line was about 2743 m/9000 ft back, something like that, and it just kind of walled out, ran out of flow.I knew I must have missed the flow somewhere.

I had spotted a restriction 61 m/200 ft from the end of the line.

It was very low, but wide. There were ripples in the sand and a lot of flow coming out. It was only about 28-33 cm/11-13 inches tall, and maybe 2.4-2.7 m/8-9 ft wide. Jason Richards and I started laying line in there, and when we got to where it opened up a little bit, we were low on gas, so we tied off and exited the cave. The next day, or the next dive, we were going to go back and survey that 91 m/300 ft of line and then continue our exploration.

That was the plan. The passage started at about 1524 m/5000 ft back. The year was maybe 2007, and the new Submerge Scooter N-19 had just come out with nickel-metal-hydride batteries. At that time, everyone else was using lead acid batteries, which were much bigger and much heavier.

I had in my possession two of the very first N-19s available; Jason had a couple of small Mako scooters, and I had two big Submerge UV-26s and then these two new, smaller N-19s. So, the plan was I would give him one of my big UV-26s to ride back to 1524 m/5000 ft, I would ride the other one, and we would each tow one of the new N-19s between our legs. We would drop a stage bottle at about 762 m/2500 ft, and then we would drop our second stage at 1524 m/5000 ft along with the UV-26 scooters that we had ridden in on.

Photo by Sandra Clopp

97

There were some small passages with a couple of 'bottle-off' restrictions and some real low, nasty stuff along the way. We didn't have room to take stages and scooters back there, so we opted to take the biggest tanks we had, which were low pressure 15L/121s overfilled to 250 bar/3600 PSI as our main gas supply, these were obviously side mounted. We also carried the new smaller scooters because the bigger ones wouldn't fit through the restriction.

We got through the first bottle-off restriction and then there was a low section roughly 30-45m/100–150 ft long by around 45-55 cm/18-22 inches tall. We scootered this, each of us holding our scooter out to our right side with a hand on the trigger. It was so small that it should definitely not have been scootered, but we were doing it anyway to save time against the high flow.

We got to where the passage opened up, passed a sinkhole, squeezed through another bottle-off restriction, made it through some more low stuff, and then we were back into the big stuff, scootering forward towards the 2804 m/9200 ft mark.

We dropped the scooters and were going to go into the low passage that we had laid on the previous dive. I was in the lead and Jason was behind me, surveying that line we had just put in. I was going to continue the exploration when we got to the end of the line. About 3 m/10 ft, maybe 4.5 m/15 ft before we got there, we were in this low, scrunchy, grindy section, and I noticed I was on the wrong side of the line.

The line was running along the ceiling. I got down in the sand and slid over to the other side of the line when I noticed the line was moving with me. I slid back, put one hand behind me and one hand in front of me trying to hold the line up higher so I could get underneath it. I kept doing this and then realized I was hung up on the line somehow. So, I pulled my regulator out of my mouth and

yelled to Jason, "Jason," and I pointed my finger towards my back.

Jason came up on me suddenly—keep in mind we were in about a 30-cm/12-inch-or-less tall passage—and I can feel him back there wrestling me around. And I'm thinking, "What the heck is he doing?" All I could do was try to look underneath my right armpit to see what he was doing back there. I saw this big translucent glob in his hand, which looked like a giant ball of snot. And I thought, "What the heck?" Then I realized that that was the bladder from my sidemount wing.

We had made multiple trips scootering through that section, but it was so low we probably shouldn't have. As mentioned, I had the scooter off to my right, so my right side was slightly higher than my left side; I must have been scraping along the rocks at full speed and had worn the shell of the wing thinner and thinner and thinner. On this dive, I apparently tore about a 25-cm/10-inch gash in the shell, and the bladder had floated out of my wing and somehow got between the line and the ceiling of the cave. Worse, when I was moving around trying to get myself freed, the remnants of gas (because you always dump your gas before you get to a restriction) got up in the bladder, preventing it from coming free from the line.

Once Jason had freed me by pulling the bladder out from between the line and the ceiling, he worked to tuck it back into that 25-cm/10-inch gash in my wing. He did manage to get it back in place, but it was obvious that as soon as I got through the restriction and put gas in it, it would just pop right back out. So at that point, he took his regulator out of his mouth and he said, "Give me a knife." I handed him a Z-knife and he emphatically repeated, "A knife!" I said, "That's all I've got."

Jason then took my safety reel and used it to stitch up the wing on my Dive Rite Nomad; there were some little, one-inch D-rings on

the back of the harness so he tied off the cave line to the D ring and toward the inside to a bungee and then out through another D ring and back and forth, back and forth. It took him quite a while to get it done.

Once he was finished, he got back behind me, pushed twice forward on my leg and said, "Go." So I continued on. Jason waited until the silt cleared and then he continued the survey.

When we got to where it opened up, I didn't realise exactly what had gone on, I was just kind of waiting there.

Jason finished his survey notes and I pulled out my explorer reel, getting ready to tie it on and start running new line. He saw me hooking up the line to do exploration and grunted through his regulator, "UH UH." He showed me his thumb saying, the dive is over. I give him my index finger and my thumb spread apart a little bit like, "a little bit more? Can't we just do a little bit longer?"

And he repeated "UH UH," this time a little more forceful and emphatically, and gave me the thumb again indicating the dive was over. At that point I realised he was way past his thirds and wanted to go.

Photo by Edd Sorenson

We were pretty close to 3048 m/10000 ft from the entrance and about 27 m/90 ft deep with multiple restrictions to go through.

We were also a good 1524 m/5000 ft away from our next stage bottle or backup scooters. So we scrunched through the section we had just come through again. We got back to the main line where our scooters were sitting, hooked them up, he gave me the okay signal, I okayed him back and off we went.

I was hard on the trigger and travelled less than 30 m/100 ft when all of the sudden my scooter died. I was like, "You have got to be shitting me, I don't have the gas for this!" Jason just kept going. It took him twenty seconds or so to figure out I wasn't behind him anymore. He circled back around, came over and he had these big eyes and his hands were spread apart as if to say, "What are you doing?"

I gave him the "It's broken" signal for my scooter. He hooked me up to him and proceeded to start towing me out of the cave. We went less than 15 m/50 ft when his scooter died as well. Those scooters were supposed to go twice as long as we needed them to go! Jason unclipped me and we just started swimming. However, he swam much faster than I did; within a minute or so, he was out of my sight. I came around a corner and there he was coming back toward me and he had the hands out again like, "Now what are you doing?"

We continued swimming, he outswam me again, he turned around, he's got the hands out again, "c'mon c'mon, what are you doing now?"

At that point, I realised that we could be in serious trouble here. I thought, "I have one idea in my mind for how I'm going to deal with this, and apparently you have a different idea." I thought to myself, "You've got to do what's best for you right now, and I need to do what's best for me." So I looked at him and pointed at him and I gave the thumb.

"You've got to go." And he left.

I didn't see him again until we got to where the sinkhole was. And if we absolutely had to, we could have surfaced at that sinkhole. There's no way to get out, but we could've got to air. We may or may not ever have been discovered in there, but at least we would have had air to breathe, plus it's very shallow.

At that point in the cave it's only about 10 m/35 ft deep, and Jason knew that we were less than 304 m/1000 ft from our next stage and scooters, so he opted to wait for me up there where it was shallow. We met up and then continued on through the low, nasty sections and the bottle-off restrictions, and we got back to our scooters and our next stage.

I hadn't looked at his gas, or at mine. I figured it really didn't matter at that point. All I know is that when I picked up my stage at 1524 m/5000 ft, and my scooter, I went on to that stage (which was about two-thirds full), and I started scootering out. I figured I'd just keep running the stage I had originally put on until it was empty.

Finally, we got out of the cave and started talking. Both of his stages were empty and his sidemount bottles were at about 48 and 62 bar/700 and 900 psi, so we weren't direly, direly low, but if we'd have gotten back to the scooters and they were dead, I doubt he would've made it. I still had about 103 bar/1500 psi in one and 110/1600 in the other, so I likely would have made it—plus I didn't use the second stage on the way out. Now, when I think about it, I've gotta say, "Yeah, I guess we could call that a close call."

I mentioned this story to my wife Stacy the other day and told her that these things don't even stand out in my mind. To me it's just another day at the office.

And she goes, "Well, what about that time in Hole in the Wall where you and Jason were surveying and you guys got lost?"

That was a whole other story.

The plan was that Jason was going to survey all these Ts in the line. Surveying is just a one-person job, so Jason said that he'd survey and I would look for leads. So of course, the whole time I wasn't paying attention to anything except looking around corners, over rocks, in crevices. A couple of hours into the dive, he looked at me with his finger in the question mark position like, "where are we?" I looked around and signalled, "I don't know, I've been following you."

I said, "Let's go this way." And I pointed, so we went. We came to a T; there was a line arrow in two different directions and he had this concerned look, "do you know where you're going?"

I didn't, but I went, "yeah, yeah, go that way."

He scribbled on his pad, "Are you sure?"

"Yup," I answered. I didn't want him to think that I wasn't confident. This happened a couple more times and then pretty soon he was ready to swim off in one direction and I kept telling him, "no, this way."

About that time, my light was brighter than his was, and I could see our scooters about 60 m/200 ft in the distance. I said, "Come here."

He was like, "No, this way."

I said, "Just come here and look."

He came back. When we put our two lights together he could see the two black silhouettes hanging off the line and I could hear through his regulator, "Woo-Who!" Later on, he and I were talking and he said, "There've probably only been three or four times out of thousands and thousands and thousands of dives that I've been concerned." That's how he put it.

He added, "The more I think about it, every one of those times where I was concerned,

you and I were diving together. We tend to not always follow our own dive plans, and sometimes we probably go outside of where we should, for exploration purposes."

Edd Sorenson *is a technical cave diver known for numerous rescues of lost or trapped divers in the underwater caves of Florida, particularly in Vortex Springs and Blue Springs Recreational Park.*

His diving career started back in 1995, in the Pacific Northwest, and that sparked a new passion for the world beneath the water's surface. He continued his education over the course of the next year. While on vacation in Florida in 1996 to wreck dive The Spiegel Grove, which was blown out, he found his new love for cave diving at Ginnie Springs doing a cavern dive. He was rebreather certified in 1997, full cave Certified in 1998, and over the course of the following years, he has continued to become one of the cave diving community's most-known instructor trainers for several training agencies. In 1999, he was asked to join the International Underwater Cave Rescue and Recovery (IUCRR) as one of the founding members. He later founded Cave Adventurers in 2003. After joining the IUCRR, Edd did his first body recovery in 1999 at Ginnie Springs in High Springs, Florida.

Edd became a local hero in 2012 when he successfully rescued four people in three different rescues in Jackson County Florida on Merritts Millpond. Edd has been featured in Duracell's series Quantum Heroes. For his efforts in 2012, Edd was awarded the first-ever Diver's Alert Network Hero Award, Heroic Merit Award, and Instructor Trainer of the Year from the Professional Scuba Association International (PSAI). He is the Safety Director for the NSS-CDS and was awarded a Life Saving Award in 2013. This year, at the 2019 NSS-CDS International conference, Edd received a Lifetime Achievement Award, and the NSS-CDS named an award after him "Edd Sorenson Life Saving Award".

Photo by Christopher Richardson

EDD STOCKDALE

OWNER / PARTNER @
GRADIENT SCIENTIFIC & TECHNICAL DIVING
RAID TECHNICAL TRAINING ADVISOR
& INSTRUCTOR EXAMINER, EXPLORERS CLUB MEMBER

LOCATION OF INCIDENT
HMS ST.ANGELO, MALTA

I have been fortunate enough to visit many places around the planet as a result of my job—working with research expeditions, searching for new caves/mines/wrecks, as well as teaching and guiding divers. Each of these, whilst applying the same diving skills and knowledge, require a different outlook as well as specific experience.

The following story took place while I was working in Malta, an amazing destination for training, relaxed diving, and easily-accessible historical wrecks.

That was when I, as a young aspiring explorer, had a "wake up call" that changed many of my approaches to advanced diving. The company I was working with did offer a range of technical options but, for the most part, us technical instructors mainly guided visiting divers.

We were there to keep them safe while showing them the highlights of various wrecks, the majority of which were in the 50-65 m/165-196 ft range. As expected, when diving at these depths day after day in clear warm water, a level of comfort and complacency developed, something which was undoubtedly a major factor in causing the incident.

It happened on one such typical trip, guiding a CCR (Closed Circuit Rebreather) client to a lesser-dived wreck - the HMS St Angelo - lying in 49-55 m/165-180 ft. The wreck is not particularly large, but it's in good condition, with many nice points of interest.

Three groups were diving. I with the CCR diver and two of my colleagues with open circuit groups. With staggered entries, my team entered the water second.

Photo by Tiffany Norberg

During our descent and bottom time everything went as planned, even though my buddy was prone to swimming off on her own, paying little attention to her teammate (me). This had sadly become the norm in technical guiding.

Due to the relatively small size of the wreck and great visibility, we made our way back to the shot line. It was at this point, at 45 m/147 ft, that my unit had an internal oxygen leak. Almost instantly, my PO₂ (Partial pressure of oxygen) peaked, beyond the unit's capability to measure it, and my buoyancy became extremely positive. At this point, my training and experience kicked in. I bailed to my offboard (no bailout valve), switched off the oxygen, and vented my loop of the excess gas, all in quick succession.

But then the real problem appeared—I was breathing water. There was an issue with the regulator and nothing but water was flowing in. At this point of the story I need to explain that at that time our routine on diving days was to meet in the morning, analyse our gas, set up our bailout stages with regulators, and do a positive and negative test at the dive centre.

Our stages were then loaded onto the truck and driven to the boat. Normally we would check our bailouts at the bubble stop depth of -6 m/-20 ft, but this time, due to strong surface currents, we decided that it was not possible. In hindsight this was a mistake.

So there I was, at 45 m/147 ft with no gas, my loop gas in a non-breathable range, having just exhaled trying to clear my regulator of water. Because of the good visibility, my buddy was distant from the line and with her back turned to me. That forced me to ascend on the shot line towards the OC (Open Circuit) team above me.

My rapid ascent signalling out-of-gas resulted in the clients on that group letting go of the line and swimming out of the way. Thankfully my colleague, who was guiding them, got to me in time and shared his gas with me while establishing a firm contact with me and the reference line. He stayed with me on point until I got it together again, and by this point, I had spent around one minute without breathable gas. Finally I established a breathable gas in my CCR unit and returned to it, fluttering the O₂ as I went.

Photo by Tiffany Norberg

During my ascent all the way to the surface, I felt very thankful. To put it mildly, I had a valid subject for discussion with the team after returning to the dive centre!

So: in the final analysis, what really went wrong?

On the boat journey home we examined the leaking bailout regulator. It turned out there was a crack next to the exhaust valve causing a shard to jam the flapper open. Bearing in mind that all our regulators had been checked that morning, it must be that the damage had occurred during transport. Lesson learned: never setup regulators before transport. Do it on the boat or at the dive site. Our technical team changed protocols about this that same day. All of us still teach it like that, to this day.

Next up was the lack of reliability in a new, ad hoc 'team' when guiding a client diver for the first time. The client frequently assumes that you, the guide, will be fine; similarly, as the guide, you have the illusion that an advanced diver will be there to help you when you really need it. Lesson learned: team diving requires trust and reciprocal reliability to actually work.

Finally, the biggest issue in all this: me. Diving every day in these depth ranges, on the same wrecks, caused a complacent overconfidence and sense of comfort to develop. This was the most important element and one that changed forever after this incident. I survived unscathed but with a renewed respect for operating in a hostile environment with only my equipment, procedures, and skills to rely on.

This respect doesn't mean fear of taking risks or doing bigger dives, but it does mean a better focus on the proper procedures to do these big dives safely. It's a thought process that allows me to improve on each dive, whether a simple shallow one or a deep overhead penetration. The advice I would have given to myself back then, or to any diver for that matter, is the same:

Take it slow, do not become complacent, develop and maintain a proficient skill base, and dive with a solid team as much as you can. Wrecks, caves and mines, fish or reefs… they will always be there another day.

None of them are worth losing your life over.

Edd Stockdale *has more than 5500 dives and 20 years in diving. He is an instructor examiner with RAID, a member of The Explorers Club, a writer for training agency course manuals, and often presents at diving conferences such as Baltic Tech, ADEX, and Oztek. In 2016, he was nominated for the Eurotek Discovery Award for his work in wreck exploration.*

He has a degree in marine zoology and worked for many years as a researcher with various institutions publishing in the fields of physiology and biophysics, for which he won the 2008 French Academy of Science Jouvance Medal in marine biology. Shortly thereafter, Edd started concentrating predominately on both technical and scientific diving, combining the two for the purposes of research expeditions.

He has worked in the capacity of Dive Safety Officer for the Universities of Oxford, University of Essex, and University of Malta on various expeditions. In these roles he has helped develop undergraduate field work training programs, the application of rebreathers to ecological research in the mesophotic zone, and helped successful expeditions looking at un-dived wrecks. When not teaching or exploring, Edd works with research institutions in the capacity of dive safety officer and technical diving consultant. He is involved in exploration projects in various areas and can often be found diving in the many mines or wrecks in and around Scandinavia.

Photo by Danny Barber

EDOARDO PAVIA

OWNER @ SEA DWELLER DIVERS / APD ITALIAN
DISTRIBUTOR / CCR IT / UNDERWATER EXPLORER

LOCATION OF INCIDENT
CARPATHIA WRECK

Everybody knows the dramatic story of the *Titanic*, and some, but not all, have some knowledge of the *Carpathia*, the main rescue ship in this epic disaster.

The destiny of this little big ship was decided by the U-55 on July 17, 1918, about 298 km/185 miles west of Lands End, while she was part of a convoy; her stern was seen on the surface for the last time at 02:45.

In 1999, an expedition guided by Graham Jessop announced the precise location of the wreck, and in the spring of 2000, Clive Cussler, with the non-profit Agency NUMA, visited the wreck with a survey expedition.

In August 2001, Richard Stevenson led the first expedition of technical sport divers on top of the shipwreck. On the 21st of that month they did the first and only dive on the *Carpathia* since her sinking. The deep team was composed of Richard Stevenson, Zaid Al-Obaidi, Ric Waring, and Bruce Dunton.

From a diving point of view, in 2001, it was like walking on the moon. Just to compare this dive with mountaineering, *Britannic*, at that time, was the Everest of technical diving, but *Carpathia* was the K2; many people have climbed Everest, some have tried the K2; few have returned to it. Logistics, depth, weather conditions, rescue plans, all were extreme.

I was invited to participate on the second expedition in 2004.

The second expedition to the *Carpathia* took place in July 2004, from the 9th to the 21st. This bunch of great divers, which was composed mainly by the Starfish Enterprises divers, with Richard Stevenson, Carl Spencer,

Leigh Bishop, Teresa Telus, Kevin Pickering, Christian Malan, Dave Cooper, Barry Smith, and Rich Waring, had decided to go back to Lucie. I was invited to participate on this expedition, along with Antonello Paone, my diving partner on the 2001 Britannic Expedition, a great friend and a great photographer. This would most assuredly not be child's play!

Again, the weather was to have the last word on this expedition; the single, most scary thing was the rough sea, and I mean it. We took shelter in the Scilly Islands and made a second attempt to get to the spot, but our boat, the Loyal Watcher, a 24 m/79 ft ex-Royal Navy fleet tender, seemed nothing more than a lifeboat - no chance. We had to turn our bow towards Plymouth.

As we cruised somberly back to Plymouth, we all thought that the prospects of completing a dive on the Carpathia were disappearing like the white stream of bubbles behind the stern of the Loyal Watcher.

In 2007, our team leader, Rick Waring, decided to set up another expedition. I leapt at the invitation; it was probably one of my last chances to visit Lucie. Rick gave me the opportunity, not only to be part of the team, but also to bring a friend of mine from Italy. The Carpathia is a very deep dive, and you really do not want to be paired with someone with whom you haven't dived regularly.

Antonello, my regular dive buddy, was not keen on taking all those risks again, so I called Andrea Bolzoni, an IANTD Italian Instructor and excellent deep diver. To cut the story short, with my little van, I drove from Rome to the north of Italy where I met with Andrea, and then we travelled together all the way to Plymouth, where the adventure was about to start. After a day and half cruise, on a fresh, gloomy Atlantic morning, we reached our spot. The sea was not calm, and the ride had been quite uncomfortable, but for the first time we were on top of Lucie.

Let me introduce the Team: Ric Waring, Carl Spencer, Edoardo Pavia, Helmuth Biechl, Tim Casham, Jeff Cornish, Richard Stevenson, Andrea Bolzoni, Mark Elliot, and Duncan Keates, a great bunch of friends and all excellent, expert wreck divers.

Day one, first dive, three pairs this time: Ric and Jeff, Richard and Carl, and finally Andrea and me. Like everyone else, I was taking three bailout cylinders (deep gas), and also a massive Gates housing, plus lights for my camera. Andrea was taking the same dive configuration, plus a UV-18 scooter with a massive Death Ray light, capable of enormous illuminating power. The surface was rough, the current was ripping like mad horses, and our boat, the Janus II from Comex, was not really in the right position for our descent, but our 150-155 m/492-510 ft dive was about to begin!

We had to pull ourselves down the shot line, as the current did not reduce in intensity down to 40 m/131 ft. I was already over-breathing my unit, and Andrea was right behind me, probably struggling to regain control of ventilation as well.

We had a little stop and after an ok signal, we continued our descent, this time at a much higher and more comfortable speed. It was our first dive at those depths, and once the gauge signalled the 100 m/328 ft mark, we knew that there were fifty more meters still to come; it was a very long and very dark descent. The ambient light dimmed away from 100 m/328 ft onwards, so for this reason I decided to place my Jotron strobe light on the line somewhere around 120 m/393 ft. When it passed out of view behind us, we really felt alone in the heart of the ocean.

We reached the bottom after eight minutes and got through all our signals and checks safely; our exploration was going to start.

The first mistake I made was to not ask Andrea to deploy a line from the shot; I was filming

and he had the scooter with light, so it would have been easier for him to do so, but as you can understand, something was missing from the beginning.

We filmed around the bow area, probably the region with most damage, and after about fifteen minutes into our RT, I decided it was time to return to the shotline, but where was it? I looked at Andrea and with the typical squeaky voice I asked him: "Where is the shot line?"

Andrea looked at me, and probably thinking the same thing, answered back: "I don't know!"

My heart started to accelerate in my chest; we were in the Atlantic, at one hundred and fifty five metres, with at least four hours of deco and a ripping current at the surface, nothing to be happy about! We looked around hoping to find the Holy Grail, but the clock was ticking, and all we could see was a mass of twisted plates and no sign of the shot line.

We knew (it's a big word) that our scrubbers could not handle this depth for much longer; we had planned twenty minutes RT on the bottom with the descent, and it was now twenty two minutes into the dive; it was time to do something. At twenty-five minutes, I looked at Andrea and told him to start a free ascent in the pitch-black water; better to handle one problem at a time.

As we started to go up, the only thing we cared about was the depth gauge; we had to do a controlled ascent, no panic at this depth. After about thirty metres into our ascent, I remembered the strobe to be at 120 m/393 ft, and we were getting close to the mark, so I literally screamed at Andrea to turn off the super light of his Death Ray. I hurriedly did the same with my camera lights. A few seconds later, the shotline appeared in slight current in front me and Andrea, and five or six metres above us the good old yellow Jotron, was signalling a safe port for ships in the storm; we were safe.

Photo by Stefan Panis

At that point, we started to cry and scream with joy into our mouthpieces.

Just above us, the other two pairs were looking at us like we had some sort of mental problem, or maybe this was some sort of Italian voodoo to keep the ghosts of the abyss away during our long deco! I guess that does make for some pretty good stories.

Edoardo Pavia *was a free diver for fifteen years before he started scuba a decade later, in the mid-80s. Very quickly he was converted to diving closed circuit rebreathers (CCR). On the onset of the new millennium, he established the Sea Dweller Divers company, both a scuba shop and diving school, specialising in technical dive equipment and training. In 2002, he became the Italian distributor for AP Valves' CCR diving units in Italy.*

He rapidly began a career with the leading technical agency IANTD as an instructor and then as an instructor trainer across Italy and Europe. At present, he is still committed to deep diving and especially underwater filming.

Edoardo Pavia has had the honour of participating in some of the most challenging expeditions to date, including: four times on the Britannic, the Andrea Doria and the incredible warship HMS Victoria in Lebanon. He has also extensively dived on the Italian liner Viminale and once (which he believes is enough), on the Carpathia (155m+ depth). He has also dived in Antarctica for an Italian TV documentary.

Edoardo is also a cave diver and has dived with some of the most experienced cave divers in the world, like friends Rick Stanton and Gigi (Luigi) Casati. Often a speaker at prestigious international conferences, he resides in Rome with his wife Gaia and their children Guglielmo, Matilda and Leonardo.

EMMANUEL KUEHN

BUSINESS DEVELOPER
FACTORY INSTRUCTOR TRAINER @ AZOTH SYSTEMS

LOCATION OF INCIDENT
CARRIERE DE PERLONJOUR – SOIGNIES, BELGIUM

I should have been dead!

I tell this story not as a victim, but rather as a survivor. It was October 22, 2000, I was 33 years old and suddenly I was on the way to my Earthly end.

To back up, the instructor trainer who had previously trained me requested that I take over a training from him. He could not do the dive, as he had already planned a trimix dive. He knew I would agree to help. I said yes, but deep inside, I wanted to say "NO!"

The objective was to supervise the final dive of an IANTD Advanced Nitrox training. I would be diving with three divers: a divemaster, an assistant instructor, and a master instructor.

On October 21, the day before the dive, and as I do my preparations, I am not feeling well.

I experience some fear. My head cannot figure out what is going on, but my gut is telling me that something is not okay. It's like I'm being warned not to dive. My head overrules my intuition.

The plan is to dive on air to a maximum depth of 30 m/100 ft for fifteen minutes, then to deploy our SMB and ascend at 9 m/30 ft per min to 4.5 m/15 ft, switch gas to EAN50, and do our deco accordingly. The dive will be in a quarry named la Carrière de Perlonjour, near the town of Soignies in Belgium.

The dive site is new to me but, unusually, I am not excited at the prospect of discovering it. Why am I so anxious for a dive like this? In the evening, as I am preparing my gear, I am constantly going through the steps of the dive plan in my head, and the night hardly brings any improvement.

Photo by Victor Chikhachev

I get up at 4:30 am; I have to drive to the diving center to collect dive cylinders.

I'd left my tank there after a dive using EAN40; they've filled it up again to 200 bar/2900 psi with the same mix. Did I inform the shop owner that I would be needing air instead? I'm almost certain I did. Anyway, we are late and emptying and filling my 15L (with dual outlet valve) with air will take too long. I decide to dive with EAN40; IANTD allows a max. PPO₂ of 1.6 bar, and as the planned max. depth is 30 m/100 ft. It should be fine.

We load our gear and drive towards Belgium.

On arrival, the protocol keeps repeating itself into my head, like a mantra. I meet with the three divers on the shore and we go through our pre-dive briefing. I tell them that I will be diving with EAN40. No comments!

We start our immersion. I instantly feel the cold on my face. It is colder than I had expected. We descend in pairs; my buddy is the master instructor. At a depth of seven metres, I suddenly feel an intense pain. It feels like someone has just stabbed an icepick right through my left ear, deeper into my brain. I give the signal to stop. I am in pain and trying to equalize the pressure by doing the Valsalva manuever. I normally never do that, as my anatomy is such that by simply swallowing, I cannot equalise my ears. I give the signal to ascend.

We surface, and I try to clear my nose. It is painful. Many scenarios are spinning through my head.

Although my gut feeling is that I should cancel the dive, I ignore it and trust my head instead. I cannot and should not disappoint those people. They have had to drive nearly four hours to reach the dive site. This is the last dive before their certification. I decide everyone has to prepare for diving again.

We begin our descent. 7 m/23 ft, 10 m/32 ft, 20 m/66 ft, then 30 m/100 ft.

This should be our bottom depth. It is pitch dark.

Before I understand what is going on, Murphy's well-known law comes into effect. Everything suddenly goes wrong; a chain reaction of problems occurs.

I experience what feels like a fireball moving at lightspeed from my heart to my head. I feel sick, dizzy. It's like I've just landed in a slow-motion movie. I am now the spectator of the movie of my own life.

I see one of the divers starting to ascend. What is going on? I have not given any signal. I grab the tip of his fin and try to stop him ascending. It is too early - we still have to spend more time at current depth before starting our ascent!

I slowly realise that he is not ascending at all. I am descending. I let go, nothing else. I can see what happens, but I am not able to act. My buddy is with me. He is looking at me with wide-open eyes. He gives me the OK signal and for some reason I answer with the OK signal.

I can see fear in his eyes. What is going on in his mind? We reach 40 m/130 ft,, and I inflate my BCD to stop descending. Forty metres deep, this is the depth we are at. The darkness and cold rise like armies smelling victory.

Murphy continues showing his power. The PPO₂ of the mix I am breathing has now reached 2 bar!! Everything cramps in my body. I am hit by oxygen toxicity. Spasms develop in seconds. I am shaking my head uncontrollably back and forth. I have nausea and I'm gasping desperately.

My regulator starts failing. I cannot breathe, I am getting water in my mouth.

Am I drowning?
I need to breathe to survive.
I have a second regulator and an Air2 on my BCD, but I don't reach for it.

I am not able to do what I have been trained to.

My buddy is petrified but does nothing. I am moving towards him and give a hand signal that I need immediate assistance. He is like a statue. His eyes are nearly popping out of his face.

I am about to die.

On one side I am at peace, it is my destiny. On the other side, a voice tells me it is too early to leave!

A primitive instinct for survival starts to take over. I figure out that shooting like a rocket towards the surface is the only way to get fresh air into my lungs. My lungs will probably explode as soon as I surface. Can I make it?

What is my other option? Do nothing?

I am facing death, playing Russian Roulette. The rules are different though. Instead of one round in the chamber, Murphy has loaded the gun with five, leaving one chamber empty. The barrel starts spinning as I start my journey back to the world.

Without removing my weight belt, I inflate my BCD and shoot up like a rocket. I am looking up, trying to spot some daylight. I am still in darkness. The ascent lasts for ages. I see a retrospective movie of my life.
Am I already dead?

Photo by Eelco Borsboom

The ascent does not stop. How can I exit the inferno I am in? Will Murphy leave me alone? I feel a rush of adrenaline rising. I am fighting for life. I will not lose the battle. Suddenly I am exiting darkness. How long will that take? Time passes and I keep on drowning, I am screaming for help, I am not going to make it. I am now surrounded by light. I am feeling so well. Is this what death is?

Then I am back into darkness again. Unconsciousness.

I am floating at the surface. I am bleeding from my nose, my mouth and my ears. Fortunately, there is an unknown diver who has just surfaced.

He notices me and drags me towards the shore.

When we reach the shore, I am taken out of the water. I am resuscitated with my own oxygen bottle.

Thirty minutes later, a trauma team arrives.

On our way to Brussels, the doctor calls the Military Hospital. I can hear him saying, "We are losing him." The oxygen saturation in my blood is 82%. It is too low. I am given all types of medications and injections.

At the hospital, I am treated by Dr. Peter Germonpré, Medical Director DAN Europe Benelux and head of the Hyperbaric Center. He and his team save my life.
To date, I still have not spoken with those three divers. What happened to them? Still unanswered questions… I can blame myself, not them.

Photo by Eelco Borsboom

I ignored basic safety rules. I underestimated the risks. Despite the multiple signals and the pain in my ears, I decided to re-start the dive. There are many things I could have done differently. Should have done differently.

Ultimately, it all started when my intuition sent warning signals and I ignored them.

I have replayed the movie of what happened thousands of times in my head. Why did it go so wrong?

Part of the mystery was unraveled in 2012, when I had a stroke (VCA). It turns out that I had a congenital heart defect called an Atrial Septal Defect (ASD); the Cardiologist's conclusion was that my ASD would have been the cause of both my diving accident and my VCA.

An ASD is a hole in the septum between the two upper chambers of the heart. The cardiologist told me that people with an ASD can have what is called a 'Paradoxical Embolism'. I'll leave you to Google what it means.

Is that what happened to me during the dive? Was I the victim of a Paradoxical Embolism? Would a clot in my venous system travel through my ASD into my arterial system and then reach my brain? Was this the clot I described as a ball of fire going at lightspeed from my heart to my head?

In 2012, I experienced the same feeling. Finally, my ASD was closed, and I stopped teaching diving. I have asked myself a lot of 'WHY' questions. In fact, 'WHY' questions are rarely answered; the 'WHAT' questions are the ones to be asked. They offer the possibility to find new pathways. As a survivor, my experience has been a life-changing event. Safety has become my life mission.

I am working with a French company named Azoth Systems (www.o-dive.com). They are the inventors of O'Dive, the world's first technology that allows divers to personalise their diving practice by taking into consideration the severity component of the dive and the bubbles detected in their venous system after the dive.

I am working with them as a Business Developer and Instructor Trainer.

My goal now is to partner with diving agencies and develop a dedicated diving safety training that is different from what is available today.

Emmanuel Kuehn *is the International Business Developer & Instructor Trainer at Azoth Systems. He is a dual national (Dutch/French) who lives in The Netherlands. His passion for the underwater realm started when he was a kid. Like many of us, he was fascinated by Lt. J.Y. Cousteau and his team aboard the Calypso. His diving history started in 1989 in France, where he was taught to dive according to the CMAS standards. In 1994, he became a PADI Instructor and later, was trained as a DAN Oxygen Instructor and as an IANTD Instructor.*

His goal was to become an IT in technical diving. He was an avid reader of Michael Menduno's amazing magazine, aquaCORPS. After he survived his accident, he stopped teaching diving.

Since 2008, he has been working as a trainer & coach, focusing on safety leadership. He has been telling his story to thousands of people in corporate organizations of all types. Although the majority of people he trained have never dived, his story inspired others and unlocked some consciousness related to safety behavior and culture. His specialties are safety leadership, culture transformation, and international business development.

EUGENIO MONGELLI

TRIMIX/REBREATHER INSTRUCTOR
PRESIDENT @ DE-OX TEMC
ACADEMY AWARDS INTERNATIONAL ACADEMY
OF UNDERWATER SCIENCE AND TECHNOLOGY
.

LOCATION OF INCIDENT
TARANTO, ITALY

I believe that skilled and responsible divers should try to prepare for their dives by considering all the aspects of logistics, dive plan, scuba gear, gas management, properly-maintained equipment, and human factors.

It is like managing a chain of activities with the strength of the whole thing tied to that of the weakest link. Any one failure may cause a small issue to begin with and lead progressively to a disaster. There is "Murphy's Law" waiting just around the corner for each activity.

After decades of diving all over the world, I learned that you can minimise the impact of any unexpected failure if you plan properly. The worst scenarios occur when you have not planned every aspect of the dive, exposing you to the worst nightmare of your life: the close call, and for sure you will never forget it!

This story concerns the malfunction of my dive computer during a deep solo dive. I have experienced this issue three times in my diving career, but the first incident is the most interesting to talk about. Twenty years ago, in August, I was at my favourite diving spot in Apulia, within the Taranto Sea Gulf, searching for red coral colonies.

These were some precious spots where red coral was still alive, florid and luxuriant. Solo diving was my personal choice, because the spot had to remain secret to prevent irresponsible divers from committing coral robbery on the site. Sadly, the red coral of this area is among the best in the whole Mediterranean sea for colour and is known for its hardness and financial worth.

On that day I dove a 2x10 litre twin air set, fully equipped and supported by a boat on the surface.

Photos by Eugenio Mongelli

The original plan was to dive from 40-60 m/131-196 ft in the range of 20 to 45 minutes bottom time and to decompress using the computer. The aim was to find the spot's coordinates and explore it.

The site itself was new to me; all I knew were some rumours and secret tips from local fishermen in the area, who said this was a real "magic spot." The only reliable source of information was the nautical chart, which reported an isobathic at 50 m/164 ft, but the characteristics of the seabed could have ranged from a wall cut to a smooth downhill or a steep slope. Such is the pleasure of exploration!

We arrived at the dive spot using GPS and anchored the boat in a depth of around 40 m/131 ft. After a quick check of my gear, I went down to explore the coral.

A moderate current greeted me, with a good sea visibility of about 40 m/131 ft. I continuously checked the dive computer and the watch to verify that there was no problem.

The depth went from 40 m/131 ft, then 51 m/167 ft. I worked my way deeper until finally I reached the wall cut in the sea bed with some small cavities full of red coral! What phenomenally beautiful coral branches! During my exploration, I was keeping check of instruments, tank pressure, depth, dive time, and managing the narcosis. I had accumulated around 33 minutes of deco time when I looked at the computer and saw the display was suddenly completely off! There were no more numbers, no prior failure signals, nothing. I was very upset, and my first instinct was to surface.

But my training stopped me. I realised that I did not have the written dive plan with me. But luckily, I always carry my watch with a depth meter (even if it has no memory of maximum depth), and I always turned it on before starting the dive. Then, in my BCD pockets I always carry a set of dive decompression tables, both Buhlmann and US Navy. I have to thank my military and diving training, where the words "stop-breathe-think-act" worked successfully in that situation.

After that first moment of shock, I understood how the potentially critical situation could be successfully sorted out. I immediately went back to the anchor line and started my ascent. But which decompression plan to execute? Which pair of depth-time to consider?

"Be conservative," I decided.

So, I stopped at half depth and consulted the dive table. Luckily the 'deep stop' theory had already been developed, and I knew I could safely stop there, buying time to think in a better narcosis situation. I chose the US Navy tables as they are less conservative compared to the Buhlmann. The max depth, I remembered, was calculated from the time when I last found the dive computer working, which indicated total decompression time to be around 40 min. So I started the deco plan with a 51 m/167 ft depth, 25 minutes bottom time and a total of deco 32 minutes; I also decided that I would continue my 5 m/16 ft deco stop until my tanks were empty. I could not be too conservative though, because my air was limited.

During the deco I was checking carefully for any possible DCS symptoms, breathing calmly and reflecting on what happened during the whole process. After 70 minutes' run time, I finally emerged with completely empty cylinders. I was still somewhat concerned, so I followed the no-stress, no-heavy-work, drink-lots-of-water-rules.

Was that my close call ?

I don't really know, but since then I always dive with two computers!

One valuable lesson from this experience: I found out that lithium batteries can betray you, as their voltage levels can remain high until the last minute, even though they are actually nearly empty. In my case, this problem was exacerbated by intensive use (due to extra energy required for processing the calculation of decompression underwater). The battery may suddenly turn faulty without any warning

on a dive. So, never trust the battery check of your dive computer, keep note of the usage, and replace/recharge the battery when you believe it is about time.

Eugenio Mongelli *was born in 1965 in Rome, Italy. Since his childhood, he has always been deeply attracted to the sea, diving, and scuba gear technology. A scuba diver since 1982, he first dived with a closed oxygen rebreather in 1984, and from the mid 1990s he started using electronic closed-circuit rebreathers.*

A diving instructor since 1991, he is a freediving and scuba diving master instructor, and a rebreather and trimix instructor with FIPSAS CMAS and TDI. During his dive career, he has known and joined many agencies worldwide. The discovery of aquaCorps magazine in the early 1990s shocked his life, opening his mind to the new horizon of diving that has become his life path.

A doctor in management engineering, he founded TEMC DE-OX Company in 1996 with the intent of providing digital gas analysers specifically designed for the diving industry. Since then, he closely follows the development of technical diving in all aspects of training, learning, designing new gear, and being an active part of the global community. As a former navy officer, hyperbaric and commercial saturation diving within the context of military diving are substantial parts of his company's asset technologies.

Leading TEMC DE-OX, Eugenio continuously travels around the world, catching up with as many friends he can and diving in all kinds of environments. He wishes he could dive more often, given his busy schedule! Eugenio also had experience organising the Olympic Games in Athens, Turin, Beijing, London, and Rio de Janeiro as part of the broadcasting department, where he developed skills for organising large events worldwide.

EVAN KOVACS

DEEP SHIPWRECK EXPLORER
UNDERWATER CINEMATOGRAPHER

LOCATION OF INCIDENT
ENGLISH CHANNEL

It was the summer of 2003 when I started diving CCR, and my first unit was a PRISM Topaz. Like all firsts, I instantly became infatuated with the capabilities of the system, and I had the good fortune to be able to dive it for both pleasure and work.

Right about the same time, I started working in television on a show for the History Channel called Deep Sea Detectives, which involved traveling all around the world. As part of the show sponsorship, we were trained on the Inspiration CCR and often dived that unit, which was one of the most consistently reliable units I had worked with.

For several years, I logged hundreds of hours on both the units—PRISM and Inspiration—and became fairly proficient in going back and forth between the two. The loop directions were different and needed different hand actions to work the add valves, so anytime I was going to switch to the other unit, I would get on the treadmill and practice the appropriate motor memory for different scenarios. I don't know why, but the treadmill helped me focus and burn in the muscle memory.

It's something I still do to this day when I need to focus my thoughts and think through issues, even on projects that are not dive-related. For the most part, I would dive the units interchangeably, but I always preferred to dive the PRISM on deeper wrecks or caves. I felt that the work of breathing (WOB) was better, I liked the radial scrubber, and even though the build quality of the PRISM was terrible (comparatively), and the system needed a little bit of special TLC or parts of it might break apart, I still dived the unit and trusted its simplicity.

Photo by Evan Kovacs

After several years of doing dive logistics and underwater lighting for the show, I was excited when I was asked to shoot lead camera for some deeper dives in the English Channel. I was regularly traveling with eight to ten pelican cases, and one of the best things about diving the Inspiration at the time was that you could just throw it in the box and pull it out on the other side, and it was always there, working and never broken. For this particular set of dives however, I decided to dive the PRISM, since we were going to be diving some deeper wrecks, and I wanted the better WOB when pushing the camera around at depth. In addition, we were going to be using full face masks (FFM) for the shoot so we could communicate effectively.

We used FFM regularly, and since they were always a little heavy breathing, I again opted to use the PRISM. I wrapped the unit in a sheet of soft foam, packed it in its case, put a note in for TSA saying it was life support and to "please be careful," and off I went across the pond.

Our usual crew of about ten people was there, and after schlepping all the gear to the hotel, I began to set up cameras. Finally about 9 PM or so, I got to my rebreather. I'll never forget opening the box and seeing the broken pieces from various parts of the unit. I had packed it adequately, except I had forgotten about my good friends at TSA. While I was waiting at the airport in Newark, I had been called by a gate agent to answer a few questions by some TSA agents about the "items in the case that looked suspicious." I explained that it was life support and asked that they carefully handle everything.

The fellow nodded his head assuredly, didn't listen to a word I said, and apparently went back to try to fully disassemble the unit with a hammer—even the parts that were not supposed to come apart. After they were done with the unit's cavity search, they threw it back in the box without even wrapping it up on the foam, and after careful handling by the rest of Newark and Heathrow's baggage dept, all the broken pieces of the unit safely arrived in my hotel room.

Although I was upset, I had nothing to do but to try to fix the unit. Actually I had a much better option, which would have been to call Martin Parker and sheepishly ask if I could borrow a unit for a week or so, but that didn't even occur to me at the time.

Our routine was to land and dive the next day, and this shoot was no different. I made some coffee, pulled out the epoxy and glued the various bits back to the unit from the bucket and head. It actually went fairly well, and I was quite pleased with myself until I turned the unit on and none of the cells registered. This particular CCR had an analog gauge for reading the cells one at a time, and as I scrolled through each cell, my heart sank as not one cell turned on.

When I looked inside the head at the wiring harness—a series of crimped connectors that plugged onto the sensors and the head—all I saw was a jumble of wires that some TSA handler had literally ripped out and apart. Frustrated again, I didn't pull out the spare harness—a $15 part—because I didn't have one. Instead, I made some more coffee, pulled out the soldering iron, and started soldering the wires back to the crimp connectors.

In hindsight, I should have just soldered everything together directly and not tried to actually solder broken crimps—or called Martin—but, of course, I didn't do either. By 3 a.m. the job was done, and I fell asleep with the all too familiar smell of burnt wires in the air.

For the next three days, we dove wrecks off the coast and everything worked flawlessly.

Although I had received a lot of good-natured ribbing about the homemade fixes and CCR held by glue, I didn't care and was quite happy to make some spectacular dives with the unit and capture beautiful images over the next few days.

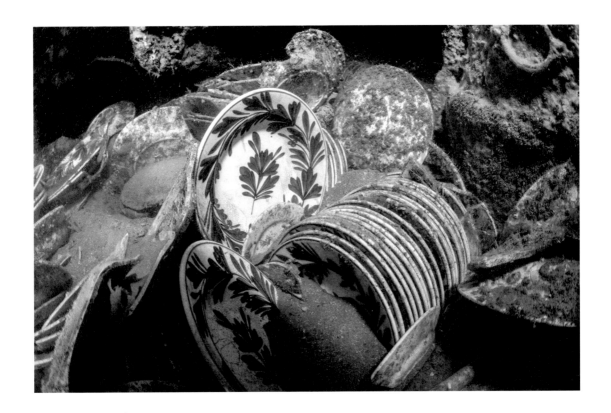

Finally, on the fourth day we were diving the Duke of Buccleuch, a steamer that sank in 1889 while laden with goods bound for Calcutta. It was business as usual, and with one giant stride, we were on our way.

As cameraman, I usually descended first and set up for the shot. As we descended, I scrolled through the PO$_2$ on my sensors and confirmed my Heads-up Display (HUD)–which I could not really see without actively pushing up on the loop in the FFM.

I landed on the bottom and set up for a nice shot over a pile of beautiful china. The guys came down, and I filmed them landing and swimming off into the distance. Once the shot was done, I made one power-kick off the bottom, and I thought someone whacked me in the head from behind. I dropped the camera (I don't remember doing that) and my right hand instinctively, through muscle memory, went to the diluent add valve.

It was only a matter of a few seconds, but I couldn't see my HUD so I fumbled for my O$_2$ gauge, which was hampered because my vision almost disappeared, and I seemed to be looking through tiny slits.

My head swam and I felt very ... switched off. Suddenly my vision seemed to get better as the diluent worked its way into the loop, and I could start to read the PO$_2$ cells once again. I started hearing Richie Kohler, one of the presenters, in my head but could not answer him.

As my brain fog started to clear, I realised Richie's voice was in my ear bud. It had taken several seconds, but I started to recognize that there was something seriously wrong. One of the best (or worst) things about working in TV is that everything is recorded so that when you fail, it is there for all to see or hear. At a minimum, it helps to keep you honest and true.

Photo by Leigh Bishop

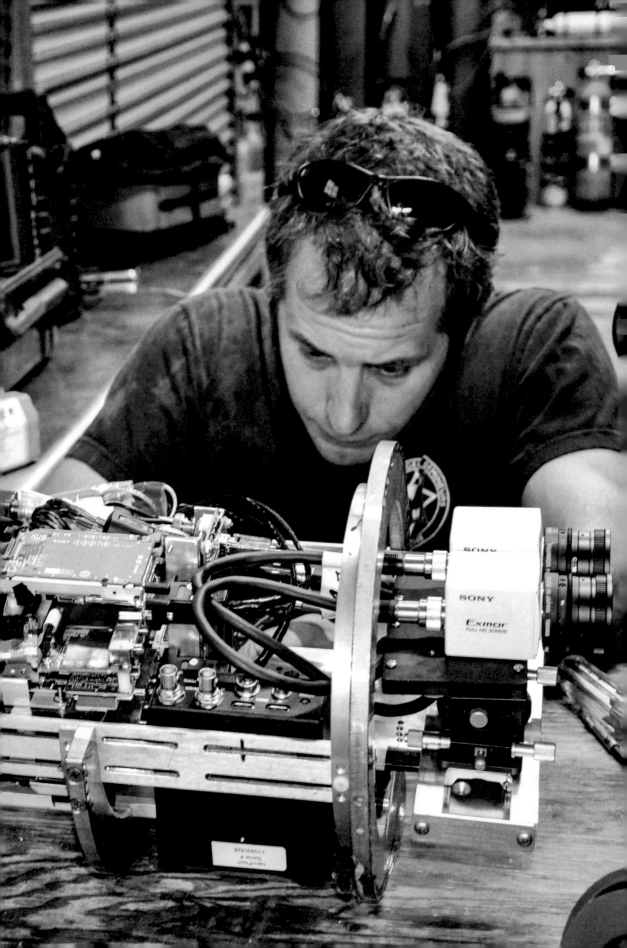

Below are a few lines from the transcript:
Richie: "Evan, are you OK?"
Evan: Garbled sounds
Richie: "Evannn, are you OK?"
Evan: "Huh? I think so."
Richie: "What's the matter?"
Evan: "Well, one cell is high, one cell is low, the third one is dead … and I don't feel so good."

Shortly after that I bailed out and our safety diver Mark Bullen came to the surface with me.

What went wrong? My soldered mess (the harness) came apart shortly after I looked at it on the descent. I don't remember anything special happening to cause it to fail, which means that it was probably marginal and failing repeatedly over the previous days, which I missed because I could NOT see my HUD. Of all the dumb things I have done, that one still blows me away.

I remember my 'logic', which was that it was just an inch out of eyesight and the loop would be pushed up by the camera most of the time anyway. Much of the time it was, and I could see it, but I had grown complacent and a little too trusting in my electronics and too confident about my repair abilities.

I think that the PO_2 in my loop was about .12-.13 when I power-kicked off the bottom, and that was not enough to keep the lights on in my head, so to speak. I am fully convinced that if I had not spent time constantly going through my emergency loop procedures on the treadmill, I could have made the wrong move–possibly hit the wrong valve–and passed out on the bottom.

That's about the only part of the story that I did right.

As someone who now builds cameras and shoots with them, I consider it a miracle that the harness I soldered survived or worked at all in the first place. That harness is now in a box with a series of other 'mementos' from assorted dives gone wrong, such as

the remains of the tattered camera tether that was run through a prop and ripped me from 110 m/360 ft to 76 m/250 ft in about six seconds.

They are good reminders that things can happen, sometimes from our own mistakes; other times due to circumstances beyond our control. Most of the time we survive, even if just barely, but what is most important for me is not to make the same mistake twice. I just wish there were not so many things for me to f*** up on!

Evan Kovacs *is a diver, passionate explorer, and underwater cinematographer, who began his underwater filming career in 2002 while working with the History Channel. Since then, Evan has run high-stakes multimedia projects around the world for National Geographic, Discovery Channel, PBS, NOVA, CBC, NHK, and others. Beginning in 2006, Evan collaborated with Woods Hole Oceanographic Institution on next-generation imaging systems.*

He has been involved in numerous expeditions utilizing remotely operated vehicles ('ROVs') and submersibles to survey and film everything from the Apollo 11 engine recovery to deep sea hydrothermal vents. Evan not only builds camera and lighting systems for these jobs, he is one of the few professional cinematographers qualified to use these systems at depths to 152 m/500 ft and is one of the few people to film extensively on both RMS Titanic and her sister, HMHS Britannic.

In 2010, Kovacs formed Marine Imaging Technologies, a subsea imaging company to develop innovative ideas for subsea imaging systems and robotics, including Pixel, the first Cinema Class ROV, and Spooler, a new style of penetration class ROV. Evan continues to film, consult, and build equipment for projects all around the globe.

DR. FRAUKE TILLMANS

RESEARCH DIRECTOR @ DIVERS ALERT NETWORK (DAN)

LOCATION OF INCIDENT
SOUTHERN GERMANY

I am lucky enough to say that I haven't experienced a real 'close call' myself, but don't we all have some dives that stay stuck in our heads even though they didn't necessarily have a bad outcome? Those sorts of dives fall into different categories, but in particular we tend to vividly remember any dive that we associate with feelings.

On the positive side, those feelings might include awe at the absolute beauty we saw on that one reef, or fascination with a curious marine creature that decided to interact with us during a dive, but there are also less enjoyable feelings that can be associated with some dives as well.

These more negative feelings can stick in our brains just as well, and those are the ones that can teach some great lessons. They teach you because you knew something wasn't quite

right; you knew you weren't quite ready for the challenge, and one little thing could have blown it all up. You knew you should have called the dive before your giant stride off the boat. Or you should have thumbed it right at the entry of that cave—but you didn't!

I want to share one of those more memorable dives. I can't say that I was particularly young or inexperienced at the time, so I won't try to make an excuse for myself. I was just over a decade into a very active diving career, was used to thinking and multitasking under water, and had made it to instructor level and dive safety officer.

I had just purchased a new dry suit–my first ever custom-made–and was beyond excited to finally take it out in the cold. The opportunity arose two weeks after it had been shipped to my door, with a dear friend who

invited me to join him and his public safety dive team for an ice dive. The lake–not more than 12 m/40 ft deep and a fishing hotspot when not covered in ice–was completely new to me. I had heard enough about it that I absolutely wanted to go, especially because lake access was normally restricted, and the county opened it only for this one group to conduct their training dives, which was the reason why I had never been. Everyone in the team that I was now going to meet already knew the dive site.

One additional requirement for participating in the operation on that day was that I had to dive a full face mask.

We prepared everything; the dive operation–a normal training day at the lake–was busy but not hectic. People seemed to know what they were doing, and I followed through, got my gear ready, checked everything, got in the new suit including the new three-finger gloves, geared up, and made my way to the ice hole we had made before. We went through all the line signals once more with the surface team, and everything went very smoothly.

It was only when I felt the water surface closing over my head that I realised that there were a few more new variables in this dive than I felt comfortable with, and that was also the moment when my brain started working and coming up with all the "what ifs:" What if the dry suit behaves different than the old one with the new undergarments? What if I lose my buoyancy and drag my teammate (who was connected to me through a buddy line) up under the ceiling? What if the mask floods and I don't get it fixed with the bulky gloves I had never used before?

What if something happens to my teammate and I–already task-loaded with my new equipment–have to drag him back to the entry in an overhead environment I hadn't even been in under normal conditions, and then get him out with a team I had not worked with before?

We continued the dive, as I did not turn the dive there, although I felt really uneasy. If anything, I was annoyed with myself for feeling–what I determined unnecessarily–task-loaded.

I got more comfortable with the gear as we moved through the very clear water. It was a good dive, and when it was time to turn the dive, I signalled my teammate and then wanted to signal the surface crew that we were coming back.

The line was a bit too loose for my liking, and when I turned to check it, I saw that it made a huge bow, which meant that there was no way any signal would have gone through at that time. I collected the spare line, about 15 m/50 ft, until I finally felt a connection resume and had a chance to signal again. We followed the line back, but because it wasn't pulled in by the surface team, we kept collecting it on the way.

I was relieved when I saw the entry hole and surfaced immediately, throwing the pile of spare line on the ice in front of the line operator. The dive safety officer must have seen the look on my face and the confusion in the line operator's eyes, and within the next five minutes I learned that the person who had been running the line had changed during our dive and that it was her third day with the team and the first time she had put hands on a signaling line.

Luckily, what happened was what usually happens: nothing.

On the drive home, I mentally went through all the things that were new on the day and could have caused trouble: a new dry suit; new, thick, three-finger gloves; a new model of full face mask that did not even belong to me; a new dive site; a dive team I had just met that weekend; a change in surface support crew during the dive; and a team member who was just being trained.

In retrospect, I can justify to myself why every single one of those factors that only started worrying me underwater or that just became apparent after the dive separately were not a "big deal" for me, and why it made sense to keep rolling with them.

None of the 'what ifs' became an issue that day, but the dive stuck in my head, and I thought about it again and again over the next few weeks.

Something changed that day, and I started questioning myself and my teammates more about the way we did things and the way I made decisions. I can say that it was one of my best learning experiences and one that is difficult to teach and bring across in a classroom setting; we can only share the stories that ultimately made us a better diver.

Frauke Tillmans *is the Research Director at Divers Alert Network (DAN). She holds a degree in Human Biology and a PhD specializing in oxidative stress, which is involved in acute diving injuries and may affect the long-term health of divers.*

Throughout her career she has participated in global collaborative projects covering decompression stress, inert gas narcosis, and oxygen toxicity.

Before going to DAN in 2019, Frauke conducted her research in the Experimental Medicine Section of the German Naval Medical Institute.

In addition to her research experience, Frauke is also an experienced public safety diver, diving instructor, scientific diving supervisor, and dive safety officer, and has recently developed a passion for cave diving.

Tillmans' commitment to safety is apparent in almost every activity she pursues, and when she is not diving or supervising researchers, Frauke is an active volunteer firefighter who enjoys endurance and self-defense training.

GABRIELE PAPARO

ITALIAN NAVY DIVING TEAM COMMANDING OFFICER
OC/CCR DIVER / EOD / PARATROOPER
TEK DIVING & CCR INSTRUCTOR

LOCATION OF INCIDENT
JACKSON BLUE SPRING, FLORIDA, USA

I am in the Italian Navy, and I was involved in training with the US Armed Forces. In 2004, I moved to the United States for work, spending five months in Texas and another six in Florida.

During my stay in Florida, I had the opportunity to complete my cave diving training–from the 'Intro to Cave' level, all the way up to the 'Full Cave Diver' certification–with an experienced fellow instructor from Alabama.

I was already a CCR diver, and all my diving gear (including my rebreather) was with me. However, back then in 2004, no instructors were available to teach Cave classes using a CCR; I had to do all the training dives on OC (doubles + stages), while all my experience dives were completed diving CCR.

After completing the Full Cave Diver training, I found myself completing multiple cave dives every single weekend (often setting my camping tent at Ginnie Spring) and sometimes during the week as well. As luck would have it, I lived pretty close to Jackson Blue Spring, where my friend and cave diving buddy Edd Sorenson was operating his dive center.

Even though most of the time I was diving using the buddy system (mainly with OC buddies and sometimes with my friend John, an Inspiration CCR diver from Atlanta, Georgia), I found myself solo diving on several occasions, either for lack of buddies or because I was planning 'special dives' (meaning longer than usual) with deeper penetration into the cave.

At the beginning of October, I planned a solo dive at Jackson Blue Spring, one of the most beautiful caves I used to visit.

At that point, after performing many dives with various jumps and paths, I was confident about my knowledge of the different sections, side passages, and jumps of that cave.

That day I planned a special dive, using 4 hail-out bottles (my standard two nitrox S80s, an additional S80, and one Oxy S40) to complete a circuit entering the main tunnel and exiting from one of the side passages. In order to do this, I would need to place a jump spool from the main line to connect to the side passage I was supposed to exit from. I was going to do this before proceeding to the farthest part of the cave.

For this dive, I was taking a single scooter, my Submerge Uv26. At the time, this was probably the best DPV available, with approximately 130 minutes of burn time. According to my plan, I was supposed to scooter fast for about 50-55 minutes on the way in, stage the scooter, and swim around to explore the end section of the cave.

Then, on my way back, I would swim for about 40-45 minutes in the 'circuit' section of the cave until I reached my jump spool. Once I reached it (and therefore the main line), I would scooter to the exit of the cave in about 25-30 minutes. Yeah, the "thirds rule" in the use of the scooter was not strictly applied; I was intending to use just a little more than two-thirds in total, which would allow me to avoid carrying two scooters. Back then they were pretty big and heavy (lead-acid batteries), so moving with less drag, especially in the narrow section of the caves, was preferable.

Before I started my dive, I asked a fellow on the beach to take a picture of me in the water ready to dive. I told him, "I am entering for a long solo dive, see ya later!" Probably, since rebreather divers were so rare, he did not realize that "long" for me was a three- to three-and-a-half hour dive. For standard OC divers with double 120s and double stage, the average was more like two to two-and-a-half.

I started scootering after staging my oxygen cylinder in the cavern, tying it to the main line. Scootering in with three S80s was a little trickier than expected–and obviously a little slower. I reached the point where I wanted to stage my first S80.

Everything was fine, and I continued with less drag to the point where I planned to place my jump spool. Once done, I continued scootering almost to the very end of the cave, searching for the correct side tunnel I was planning to exit from. I had to find the one on the right-hand side that would allow me to swim back to my jump reel. At this point, already running behind time, I was more than 70 minutes into the dive but decided to continue anyway with my original plan: exploring the end section of the cave before heading back and completing the circuit (as far as I knew, nobody had done it before since Edd never mentioned it to me). I staged my scooter and one of my nitrox bailouts and started advancing into the 'Stratosphere', 'Banana room' and 'Terminal room'.

After completing this leisurely swim, I finally reached my DPV and nitrox bottle, recovered them, and called the dive. I knew I had taken longer than expected, but I figured this was fine anyway (nobody was waiting for me at dinner!).

I started swimming back with my two S80s on my side, towing the scooter behind me. Everything was going well. I came to a familiar, tapering section of the cave and swam on until I reached a point where I had never been before; usually, once I reached these side passages and narrow sections, I would turn around and go back the way I came to exit on the main line. On this occasion I stayed and began to traverse tunnels that I was visiting for the first time.

In the beginning it was fun–I was without worries, curious, and enjoying the new view. Even though I was more than two hours into the dive, I wasn't tired and was still very attentive.

But soon the problems started to arise.

My current cave section began tapering even more in a "no stream" area, where the bottom was light and volatile enough to make a dangerous silt-out behind me very likely. To avoid this, I took my scooter from my back and pushed it in front of me instead of towing it.

I was having to concentrate much harder to focus on my trim and propulsion technique, and I was still swimming in an unknown area without any idea of how far I had to go to get back to my jump reel. The farther I swam, the more this section became a labyrinth. I continued passing T's after T's, placing my clothes-pin markers on each split in case I was forced to turn back instead of continuing forward. I hoped that a situation like that was unlikely but "you never know," and I was applying a safety rule. However, once my dive computer counted three hours into the dive, and I was still in this low section of the cave, having passed so many T's in an easily silted-out area …

I started to become very worried! I began to ask myself, "Am I going in the right direction? Did I take a wrong turn into a blind tunnel? How far am I from my jump spool/main line?" After more than 180 min of precise trimming and swimming, carrying two stages, and towing/pushing my scooter I was exhausted! I had the option of using the scooter in that section to be faster and conserve my own energy, but doing so would create zero vis behind me, making it impossible to swim back if I ended up needing to.

The only tool I had to help me navigate was my compass; after every corner I was hoping to find my spool or a familiar tunnel. At every new T-junction, I was praying that I would choose the correct direction. There was no more room left for error. I was on the verge of giving up. The only alternative remaining would be to swim back through all those tapering passages, back to the end section of the cave, and then scooter along the main line to the exit. This solution would bring my dive time up to an unplanned six hours, without enough oxygen to do it and dangerously

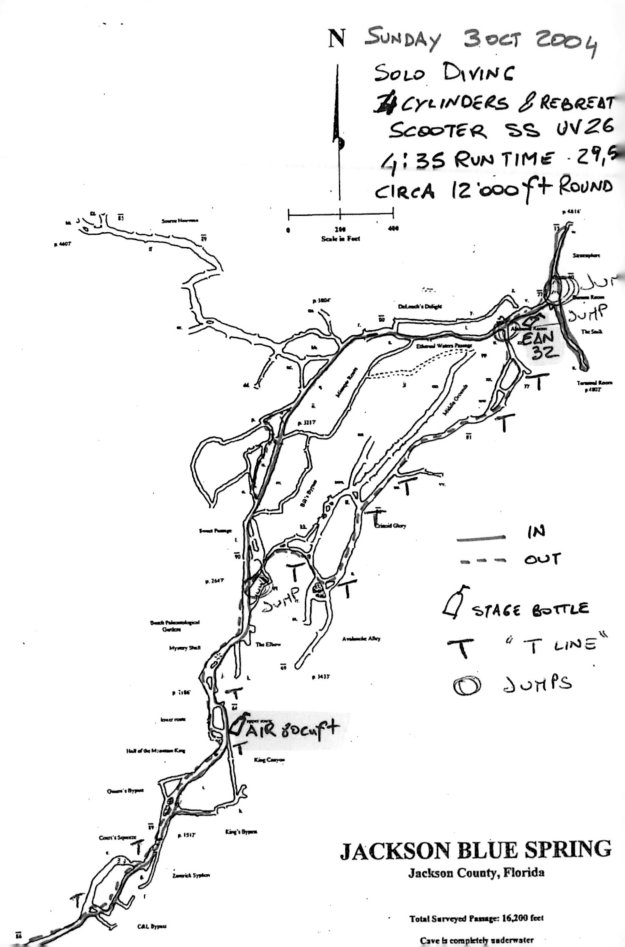

N SUNDAY 3 OCT 2004
SOLO DIVING
4 CYLINDERS & REBREAT
SCOOTER SS UV26
4:35 RUN TIME · 29,5
CIRCA 12'000 ft ROUND

Scale in Feet

IN
OUT

STAGE BOTTLE
"T LINE"
JUMPS

EAN 32
AIR 80cuft

JUMP
JUMP

JACKSON BLUE SPRING

Jackson County, Florida

Total Surveyed Passage: 16,200 feet

Cave is completely underwater

pushing the scrubber way longer than the stated limit of three hours.

Having considered all of this, I decided to continue on the circuit, forcing myself to stay mentally focused and physically maintaining a good trim and propulsion technique. I zeroed in my attention to every detail of the cave and the direction I hoped I was swimming toward.

Now three-and-a-half hours into the dive, I was clearly past the 'point of no return'. Physically drained and mentally exhausted, the seeds of doubt began to sprout in my mind. I thought I was not going to find the exit. I thought I was not going to make it this time.

Finally, after one last turn, my powerful light reflected off a glimmering piece of metal in the distance: it was the carabiner of my spool reel! A feeling of immense relief washed over me–finding my spool meant finding the exit of the cave.

After recovering it, I started scootering to my staged bailout bottle and to the cavern for deco stops. My decompression was longer than expected, of course. The max depth had been about 30 m/100 ft, but my dive time was pretty long on a 1.2 PpO₂ setpoint but I was safe!

While in the cavern section, I started thinking about the guy who'd taken my picture. I probably would not see him again because it was so late. In fact, I did not meet any other diver in the cave or cavern while decompressing.

I thought, "Well, it is Sunday,and people go back home early." The total runtime was 275 minutes when I surfaced. I expected to find nobody, but I was wrong. The sheriff and the county rescue diving team were there. They'd just arrived and were getting ready to start a dive to "recover the body of an Italian diving a Rebreather."

The guy who took my photo had noted the time-in and after two-and-a-half hours he

started to be concerned. After three hours he was asking other divers about me (nobody had seen me, of course), and shortly thereafter he called the sheriff's department to report a "missing diver." I was fine, just pretty tired and very embarrassed. My excuse was, "I told you I was going for a long dive!"

Gabriele Paparo *is an active scuba diving instructor and technical/rebreathers diving instructor for several scuba diving agencies (TDI – PADI – IANTD – RAID and more). He is also currently on active duty as an Italian Navy EOD/Diver Officer, as a CO (Team Leader) of the Divers/EOD Unit detachment in North Sardinia (Italy). He has logged over 3000 recreational and technical dives and over 1500 logged commercial & military dives over 23 years of continuous activity.*

He first began his recreational scuba training in 1992 and later began his training as a Navy diver in 1994. He worked as a commercial diver for PCS (Italy) and as a dive master for diving centers in Southern Italy before re-joining the Navy.

Gabriele worked over 10 years at the main base of Italian Navy divers & Special Forces (COMSUBIN) as a diver, diver supervisor, explosive ordnance disposal technician, ROV / ADS pilot, Search & Rescue operator, and hyperbaric chamber operator/technician. He has been part of the inspection and recovery of shipwrecks, submarines and aircraft including: Canadair – Palermo 1996, F104 –Trapani 1996, TOTI Submarine – Cremona 2005 and Ardena Shipwreck – Greece 2009. His national & international mission activities have included: Enduring Freedom – Persian Gulf 2002, Bilateral training Bulgaria 2003, Lake Garda Clearance diving 2002 – 2006 and SNMCMG2 – MedSea 2009.

He has participated in several national and international/NATO exercises including: Deep Divex – Curacao 2008, Deep Divex – Portogallo 2010, Ex with USNAVY in Sigonella 2010, Ex Mare Aperto 2008, Ex Loyal Mariner 2009, Deep Divex Canada 2011, Deep Divex Italy 2013, Deep Divex Norway 2015 and other.

GARETH LOCK

HUMAN FACTORS IN DIVING SPECIALIST / DIVER
SPEAKER / UNDERWATER PHOTOGRAPHER

LOCATION OF INCIDENT
MALTA

In October 2009, two technical divers travelled to Malta to undertake a number of advanced trimix dives on the wrecks of HMS Stubborn (55 m/180 ft), La Polynesien (65 m/213 ft), HMS Southwold (68 m/223 ft and 73 m/239 ft) and Schnellboot S-31 (66 m/216 ft). They had visited Malta earlier that same year and were returning to capture more photographs of the intact wrecks that lie at these depths in the clear Maltese waters.

The dives on HMS Stubborn, La Polynesien and the two sections of HMS Southwold were undertaken without issue. The team were diving using GUE standard gases, as both divers were GUE Tech 2-trained and also used scooters where possible to get around the wreck sites.

The final diving day was due to be on the Schnellboot S-31.

The S-31 was a German fast motor torpedo boat which sank on May 10, 1942, while laying mines in close proximity to the Grand Harbour, Valetta. Thirteen of the crew were lost, while the other thirteen were rescued. These days a permit is required to dive the wreck; in 2009 that requirement had not yet been put in place.

The dive team prepared their gases and dive plan and set off for the dive site. One of the dive team was also there with his girlfriend. She stayed on shore while the team travelled out to the wreck site, which was only 20-30 minutes from the harbour.

The weather was pleasantly warm, with surface air temperatures in the mid-20Cs, but bottom temperatures were approximately 12 C/54 F, so the team wore relatively thick undergarments.

Photos by Gareth Lock

The team of two divers and guide descended the shotline to see the beautiful wreck laid out beneath them. They started to move around the wreck, taking numerous photos including shots of the torpedo tube that still has a live torpedo in it, the upright bow which looks like a ghost ship, and the anti-aircraft gun on the upper deck with ammunition still dotted around.

After 20 minutes or so, the guide left the two divers on the wreck and started a solo ascent. After the 30 minute planned bottom time, the two divers started their ascent and carried out a standard 'ratio deco' ascent which involved decompressing using 50% and 100% gases. After their deco cleared, they boarded the large RHIB via the steps at the back after handing up their three stages (bottom stage, 50% and 100%) and the camera equipment.

Once onboard, the photographer took off his twinset and started to notice some visual disturbances. They were hard to describe, but the diver had not experienced them before. They felt no signs or symptoms of DCS and so did not say anything to their buddy or the skipper. After a little while they set off for the harbour; 20 minutes later, they were back alongside and starting to take everything from the boat up onto the quayside.

Before the boat docked, the visual symptoms which the photographer had been experiencing disappeared, and the diver had still not mentioned them to anyone. Once all the gear was off the boat, the team started to lift it from the quayside onto the back of the flatbed, ready to drive back to the dive centre.

As the photographer was straining to lift a twinset from the floor, to about chest height, they noticed that the visual disturbances had come back but much stronger this time.

Having researched DCS, patent foramen ovale (PFO) and diving incidents for a while, the diver thought to themselves that they potentially had a PFO; they knew that straining creates pressure inside the chest cavity which, in turn,

can allow a PFO to open and bubbles to pass from the arterial side to the venous side of the heart. In addition, they knew that peak bubbling occurs approximately 30 minutes after a surfacing from a dive.

However, they still did not say anything.

They carried on lifting gear and soon everything was packed away. They got into the back of the truck and started their journey back to the dive centre. The photographer's girlfriend was in the back of the truck along with their teammate. The photographer was a little quieter than normal, but nothing too out of the ordinary.

On arrival back at the dive centre, approximately 45 minutes later, there were still some slight signs of visual disturbances but no external signs of DCS. At some point during the unloading, the disturbances disappeared. The dive team then started packing their gear to fly back to the UK the following day. The flight back was uneventful.

Now, what are you thinking about the photographer and his actions?

On return to the UK, the photographer contacted their technical diving instructor to ask for the details of a cardiologist based in Bristol, a cardiologist whom the photographer knew specialised in the treatment of PFOs.

The photographer made contact with the cardiologist by phone a few days later, explaining the situation and the profile.

The doctor responded that, whilst it certainly sounded like visual auras associated with a PFO and DCS, the only way to prove it would be to undertake a PFO test. This was paid for privately, and the photographer found out that they had a PFO ('hole-in-the-heart') which was 8 mm x 12 mm/0.3-0.4 inches in size! Interestingly, the PFO only opened when a deep, sharp breath was made through the nose, a normal Valsalva did not open it.

I had my PFO fixed on February 14, 2010, in a 90-minute operation at the Bristol Heart Institute and was discharged that afternoon.

Now what are you thinking about the photographer?

I tell this story about me for a number of reasons.

First, even though I had researched diving incidents, knew about cognitive biases, and understood the risks that were present, I was not thinking rationally in the moment.

DCS has a huge stigma associated with it, and I did not want to be known as a diver who got bent (even though I followed a 'standard' profile). In addition, I did not want to stress out my girlfriend as I knew that if I went to the chamber, I would likely not be flying back the following day, and that would be a major hassle!

I didn't have any external signs or symptoms of DCS, so didn't think that this could have been the issue. Victims make terrible decision-makers! Second, when I frame the story this way, it leads people to judge others in a negative way using something called the Fundamental Attribution Bias.

The Fundamental Attribution Bias leads us to look for the personal reasons the incident or accident happened, rather than the context. We need the whole, context-rich story if we are to understand local rationality–how it made sense to us (or others) at the time. Unfortunately, the attitude of many divers is to declare that they wouldn't make that mistake and then throw metaphorical rocks that then stop the conversation.

There are many incidents or near-misses in diving, and we simply don't hear about them. Changing attitudes to telling these context-rich stories by developing a 'just julture' and understanding the influence of human factors in diving incidents and accidents has been

my goal for the last 10 years. Slowly, things are changing, and the events outlined in this book will go some way to encouraging divers to accept that we all err.

Consider learning from the conditions which lead to the event, not just the outcomes, and say "I wouldn't do that."

Gareth Lock *is a retired Royal Air Force senior officer navigator of 25 years, who was both a senior supervisor and a tactical flight instructor on an operational C-130 flying squadron. He has a MSc in Aerospace Systems from Kingston University.*

Gareth is an GUE Open Circuit advanced trimix diver and normoxic TDI trimix CCR diver with around 800 dives over 12 years of diving. He is also an accomplished underwater photographer with a deep interest in cold, green-water wreck diving.

In 2012, Gareth started a PhD, examining the role of human factors in scuba diving incidents. He is published in a number of magazines and journals, has acted as the lead SME to a review of military diving, and has presented at numerous international diving conferences on human factors in diving, how they contribute to incidents, and what can be done to improve diving safety.

Since January 2016, he has run The Human Diver, a company focused on delivering training and consultancy around human factors, non-technical skills, and 'just culture' in diving. Since he started, he has trained more than 350 students around the globe and won an innovation award for his online training, thehumandiver.com

GARRY DALLAS

TECHNICAL DIVER / INSTRUCTOR TRAINER
PHOTOGRAPHER / CAVE EXPLORER & PRESENTER

LOCATION OF INCIDENT
DOROTHEA QUARRY, UK

Living in the north west of England, not exactly land locked, but a fair old drive away from a good sea dive, so Dorothea quarry it had to be.

I'm in my mid to late 30s here, an avid diver in all weathers, all year round with a small group of friends who make weekends really interesting and fun. I took up diving in my late 20s and got the bug for anything that involved water, wrecks, eventually caves, CCR, and even photography.

Progressively over 20 years, I trained for these and was never phased by a bit of a challenge. I took things in my stride with some confidence that I matured throughout practice and perfection, or at the least OCD or CDO.

Out of all the inland quarries, Dorothea has had the most controversy, probably the most deaths—most of which are not attributed to diving—and yet appears to many to be the most daunting of all dive sites. To me and some of my friends, it's one of the most interesting and picturesque places to dive.

Situated in the Snowdonia National Park, Northwest Wales, adjacent to a little village called Nantlle, it has dramatic hills and mountain slopes, mostly covered with discarded excavated slate rock.

Some of the discarded slate was carefully rebuilt to resemble huts and workspaces around the quarry, houses used for the workmen and their families or to house winches and the huge pumps that removed water from the depths when it flooded. From old images and photos, the site is pretty jaw-dropping. For diving, we have plenty of levels to choose from in this huge body of water.

Shallow, 5 m, 15 m, 25 m dropping to 35 m, 45 m, following contours and walls down to 65 m then sheer drops to 95 m and eventually reaching the bottom around 105 m/345 ft. All of which sounds great except for the logistical issue sometimes of the 30 degree, 100 m walk down to the entry point from the car park area.

But once you're there, you've got all day!

So, one day my friend and I decided we're going to do a 60 m/197 ft dive just off the 40 m pinnacle wall past the 56 m tunnel entrance. Back then we were diving 12ltr steel twinsets and ally80 stages. Trimix bottom gas and deco gas was calculated and agreed for the decompression. It was quite customary for us to use wings mainly for buoyancy and just remove the squeeze from the drysuit with our offboard gas.

Our dive discussed, our gases filled, and our route planned, we headed on the journey, which was like an adventure day out, 2.5 hrs drive to get there, picking up BBQ food along the way.

We took things nice and easy as usual, going through our safety checks on the surface whilst kitted up and standing in the water and signalled okay, both of us comfortable and happy to commence. We surface swam to the 40 m buoy where we would then descend to 6 m/20 ft, hold, and do a final bubble check and S-drill, just to really get in the "Zen".

Everything was going as planned during the descent; my friend seemed a little slower than usual, but he showed no other signs at all that he was uncomfortable. So, I added more gas to my buoyancy to hold position with him along the way.

These dives were generally around the 4-6ºC temperatures below 20 m/66 ft. Only in the summer would you be lucky to get a balmy 16ºC, and that's only near the surface. However, this day was a cold one, and as such we were prepared and layered up for it.

Oddly, we both seemed to manage quite well in those days with just a pair of 5mm wet gloves, even at lower temperatures as 2ºC / 35F, for a two- hour dive.

We descended further, and as planned, decided to go down the wall this time, rather than follow any ridge contours, because it just made a nice change, and we'd done this dive many times before. Over the ledge we went, not stopping until arriving close to 60 m/197 ft, our target depth.

For some strange reason, I wasn't slowing down much. My buddy now seemed to be just higher than me (as he seemed most of the dive), and was waving his light wand at me a bit concerned. I acknowledged and checked my depth repeatedly, adding gas to my wing and to my drysuit, by now a little bit too frantically, but it just didn't seem to stabilise my depth, I was still sinking! All I could think of was how do I stop myself hitting 90 m/295 ft breathing this gas.

At one point, I had my hand on my wing inflator pressing it constantly and yet still sinking. It probably didn't help that in trying to communicate to my friend, who by now was a few more meters above me, I had adjusted my angle too much when looking up and lost some gas from my drysuit dump valve, but I quickly closed it and re added it... but I was still sinking! At this point, I panicked and just swam over to a rock ledge on this vertical sheer wall and held onto it for dear life!

What the hell had happened??

I could not understand. My heart was beating like a war drum. My breathing had escalated and knew I had to calm this shit down. I didn't even recognise any torch signals. What seemed like an eternity, was merely only a few seconds. All I remember was holding onto that ledge and nothing else mattered.

I began to control my breathing a bit better, (or was it my adrenalin?) enough to know that I had to get out of there soon.

I made sure my drysuit dump was closed, mask cleared, gas pressures okay and started to add more gas to my wing again. Everything seemed okay, added gas to my drysuit—no problem.

By this time, my good buddy came to me at 70-ish meters. He signalled OK, ascend, and he watched as I got neutrally buoyant. Then he signalled there was a problem with my wing dump valve venting.

He checked if it might be loose, which it wasn't. In the end, I simply added more gas in my drysuit, even though it felt much more inflated than usual, obviously compensating for the gas escaping from the wing dump, but I felt stable enough. I could now let go of the ledge and that rock that saved me and ascend with my friend. He monitored my wing dump valve all the way back up to our stops, following the contours along the way.

At the last stop, on a flat 6 m area, still a chilly 6ºC / 42.8F, my buddy attempted to remove the dump valve cover and see inside as to what might be the problem. He wasn't 100% sure, visibility wasn't great, but thought he saw what appeared like a very thin twig or something fall out of the seal.

This would explain the problem at depth. More dense gas escaping out than going in, and maybe why it was less noticeable at the bubble check at 6 m.

However, ultimately, I am responsible for checking/servicing my own kit and how I look after it, e.g. laying it down on a wooded area prior to a dive. In some countries, things crawl inside your kit when it gets left on the floor!

This was one of those ass-clenching moments I would not want to repeat. It really sends home the message of kit checks, then check properly and double check properly, otherwise Murphy and his law joins you on your dive!

Garry Dallas, *known to many as 'Sidemount Bob' or 'Chewie,' is indeed fascinated by the underwater world and is equally happy being mesmerised by the gracefulness and beauty of marine life as he is with the eerie silence of the deep and caves. For over two decades, he has been imparting his infectious passion for diving, knowledge, and skills whilst making scuba liberating and fun!*

Credentials: Cave, technical, and recreational Instructor Trainer through RAID. Additionally, he's a CCR instructor, technical advisor, co-author in RAID diver training manuals, product tester, and ambassador for Fourth Element, Divesoft, Otter Drysuits, X-Deep, Ocean Reef Inc, Ammonite Systems, and other great manufacturers.

In his diving career, he has trained with most major training organisations, served as director of training for RAID UK and Malta, and is a published photographer and writer.

Exploring mines and caves whenever possible, he has developed practical environmental skills for OC and CCR in Sidemount, for which he is globally reputed.

A keen conservationist and an honorary member of "Artic on the Edge," a contingent of the Royal Canadian Geographical Society, promoting protection of all marine life through media while presenting at schools near home and a speaker at national and international dive show events.

His dad introduced a pair of Jet fins, snorkel, and a round face mask to him when he was 13. Since 2011, Garry has been the director of Simply Sidemount & Simply Tec, travelling and teaching locally and globally throughout the year, sending passion through vibes on media channels wherever he goes.

GERMAN "MR.G" ARANGO

DIRECTOR TECHNICAL DIVING DEPARTMENT
MARINE ECOLOGIST / TECH INSTRUCTOR

LOCATION OF THE INCIDENT:
BONAIRE, DUTCH CARIBBEAN

It was all about excitement back in the spring of 2010, when I first heard about the idea of supporting a pair of freedivers on their attempt to break a 'Tandem No Limits' world record here on Bonaire. Our job? To be deep safety divers during the attempt.

But let's contextualise what freediving is a little better and what the most extreme discipline of the sport actually is. According to the Cambridge Dictionary, freediving is "to swim as deep as you can underwater without using breathing equipment." Ten years ago, we were part of the safety team supporting a Tandem No Limits world record attempt. No Limits is defined as the discipline in which the freediver descends and ascends using the method of his or her choice. Typically, the divers descend by means of a heavy metal bar or 'sled' fixed to a line, enabling them to reach great depths.

The most common ascent assistance is via an inflatable lift bag, which the diver inflates and uses to ascend rapidly to the surface (remember this!). This form of diving is considered extremely dangerous by diving professionals, for good reason. No Limits Apnea has claimed the lives of some of the most talented freedivers in the world; by contrast, there have only been two fatalities in more than 30 years of traditional freediving competition.

One of our first tasks was to find a suitable dive site–a place deep enough for the record. We were looking for at least 150 m/492 ft of uninterrupted water column with easy access, 'predictable' conditions, and located close to emergency facilities. We decided that the best place for the record attempt would be the channel between the island of Bonaire and its sister island, Klein Bonaire.

Photo by Kirill Egorov

The maximum depth in the channel was about 200 m/656 ft, and it was close enough to our dive operation, so it was the absolute perfect place. Once the freedivers were on Bonaire, we conducted a series of meetings over the subsequent days to discuss our specific task during their dives: how deep to position ourselves, how to react if anything went wrong, and what specific equipment that we would need to handle/carry during their dives.

The freedivers conducted a series of 'shallow' dives a few days before the final attempt, but we were not involved with those because our main task was to support the real deep dives– their world record plan was to dive to 121 m/396 ft.

However, as we later learned, not getting actively involved on the shallow work-up dives was one of our first mistakes, actually a critical mistake. Our support dives would be to 60 m/196 ft, and required us to hover near the line in midwater while a diver went down and soon after came back up. It seemed too simple and easy, and yes, this evaluation was our second mistake; we underestimated the task and the risk involved.

Ready To Dive
The world record attempt day arrived, and my dive buddy and I were ready for the dive. We choose to dive a double set of Al 80s (11 ltr x 2) with trimix 18/45, one Al 80 with nitrox 50% and one Al 40 with 100% oxygen. Our calculated bottom time was 15 minutes followed by 50 minutes of deco. We had contingency plans, but we were confident that we would not be spending a lot more time at depth.

The plan was to dive to 60 m/196 ft and just 'sit' right there, waiting for the divers—a piece of cake! We started our descent five minutes before the freedivers started theirs, and the first thing we noticed after passing 40 m/131 ft was a super, abnormally strong current, which only got worse as our depth increased. It was like a river down there, as if we were going into a high flow cave.

What an unsuspected surprise, considering that we were hovering in the blue, working as hard as we could to stay in position, trying to stay close to the line without holding it, and keeping an eye out for a super-fast moving object that could be coming from the surface at any time! In the meantime, we were accumulating lots of inert gas and loads and loads of CO_2 together with a huge responsibility: We were the first line of defense in case anything happened to the freedivers at depth, making them unable to ascend. At this point, we were already stressed enough, and our heads were more than busy considering all the uncalculated factors. But we carried on.

Finally, the freedivers began their descent into the blue at a fast rate and passed in front of us. In a few seconds we couldn't see them anymore except for the lingering trace of micro bubbles indicating their trajectory. Now we had to hold position, start our timers, and wait for them to ascend past us toward the surface. We had to be very close to the ascent line because, if anything went wrong, we would have to clip a carabiner with a lift bag to the main line in order to bring the freediver(s) up, so time and position were critical.

We had already been working hard and just wanted to start our ascent. Finally, we saw something coming up from the blue depths, but it didn't look like a freediver. It was more like a miniature underwater volcano had exploded, creating an insane amount of bubbles like the mushroom cloud of a nuclear explosion; it was coming up fast and getting closer and closer to us.

This incredible effect was in fact created by the expansion of the air in the 50 kg/110 lb lift bag that had been fully inflated at the bottom by the freedivers. We had to move, and we had to move fast before it hit us.

In a matter of seconds, we were in the middle of the bubble cloud, not knowing how deep we were, where the line was, and where each other or the freedivers were. I just knew that we drastically changed depth and position, but I couldn't tell how deep I was because I couldn't read my instruments at that moment.

After a few seconds, things started getting back to 'normal.' I looked up, or what I thought was up, and I saw the silhouette of the freedivers continuing their ascent, but when I looked around I couldn't see my buddy; I could barely see the ascent line in the blue. Now it was time to assess my current depth: 45 m/147 ft, and I was supposed to be at 60 m/196 ft. What the f***! Where was my buddy? Well, he was deeper than I was and also very confused, and now what?

Making Our Way To The Surface
We both went for the obvious: let's try to communicate and reunite. My buddy finally saw me and intuitively he came up and I went down. We were at about 50 m/164 ft with no reference line anymore, just water around us. We tried to re-adjust our decompression, but it was hard to tell how much these rapid ascents would impact our profile, especially after working so hard at the bottom. We decided to look for the line because that was our way to safety and the rest of the team. We worked hard, very hard, and were lucky enough to find our way back to the line, but of course at that point our original plan was a thing of the past.

By now, we just wanted to get out of the water. We started our ascent and the vision of the boat hull brought us comfort. We were getting closer and closer. Our gas switch to nitrox 50 was pretty uneventful, but the possible impact of the drastic depth change weighed on my mind. We finished deco and decided not to add extra time at the oxygen stop; we just wanted to get out. Unfortunately, this was another critical mistake.

We finally surfaced and both felt like we had run a marathon. We were so tired and stressed that we preferred not to talk about what happened with anyone. Everybody on board was celebrating: a world record had been broken! We smiled for the picture and moved aside, being alert for any symptoms of decompression illness.

Unfortunately, we didn't have to wait long. Within 30 minutes, my buddy got a rash indicating skin bends, and I got temporary numbness in the fingers of my right hand. We decided to breathe 100% oxygen and rest. The symptoms eventually resolved themselves, and we both took a few days off before returning to work. We were lucky. Very, very lucky.

German (aka Mr.G.) Arango *was born in Colombia and has been actively diving for the past 17 years. He has been dedicated to teaching and education since finishing his university degree in ecology, in 2004. He took his first technical diving course that year and successfully became one of the first technical divers in Colombia. In 2007, he joined GUE and moved to Bonaire, where he started working for the Buddy Dive Resort and began to develop their Technical Diving Department. This was a challenge, as the island was only known as a recreational divers' destination and paradise.*

In 2010, 2011, and 2012, German participated as a technical support diver for world famous freedivers, Karol Meyer and Patrick Musimu, as they successfully broke the world records for Tandem No Limits. Also during his time with Buddy Dive Resort on Bonaire, German has conducted exploration, documentation, and research on the deep wrecks, caves, and deep water reef systems of the island and its surrounding waters. He has planned and led dives that have opened up very interesting and exciting discoveries for technical diving on Bonaire, locations that are still under investigation and exploration to this day.

German's main goal is to keep promoting and educating divers in responsible technical diving behaviors, practices, and courses. He wants to continue the expansion of technical diving in the Caribbean and South America, as he knows there is so much more to discover, develop, and find through technical diving.

JILL HEINERTH

UNDERWATER EXPLORER & FILMMAKER
AUTHOR "INTO THE PLANET, MY LIFE AS A CAVE DIVER"

LOCATION OF INCIDENT
DEVIL'S CAVE SYSTEM, FLORIDA, USA

In 1997, I bought a Cis-Lunar MK5P Rebreather in preparation for diving on the Wakulla2 Project in north Florida. With no formal training available, a few of us early adopters became test pilots, trying to figure out how to teach others. When I look back on those first years of experimentation, I realise that I am incredibly fortunate to have survived the learning curve.

I recall one exercise held in the classroom of the scuba shop that my husband and I owned in north Florida; my colleagues Andrew Poole and John Vanderleest were visiting from Australia, helping with development of the new training protocols. We were trying to analyse everything that could potentially go wrong on a rebreather.

We spent a lot of time dwelling on the topic of hypoxia. John had previously experienced an underwater blackout when the orifice of his Drager rebreather became restricted.

He survived the event due to the quick action of his buddy Andrew, but the incident lingered in their minds. What other failures of this gear might lead to hypoxia? Could a diver detect the problem in advance and prevent a blackout?

We decided to set up and film a risky experiment with a willing volunteer. The subject would sit on the floor wearing the MK-5P rebreather, taking notes about anything that spelled trouble. The rig's oxygen supply was disabled, but the volume of gas in the loop would permit comfortable breathing.

The subject was aware that the oxygen PO_2 would be slowly dropping during the experiment, and their instructions were to write down any symptoms that might indicate a problem. The ultimate goal for the subject was to bail out by turning a rotating switch on the front of the mouthpiece block when he thought the loop was getting hypoxic.

Photo by Gene Page

We wondered, "Can you feel hypoxia coming on and prevent a blackout?"

You've likely already figured out that telling someone to write down symptoms is pretty contradictory to taking action and bailing out. If the victim feels compelled to write something down, he should be trying to save his life by turning the bailout valve to get safe gas.

Right? Well, it appears that self-rescue is not always that simple.

I watched Andrew closely and monitored his displays while John handled the video camera. I turned off the oxygen supply and told Andrew we were ready to begin. It took ages for the PO2 to drop. From time to time, the reduced volume would trigger the automatic diluent valve into flooding the loop with fresh gas. I watched the numbers tick down.

First, I saw 0.18. Andrew appeared normal.

Then 0.16. I thought, "This should be the threshold of consciousness." Apparently not. He lifted his hand slightly, looked puzzled, and set it down again. He continued to breathe, laboured somewhat, as the minutes rolled on.

The handset read 0.14, and still he was breathing. His face now ashen, he picked up the pencil. "Tingling," he wrote in a messy script on the yellow ruled paper pad. I looked up at John to let him know we were close. I checked the display to see it hit 0.12, and then it dropped another tenth.

Andrew placed the pencil awkwardly and wrote, "TW," then his hand spasmed, and he slumped forward in chaotic twitching. I yanked the block from his mouth and threw an oxygen mask on his face, hitting the demand valve and sending him a boost of fresh gas. His blueish slouching body convulsed. It was terrifying. For a moment, I envisioned that we had killed Andrew, while on the other side of the wall, people were shopping for gaudy dive skins. My heart raced.

Slowly, he came around and shuffled himself into a more comfortable position. It was a full seven minutes before he pulled the DAN mask from his face and remarked, "Sorry guys, I guess I just have too much self-preservation."

I replied, "Whatever," and pushed the mask back over his face. A few more minutes passed, and he looked confused, "Guys, what just happened? I thought I bailed out."

Photo by Jill Heinerth

152

We learned plenty from that experiment, but don't even consider trying this at home. People who develop hypoxia might not come around when you throw an oxygen mask on their face.

But on that day, another lesson was clear to me. Andrew was expecting hypoxia. He even had the cognitive ability to note symptoms. He might have appeared conscious, but he was already long gone. Andrew recalled recognizing the symptoms and thinking, "Gee, it is time to bail out." But his mind never managed to get his hands to handle the task of doing it. If he had been underwater, he would have drowned.

Weeks later, I got lucky, too. Alone in Devil's Ear Cave System, I was training myself to operate the rebreather without electronics. I wanted to know if I could get home from the back of a cave with no sensors, no displays, or any electronic means of monitoring PO₂.

For nearly six hours, I swam around the cave flushing with diluent gas and then practicing a technique called minimum loop volume. At a known depth, a CCR diver floods the loop with diluent, does the mathematical calculation for PO₂, and then tops up whatever oxygen is metabolized with tiny injections of oxygen to maintain the PO₂.

After a very long dive, I returned to the entrance of Devil's Eye to decompress based on tables that I had calculated before the dive. I was pretty proud of myself and became somewhat distracted by what I suppose was my growing ego. "Look at me in my awesome yellow box!" I thought.

But complacency can kill, and as I patted myself on the back, I swam toward the steps to exit the water. Lost in my silly sense of greatness, I failed to make the manual oxygen injections while heading down the run. For several minutes, the PO₂ dropped while I lost concentration. Mere meters from the steps, I felt a black curtain encroaching on the edges of my vision. I woke up, threw the loop into open circuit, and pulled the wool sock off my handset.

The PO₂ was down to 0.11. With a fresh blast of nitrox, the colours of the spring and the clarity of my mistake slammed me back to full consciousness. I could have died in the shallows, an arm's reach from the stairs, but instead I developed an enduring respect for guarding against complacency. We found better ways to teach important rebreather skills, but the development of these safety protocols was not always pretty.

Jill Heinerth *is an underwater explorer, writer, photographer, speaker, and filmmaker. Jill was a lead technical diver on the ground-breaking Wakulla2 project, where she piloted the first 3D underwater cave mapping device–technology that will be bound for space. A pioneer of technical rebreather diving, she led a team into underwater caves beneath the massive B-15 iceberg in Antarctica.*

From desert oases of the Sahara to the cold waters of Baffin Bay, Jill Heinerth becomes the hands and eyes for climatologists, archaeologists, and engineers. Jill serves as the first Explorer-in-Residence of the Royal Canadian Geographical Society and is a presenter on radio and TV broadcasts worldwide. Her book, Into The Planet *has been lauded by* The Wall Street Journal, O: The Oprah Magazine, *and The* New York Times. *Jill was named a member of the International Scuba Diving Hall of Fame.*

Photo by Wes Skiles

JIM WARNY

CAVE EXPLORER & DIVING OFFICER OF THE IRISH CAVE
RESCUE ORGANISATION

LOCATION OF INCIDENT
BLACKWATER RESURGENCE, IRELAND

When I started diving in the mid-nineties, rebreathers were just starting to pop up on the diving scene; as a 16-year-old sport diver, I could only dream about these machines whilst browsing the internet.

I concluded that I would have to build my own if I were to dive one. So, while still on the school benches, I started drawing up designs. Two years on and I grew hungry for more advanced forms of diving as I read about cave pioneers like Olivier Isler and Jochen Hasenmaier.

During my search for a diving club that had cave divers in it, I stumbled on a small club led by JP Bastin, and over the years that followed, JP mentored me into a cave diver. I am truly grateful I found this small group of mentors who kept me on a short leash during those early years in my cave diving career;

if not for them I'm sure I would not have the experience I have today. That early period of mentoring and informal training was hugely important during my later years of cave exploration when I moved to the west of Ireland.

Once I settled in Ireland in the early noughties, I started discovering and exploring the dark, challenging underground rivers in the Gort lowland area. Here I found my true calling and was on a roll with exploration successes every dive season. I teamed up and mentored an equally driven Polish diver, Artur Kozlowski. Sadly, a few years later he passed away on one of his exploration dives.

That night when I got the call from his friends, saying he was overdue, I instantly pictured in my head what I was going to find when I located his lifeless body.

Photo by Frank Griga

After Artur's death, I regained a new interest in cave diving, as my interest had shifted to other sports the year leading up to it.

Fast forward to June 15, 2016. It's quarter to four, my shift at work is nearly over, but then an operator calls me to his machine saying it's down again. I rush over to see if I can fix it pronto, as I want to get out of here so I can go diving.

Luckily, the problem is not that bad and the machine is back on track in no time. I clock out only a few minutes late, but it doesn't matter–I'm on the way to my playground.

Today's objective is Blackwater Rising, a resurgence just outside the town of Gort. This had been dived by a group of Polish divers to a depth of 47 m/154 ft and roughly 200 m/656 ft penetration from the entrance. I was eager to push farther into the cave, as on my previous dive here I had managed to pass this deep point and find the way on, ascending a 45-degree slope.

As I pull up to the usual parking spot, my phone rings. It's my solicitor. "Fuck!" I think, "this is not what I need now!" I am in the middle of a custody battle and divorce, so a late-day call from the lawyer is rarely good news.

The joys of fighting for your rights as a divorced father! I finish the call after a brief but still stressful conversation and get out of the van.

First on the cards is carrying my gear 500 m/1640 ft and then down a steep 50 m/164 ft slope to the water's edge. I make good progress, and within an hour I am sitting in the water with my rebreather on my back and a pair of 12 litre tanks strapped on. I slowly start descending, making a brief stop at 6 m/20 ft. Everything is going well and the visibility is the usual ~50 cm/1.6 ft. Away from all my surface life struggles, I'm starting to feel relaxed.

From -6 m the cave drops to 20 m/65 ft and averages at this depth for about another 100(ish) m/328 ft in. Ten minutes into the dive and I start feeling that something is not right. "I'm fine," I think. "I am probably just a bit tired and not in the zone with all that crap I am dealing with up there. I'll just keep going…"

Now I am dropping off slowly. At 30 m/98 ft: Still not feeling great. My PPO2 is ok, so maybe I am just out of shape! It will be fine once I hit the bottom and start. At 35 m/114 ft: Wow, fuck me, I am spinning and feel worse by the second.

Photo by Adam Haydock

At 43 m/141 ft: After following a section of line hanging on the ceiling, I find a belay point on the wall and grab it. My heart is pounding, and I'm experiencing tunnel vision. Strangely enough, my breathing seems under control, but then again, I have a weird breathing pattern from years of diving high flow caves.

As I hang on to the wall, I say to myself, "It cannot be the rebreather! Come on, it's my trusty old Meg."

Things are not getting any better. I am in serious shit now; I bail out on to my BOV and start crawling up the line hand-over-hand.

At 25 m/82 ft: I am not getting any better. It's not the rebreather, so I go back on the loop. To be fair, I am not getting worse either; I am just starting to get a headache now. A couple of meters farther and I'm starting to feel worse again; the tunnel vision sets in again, and I get this warm feeling I had earlier.

Bailout again. This time I stay off the loop until I hit the surface. I swim to the water's edge; Jesus, I am completely drained!

I roll onto my back and get my rebreather off and sit down by the water. My head is splitting the rocks! It must have been CO_2 poisoning. But the rebreather is bulletproof, right? I've been diving that MEG for ten years without a glitch! I slowly gather my stuff and make my way back to the van where I inspect the rebreather. Scrubber seems ok and was fresh before the dive.

Then I try to breathe from the BOV. This is weird. I don't get the expected sound/vibration of the check valve sealing as I breathe out. I get a screwdriver and pop off the hose to find the whole check valve assembly hanging loose and completely dislocated. My heart sinks: I was in deep trouble there.

This was a close one, and I did not even have the brain power to act properly. I put everything down to not being 'in the zone' or fit enough.

Photo by Joanna Mania

Before I left the dive site, I had a FaceTime call with my mother; she said I looked as white as a ghost and she'd never seen me this bad.

So, looking back, I do not feel proud of what happened on that dive. Diving has always been an escape from my surface life but this time it could have taken me for good. This was the first time I experienced CO_2 issues on a rebreather, but I should have known what was happening. As for the check valves, I had replaced the original valves for newer versions, but they were not the right type for my BOV and could easily fall out of the main body when subjected to vibration and bumps.

I believe if I had continued for another few seconds, I would have completely lost control and probably would not have been able to bail out. Next time something does not feel right, I will try to be more mindful and just turn the dive, bail out when needed, and stay off the loop! The cave will still be there tomorrow, make sure you are too!

Jim Warny *has been diving since the age of 12. Very early on, he was attracted to the technical side of diving, leading him into cave diving. He has explored many caves in the west of Ireland, where flow and limited visibility are the norm.*

Along the way, he has designed and built multiple rebreathers and has been diving them for about twenty years. Cave exploration is his true calling, and he remains active in both the cave diving and dry caving scenes in Ireland. In 2018, Jim was part of the rescue team that extracted the boys' soccer team from Tham Luang cave in Thailand.

JON KIEREN

CAVE DIVING INSTRUCTOR

LOCATION OF INCIDENT
TULUM, MEXICO

I've made a lot of mistakes while diving, and I am always very happy to share those stories. It's great to demonstrate to aspiring divers that, no matter what level, we all make mistakes.

However, when mistakes are made while teaching, it is far less likely that an instructor will speak up and discuss the event. It's embarrassing, may lead to some unwanted attention from the training agencies, and can spark heated debate on social media. So, most often I have to reserve discussion of these instructional follies to private conversations with instructor candidates.

However, one incident is of such great value for all divers and instructors alike that it would be a disservice to my peers not to discuss it openly. It was my worst day of teaching to date. My student ran out of gas in the cave.

It was day five of a stage cave diver course, which is normally taught over three or four days, but we elected to stretch this one out to six since the students hadn't been in the caves for a couple of months. My students were Dillon and Alex, and I had an instructor intern, Dave, tagging along as well.

I had worked with Dillon previously, and knew well what his strengths / weaknesses were. Alex and I had never been in the water together, but I had spent the previous four days getting to know how he performed under pressure. Dave and I are regular dive buddies and have been through quite a lot in the water together.

The team dynamic is important, as it sets the stage for how I conducted this particular scenario, and how my assumptions of the team's capabilities both created the issue and allowed us all to make it out alive.

Photos by SJ Alice Bennett

Dillon was a very thoughtful and cautious diver who knew his limits and was happy to remain within them. Like many, when pushed beyond those limits he struggled with slowing down and regaining composure to manage problems. Alex was a clever diver with excellent stability and the ability to slow down and think through a problem, but also like many, he had difficulty communicating slowly and clearly with his team if things went sideways. Alex's gas consumption was a bit better than Dillon's. My goal in this scenario was to highlight both of the students' weaknesses while ensuring we kept more than enough gas reserve to exit the cave safely.

The dive plan: Using standard "1/2+" stage calculation, we would enter the cave at an average depth of 10 m/32 ft for about 12 minutes, and take a T and an immediate jump down to the saltwater section which averages around 23 m/75 ft. We would be dropping stages approximately 22 minutes into the cave. We would then continue on back gas until someone reached turn pressure. Once turn pressure was reached, we would exit the cave the same way we entered. Dave and I would remain on our stages as long as possible to reserve as much of our back gas as possible to donate.

The failure scenario: Complete loss of back gas and stage failure for Dillon. While a complex drill and unlikely in real life, it is the exact scenario we use as the building blocks for our gas planning. The value of demonstrating the practical application is very powerful. My primary objective was to demonstrate the need for Dillon to maintain his composure, and for Alex to clearly communicate what needed to happen in order for the team to make it out with the gas available.

Once the dive had been turned, I would simulate a failure of Dillon's right post, followed by a left post failure later in the exit. Upon reaching the stages, I would simulate a failure on Dillon's stage, forcing him to remain on Alex's long hose until they could figure out how best to re-organise.

The best course of action would be for Dillon to take Alex's stage and switch to it, leaving Alex to exit on his remaining back gas. Their failure or ability to do so would clearly demonstrate where they stood in the course. Each of the components of the scenario had been practiced in various situations, but the full scenario had not.

Plans and expectations regarding how the scenario should play out:

Because of his higher consumption rate, I knew Dillon would have less available gas to donate, so I wanted him to be the out-of-gas diver. I knew his stage would have the least gas, so that was the one I wanted to fail. Dave would be available to pick up the 'dead' stage behind us, and be an extra safety net of available gas to donate. The stage pickup would occur in the deep section, about ten minutes from the jump back up to the shallows. The passage becomes slightly restrictive for a significant period between those two points; however, and a gas share through that section should be avoided.

How it all played out: Everything up to the turn went as planned. Dillon managed the first failure with ease and composure. The second failure came as a bit of a surprise and it was easy to see Dillon's frustration when it happened, but it was still managed with relative ease. However, communication was beginning to break down, and you could see the anxiety beginning to build in the team. As the team initiated the gas share and began to exit, I checked Alex's gas supply and verified that he was still at about 120 bar/1740 psi. All on track as expected.

When the team reached the stages, Dillon's anxiety was really beginning to show. Not anticipating that Dillon's stage would fail, the team decided to have Alex retrieve his stage and switch to it first.

With Dillon still on Alex's longhose, they would save the gas in Dillon's stage as it would be the only gas he would have "available" on him

for the exit. It was the most conservative call based on the resources available.

When retrieving his own stage, Dillon forgot to stow his primary light. With the light head still on his hand, he struggled with the light cord getting hung up and tangled repeatedly and a downward spiral began.

When he tried to pressurise the stage, and I simulated the failure, communication within the team deteriorated quickly.

Alex responded promptly and switched back onto back gas, anticipating that Dillon would drop his failed stage and prepare to receive Alex's.
When Alex attempted to communicate this through the halocline, it was clear that Dillon was not thinking clearly and did not know what needed to happen.

In hindsight, this was my chance to cut the drill, and I should have. However, this was the exact scenario I wanted to highlight, so I let it play out. I believe having Dave as a "safety net" contributed to my overconfidence here. For over 10 minutes at 23 m/75 ft, the team struggled to communicate what needed to happen and execute the stage handoff from Alex to Dillon, all while both divers were breathing from Alex's back gas. Communication had completely broken down, but things needed to get moving, so I stepped in and got Dillon switched to Alex's stage and the team began to exit immediately with Dillon in the lead.

As they swam off, I took a peek at Alex's gas supply, and he was down to around 40 bar/580 psi. I knew it was going to be close, but we would exit quickly, so I was confident he would make it.

This would have also been an opportunity to cut the drill, but with Dillon already swimming away and towards the restriction, I was worried it could make the situation worse and potentially split the team.

So I stayed close to Alex. But as they swam off, I noticed he was still struggling to stow his longhose as we approached the restriction. He seemed to be managing OK and cleared the restriction cleanly, but was clearly stressed and using more gas than expected.

As we approached the shallow section, I finally killed my own stage and switched back to back gas. As we ascended to the shallow section, I watched as Alex checked his pressure gauge, which just hung limply at his side. He got Dillon's attention and clearly and calmly signaled "cut the drill, I'm out of gas." I did not wait to see how Dillon would respond and donated my long hose to Alex. We paused for a few moments to ensure everyone was calm and ok.

I got Dave's attention and communicated what was going on, and we began to exit quickly but calmly. On the swim out, I began to re-inventory the resources in the team; Dillon still had two-thirds of his back gas, Dave still had almost all of his back gas plus 120 bar/1740 psi in Alex's stage. There was a ton of gas left in the team, just none of it was 'attached' to Alex.

We were back at the entrance less than seven minutes after Alex had signalled out of gas. We had a bit of deco to do in the entrance and just to add insult to injury, as Alex switched to his oxygen, he had a real failure of his first stage. We calmly identified the issue and fixed it, then completed our few minutes of decompression before exiting the cave. All a bit shaken, but still breathing.

So what really went wrong? Did I set the scenario up appropriately? With hindsight 20/20, I still believe the scenario was set up properly. However, I was overconfident in Alex's ability to remain calm enough to communicate and help Dillon manage the situation in a timely manner.

Between that and having Dave as a safety net, I ignored the clear signs that the team was in over its head. Finally, the fact that it was my first class back after a bit of a break and was late in the course is also worth noting. Had I been as fresh as I normally was, I might have noticed how far the stress level had risen.

As instructors, we have a responsibility to push our students just beyond their comfort zone while maintaining a safe environment. It takes extreme attention to the student's state of mind, awareness of the environment, and complete control of the resources available to the team. This is a difficult balance, and we are often walking a fine line. On that particular day, I failed in my duties. While there was constant awareness of what was happening, and ample resources to get everyone out safely, a student genuinely running out of gas is never an acceptable situation.

I will never let it happen again.

Now, the positive takeaway is that it was a great learning experience for everyone involved, as well as for whoever reads this. Dave and I learned a great deal about where to draw the line when scenarios begin to go downhill, as well as gaining a higher level of awareness of our confidence level.

Dillon and Alex learned how our gas reserves are only adequate if we manage problems in a calm, collected, and efficient manner.

And hopefully all of you reading can take both lessons away, along with an appreciation of the importance of planning and executing dives conservatively, and an understanding that everyone makes mistakes.

Jon Kieren is a cave, technical, and CCR instructor/instructor trainer who has dedicated his career over the past 12 years to improving dive training.

As an active TDI/IANTD/NSS-CDS and GUE Instructor, TDI Training Advisory Panel member, and former training director for TDI, he has vast experience working with divers and instructors at all levels, but his main professional focus resides in caves.

In his own personal diving, Jon's true passions are deep extended-range cave dives (the more deco the better), as well as working with photographers to bring back images of his favorite places to share with the world.

JOSH BRATCHLEY MBE

CAVE DIVER / BRISTOL EXPLORATION CLUB (BEC)
BRADFORD POTHOLE CLUB (BPC) / CAVE DIVING GROUP
(CDG) / BRITISH CAVE RESCUE COUNCIL (BCRC)

LOCATION OF INCIDENT
MILLPOND CAVE, TENNESSEE, USA

Having started cave diving in 2012 in the small, shallow, and poor visibility "sumps" in the UK through a desire to go further in mostly dry caves, my cave diving was very much an extension of my caving passion.

For some, expeditions play a large part of the British caving scene, and I have participated in many overseas exploration trips in the past, including locations in Asia, the Americas, and continental Europe.

Whilst I also took a strong interest in bigger and longer cave dives over the years, especially in places such as the Lot in France, my passion remained with expeditions and sump diving.

In the UK, these dives are often undertaken solo due to the conditions of the dive site (passage sizes, very poor visibility, etc.)

One such expedition in April 2019 was to Tennessee, where I had joined a group of British cavers who were planning to work with their local counterparts with the aim of extending the Mountain Eye cave system. Within the UK group, there were two other cave divers, Ben Wright and Gareth Davies, who were to be investigating the potential diving leads with me, along with Thorn Walthall, a local diver who was a great help sorting out our logistics. After much exploring in the wetter areas of the system, we had still found few prospects for a concerted diving effort, so we chose to start looking at other local caves. One of these was the Mill Pond Cave.

Mill Pond Cave had an inviting entrance pool and had been explored by local cavers to a large airbell, beyond which the exploration limit sat after a further short dive.

Photo by Tom Clayton

On April 12, the three of us had a recce of the existing passage, reaching the End of Line, but found little 'way on' from there, so exploration was carried out in another direction from the airbell. This proved fruitful for us, and another passage was entered with slight notable flow.

Visibility was poor for Gareth and me (the latter two divers), with large amounts of silt, exacerbated by open-circuit bubbles in addition to sharp rock and a low bedding section. The dive line in the cave was very thin and not what we UK cave divers were used to in the cold, fast flowing, and murky waters at home, so we decided that if we were to continue exploration at this site, we would make it homey and replace the line with something thicker.

After sourcing 4 mm polypro line for the job at hand, we returned to Mill Pond Cave in the early afternoon of April 16 and started sorting the new line onto spools. My dive had been a little chilly here in a wetsuit on the last dive, so I had borrowed a dry suit from Thorn to make things more comfortable. The plan was for two divers, Ben and me, to reline the cave during the same dive through to the airbell.

Ben entered the cave laying the new line, and I was to dive afterwards, following this line whilst removing the old one. After having some issues in the restricted section, Ben continued for approximately 50 m/164 ft before turning due to not recognising the passageway he'd ended up in and thinking he'd gone the wrong way.

In very low visibility, I followed the newly laid line, whilst spooling the old line onto an empty reel. Whilst completing this task, I became detached from the newly laid line and immediately attempted to relocate it.

After some time, this had still not proved fruitful, so with very little reference and conditions deteriorating further, a retreat was made to the airbell, the known (and accessible!) airspace.

During the next few hours, I attempted to re-enter the water and go back to try and find the lost line, but conditions had not improved, with zero vis and further complications developed throughout this period. Eventually I had to stop due to gas reserves.

Meanwhile, Ben, who had stopped laying line and exited the cave to find I was still underground, re-entered the water to return to his line end but again could not recognise where he was. In zero visibility and feeling very uncomfortable, he exited again.

After this, both Gareth and Ben and the newly-arrived Thorn waited a few more hours before diving again, but visibility had not improved. They decided to return to the accommodation, where Gareth called John Volanthen, who advised calling Cave Rescue. At this point, my caving friends on the surface initiated the call-out while Ben and Gareth took some rest.

Underground, I was busy digging a flatter ledge in the mud-slope in the airbell so that I could get most of my body out of the water. To retain the heat I had acquired whilst digging, I removed my dive kit, placed it between my body and the soft, cold mud, and inflated my suit.

The next twenty or so hours were spent listening to drips and the occasional residual bubble coming out of the sump, or attempting occasional limb movements to keep blood flowing in an uncomfortable position.

Occasionally, I would check the time on my Shearwater, and at one point I attempted to keep myself amused by recording a video, only to find that I had forgotten to put an SD card into my Paralenz.

Eventually, I saw lights in the sump pool, which was beautifully clear by this point, having had over a day to settle without disturbance. As I watched the diver come to the surface, I took some mental guesses as to who it would be: American? British?

Photo by Chris Jewell

Could it be one of my Thailand colleagues and should I therefore prepare for instantaneous, brutal mick-taking?

Surfacing was Edd Sorenson, with his sidewinder, having flown up from Florida. Very grateful that someone had arrived in the airbell, I thanked him instantly and we exchanged some short sentences before discussing the route out.

Feeling a little stiff after being relatively still for so long, but OK, I donned my mud-coated dive kit and followed Edd into the water. Having saved adequate gas for this exit, I marvelled at the much improved visibility, deteriorating quickly behind me with my bubbles rippling across the ceiling and muddy drysuit.

It wasn't long before we were back on the surface, where we met Mike Young (who'd

driven from Arkansas), my friends, and the Chattanooga-Hamilton rescue team who had all done an incredible job.

What went wrong?

This second day of diving at Mill Pond Cave was multiple days after the first, with various other projects being tackled on the days in between taking our focus away whilst waiting for the new line delivery.

On the day when the new line finally arrived, our dive plan was put together rapidly. It is, of course, clear now that doing the job in one dive, with two divers working together in those conditions (so that we could get on with the push sooner), was a mistake.

Although occasional 'team diving' is practiced in the UK, given the choice, we primarily solo dive and work alone once underwater, especially in these conditions. Exploration fever was catching the team who were finally looking at getting into an open underwater lead after a busy morning dealing with non-diving related logistics, and on this occasion we chose an inadequate dive plan.

Though there were compounding factors whilst underwater that led to my loss of the main dive line as well as complications during the search, the details of exactly what happened underwater are hazy and complex for both of us.

The visibility was extremely poor and neither diver could see the other so we therefore do not have a clear subsurface picture to describe here.

Everyone remained calm and did what they could, and no one drowned, but the primary fact remains that an improved, more conservative dive plan for this individual project would have significantly reduced the risk of this incident occurring.

The cave will always be there for another day of diving.

Photo by Chris Jewell

I will be forever grateful to everyone who contributed to getting me back to the surface that day. Especially Ben and Gareth for trying to find me initially, Edd Sorenson and Mike Young who got the rescue call, Dave Powlesland, Chris Jones, Hannah Moulton and Ian Holmes who made that call along with the rest of the UK team, who sorted the logistics with Chattanooga-Hamilton Rescue squad.

Josh Bratchley *is a British exploratory caver and diver, who is actively involved in the exploration of dry and underwater cave passage in both the UK and overseas.*

The variety of conditions in which Josh conducts his dives means that a range of configurations are used, from sidemount and backmount CCR using mixed gases, to pushing the smallest available cylinders through 'no mount' silty squeezes.

Over the past few years, Josh has found himself – among other things – pushing tight, high-flow sump passages in Wales, jamming crow bars into zero-vis boulder chokes in Yorkshire to find the way on, diving the end of difficult caves in the Picos de Europa, and camping for a week or more at a time beyond sumps in remote parts of Mexico.

During the summer of 2018, Josh was one of the cave divers sent by the British Cave Rescue Council to rescue the football team and their coach from Tham Luang Nang Non cave in northern Thailand..

JP BRESSER

GUE CAVE INSTRUCTOR

LOCATION OF INCIDENT
CROATIA

This incident happened a few years ago, during a project in Croatia where we received permission to continue documenting a cave that was no longer under active exploration.

The team consisted of European cave divers trained by Global Underwater Explorers (GUE) who had varying levels of experience and certifications. The main objective of the project was to create a detailed record of the deeper areas of the cave, comprising maps, imagery, regular video, and 360° video of the deeper areas of the cave.

These specific dives had multiple goals and, as always, the task-load grows exponentially with the complexity of the media involved. In this case the plan was as follows: we acquired a specially 3D-printed underwater housing which was able to hold six GoPro cameras with overlapping fields of view. We would then use dedicated software to stitch the six streams of video together into a full-view 360°video stream; the challenge was to start

and stop all the cameras, which had to be done one-by-one using a waterproof infrared remote controller.

We selected a team of four divers to film the deepest passage to the end of the line. The line ends at the crossing with a new, unexplored bigger tunnel; visualise a drainpipe ending in the middle of a new drainpipe. One of the team members was assigned a reel and the job of tying it in to the end of the line, to create reference whilst the other team members were engaged with the remote controller to turn off all six GoPro cameras.

Once done, two would head out of the cave, and I would remain with the team member responsible for the reel and explore the new passage; pretty simple plan, you would think. The whole dive proceeded as planned; we brought tons of video lights and made it to the end of the line without issue.

So, we start the process of turning all cameras

off, which takes a couple of minutes. I feel we are slowly drifting due to some small flow in the new tunnel and percolation is reducing our visibility. I look to my right and see my teammate who was supposed to tie us in; he's looking on with interest at what we are doing and I notice the reel clipped on his left hip D-ring. He forgot to tie in the reel!

I look around and see we are slowly drifting in a cloud of particles with no clue of the line or sidewalls; we are at 28 m/91 ft depth, and I get that underbelly feeling that something is completely wrong. I give the team member the question mark followed by a tie-off hand signal and get no response; I look at the two other teammates who realise the same thing: we lost the line.

I look around for any point of recognition, but I'm completely clueless as to where we are; the only thing I remember is that I always check my compass at every major change of direction. So I take the reel from the teammate, give the two others a "stop and hold your position" signal, and tie the line to a rock-formation on the bottom. I turn around looking at my compass, checking what heading we should go based on what I remember and start a shotgun search pattern with one teammate whilst the other waits at the tie in. To make a long story short, after close to fifteen minutes we located the end of the line, tied in, swam back to get the others, and made our way out of the cave.

In analysing the incident, it was clear that a couple of factors influenced the event: one was the pressure of the media, the pressure of producing something spectacular. Second, the unfamiliarity with the equipment, draining the general awareness of the team; third, the team-member responsible for the tie-in probably suffered from gas narcosis, breathing enriched air nitrox EAN32 at 28 m/91 ft of depth. But mainly the fact that the whole team was responsible for making sure that the tie-off was made and none of us double-checked, with the consequence that we ended up drifting, lost in a silty tunnel without a line.

The conclusion is that what we teach in classes really works. Stick to the procedures and you will find that line. Media and cave-diving is a risky combination and requires experience and overcapacity in the team.

No cave is worth dying in for the sake of a couple of minutes of video. The cave will still be there for you tomorrow to go back and film. Stop if you are having a bad day or feel incapacitated or not up to it.

JP Bresser *is an experienced technical diver and instructor with a passion for cave diving. Being an Instructor for almost 30 years, JP has been actively teaching all levels of technical diving for different training organizations and is nowadays active as a cave and tech instructor for GUE, in addition to teaching and exploring caves and deep wrecks to write articles for several international diving magazines.*

JP is known for his underwater photography and film work that has featured cave and deep wreck exploration in remote and hard-to reach locations. JP is also a member of several cave exploration teams and has worked with many projects around the world (e.g., MCEP in Mexico, Karst Odyssey and Morpheus in the Balkans and the European Karst Plain Project [EKPP]) to support and manage underwater documentation.

As a member of the GUE Atlanta team, JP travelled to the Solomon Islands to document this impressive wreck to depths exceeding 130 m/424 ft. In 2016, JP joined a International Project Baseline initiative on the Bermuda Islands where he worked as video diver in CCR teams, filming scientific work to depths exceeding 100 m/326 ft.

KEVIN GURR

REBREATHER & RELATED EQUIPMENT DEVELOPER
FOR THE MILITARY

LOCATION OF INCIDENT
DIVING SHOW, UK

My rebreather diving and designing career started around 1988, with what was essentially a hybrid of a USN MK 15 and 16, called a MK 15.5. Basically, it was a MK15 with a MK16 centre section (CO_2 canister). In the early days of technical rebreather diving, these were the weapons of choice for several explorers—although very hard to obtain and with famously unreliable electronics. I and an electronics wizard friend of mine were asked if we could develop a new electronics package to work with a MK15.5 rebreather. I said "Sure!" My second question was "What's a rebreather?"

In no time at all I had the chance to find out! My first rebreather dive was in Plymouth Harbour, outside what was then the Diving Diseases Research Centre (DDRC) at Fort Bovisand, on a prototype Mk15.5 (note the duct-tape on the picture to the left), fitted with our new electronics. As I recall, we reached the extreme depth of 6 m/20 ft.

My second dive was inside the DDRC, to a depth of 100 m/326 ft. Needless to say: the rebreather failed, and I did my first heliox bailout. Quite a day for firsts!

After a phase of development and testing, which, from a rebreather perspective, went nowhere really (although we did do some useful practical trials with experimental trimix and heliox tables), mainstream technical diving and the tech diver forums were born.

On one early forum I 'met' an ichthyologist (easy for him to say), called Richard Pyle. Richard was using open circuit to explore the deep reef zone for new fish species, and I was using similar techniques for wreck diving. We immediately struck up a friendship, and an interest in a cave explorer in the US called Dr. Bill Stone.

Bill had developed his own rebreather to explore caves in Florida and Mexico and

Photos by Kevin Gurr

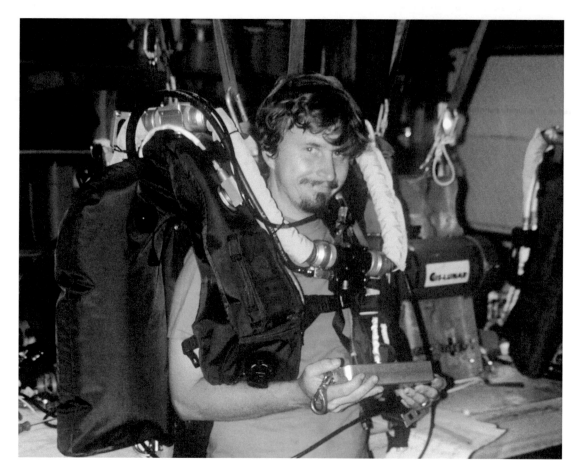

seemed to have a very advanced (and reliable) system. We had to have one!

I can't remember the date now, but the short story is I turned up on Bill's doorstep to find a guy clad in a Hawaiian shirt and shorts waiting for Bill to come home. I had started a friendship that lasts to this day. On Bill's return and after a short introduction to several Cis-Lunar (Bill's real thing is space) MK4 rebreathers covered in Mexican cave mud, Rich and I were tasked with rebuilding them over several days.

Before we were allowed to go diving, one of the 'training' events was to adopt a recognition and response for hypoxia (don't try this at home, kids). As you can see from the picture, Rich is tied onto the roof of Bill's garage by various bits of blue rope. The deal was that we went on the rig for as long as possible with

no O_2 injection taking place. Throughout the test we wrote our name on a board and had to respond to prompts.

When we felt we could no longer respond, we had to hit the manual O_2 bypass valve (and hopefully recover).

On the Cis-Lunar, the gas addition block is on the front of the left counterlung, so the response was ingrained to reach over with the right hand and hit the O_2 bypass. We lived to tell the tale, and both Rich and I had Mk4's 'issued' on loan to get us up to dive speed in our specific environments. This involved many hours expanding our horizons in terms of depth and time—Rich in Hawaii and me in the UK.

Moving on, Rich and I helped Bill bring the MK5 to the market, eventually going our separate ways, with Rich and Bill working with Poseidon and me starting my own rebreather design and manufacturing business. On my return to the UK with the MK4, I was contacted by a dive show organiser who had read some articles I'd written about the 'new rebreather technology' everyone was raving about.

"Would you do a tank demo?"

Basically, they wanted me to swim around in a glass fish tank for several hours at the dive show, waving at the audience while a commentator explained the technology. "Not too stressful," I thought—and they were paying!

The day started well, and hundreds of people turned up to the show. At the allotted time, I professionally stepped forward while the compere chatted with the audience. Trying to look like I knew what I was doing with my new rebreather, I gracefully slipped into the water. Outside the tank were the diving masses, faces pressed to the glass, all intrigued by this new device and its capabilities.

"Such small cylinders!, he can stay down for hours you know, look, no bubbles!"

I could see the amazement on their faces as I happily started my 10th lap of the (small) tank. Then it struck me: I didn't feel right and I had felt this before. But where? Then I remembered: tied into the roof of Bill Stone's garage! (picture to the left). I broke out in a cold sweat (quite a feat underwater). I looked at my handset and registered (just) a PO₂ of 0.12.

As I started to blackout, I instinctively hit the manual bypass and took in a big breath. It took me a couple of seconds to respond, and when I again looked out through the glass, I saw a level of bewilderment on the gathered faces.

Then I realised my body was slumped against the glass. That can't have looked good.

Still sweating (or at least it felt like it), I regained a level of composure and tried to work out what had happened. In short: the Cis had an auto turn-on feature, and it had failed to do what it said on the tin. Not the machine's fault really, and my first practical lesson in the importance of the pre-dive sequence. The happy faces resumed as I swam round, chastising myself for what would have been a very embarrassing death!

In the years and thousands of rebreather dives that have followed, I have learnt many lessons and seen many things; some good, some bad and some sad, but to this day, if I am lecturing on manual gas-addition drills, I still move my hand to my left shoulder to demonstrate the addition of oxygen even though none of my rebreathers since then have ever had that feature.

Kevin Gurr, *as well as being the first Technical Diving instructor outside the USA, has led and been a part of many expeditions including the first sport dives on the* Britannic *in 1997, treasure hunting in the Pacific (and several other locations world-wide), filmmaking and a dive on the* Titanic *in the MIR submarines to name but a few.*

As an engineer and diver, he has developed several groundbreaking products for the diving industry, from trimix computers to rebreathers. He is the author of the book Technical Diving from the Bottom Up.

He lives in Dorset, England, with his wife Mandy, daughters Leyla and Amberlee and various motorcycles.

LEIGH BISHOP

DEEP SHIPWRECK EXPLORER

LOCATION OF INCIDENT
NORTH ATLANTIC

Thinking back, it doesn't matter where it was, when it was or how it happened. But it did. It happened.

What matters are those lessons that life's little experiences throw at you, or in my case the one that was violently launched at me. Perhaps the reason I can think back almost two decades and remember just some of what happened on that day is because hard lessons were learnt and few, if any, close calls have occurred since. One only needs to remember once!

Back then we knew not of the knowledge we know now. It was the dawn of the new millennium, my rebreather was an early prototype, my youth drove energy through my veins, my fear was practically non-existent, and my careless attitude…well basically it stunk.

All of which was about to change as the result of one single dive.

I often wonder if it was God's way of saying, "Look Sunshine, this is the only thing you're ever going to be good at. Chill out, drop the attitude, and let's explore some great shipwrecks together."

I never had much money and because of that, I routinely cut corners, just like I did on this particular day. I used to regularly dive 70 m/230 ft shipwrecks breathing compressed air from a twinset until I grew up and did the maths, only to realise that my accumulated oxygen CNS-loading on such a dive would be through the roof! Thinking about it now: scary!

My diluent cylinder of trimix on this particular day was only half-full.

"That'll be ok," I said to myself. "I'm only nipping down to bag-up the ships telemotor and get the hell out of there." Basically, to cut a long story short, we were up to mischief. It was what wreck divers did back in those days.

Naughty scoundrels, lifting anything off the seabed that shined. It's just the way it was. On this occasion however, the item was big, heavy and respectably deep.

The wreck was big, a massive ocean liner, and the shot line had landed some distance away making quite a swim to the item in question. Big cylinders of dedicated lifting gas carried on either side made the swim a laborious drag! As I wrapped ropes around the telemotor, a connected and partially filled commercial lifting bag kept getting in my way, causing my mask to slightly dislodge itself and fill with nasty, unwelcome seawater—something I have never been too keen on.

Pausing, I tilted my head back and cleared the mask with gas through my nose.

I continued filling the lift bag now floating above me, emptying both cylinders into it. Frustration turned to anger as, despite the lift bag being about the size of one of Richard Branson's hot air balloons, the telemotor still sat firmly on the seabed! Damn this thing was heavy!

Looking for some extra momentum to get it going, I tried to lift the solid brass item off the seabed with a little muscle power. Again, I dislodged my mask and again cleared it in the same fashion. A process that repeated itself several times. I would have to use an extra bag and that meant eating into my dedicated, but somewhat smaller, bailout cylinder.

Automatic diluent valves were yet to be invented, and I relied on pressing a counter-lung button when gas in the loop dropped low. When the telemotor finally started rising slowly from the seabed, I took a sigh of relief and drew for a deep breath of gas.

What happened then hit me like a ton of bricks. There was NO gas! Nothing entered my lungs. Despite forcing the counter-lung button in as hard as I damn well could, nothing happened.

There was no gas in the counter-lung because there was no gas in the diluent cylinder! It had all escaped the loop through my nose. A combination of depth and Boyle's law had stolen the little diluent I had carried. It just so happened to be at the very point when I actually needed to breathe but there was nothing, zero gas. I couldn't breathe air, I knew I couldn't breathe water and quite frankly I didn't like it! The contents gauge on my tank read zero and its hose was floppier than a floppy thing.

In classic English slang and in the words of the good Lord…. I fucking shat myself.

My expression of relief changed to sheer panic quicker than Katy Perry changes outfits on stage! A gathered group of onlooking divers took the incident in with a degree of amusement as I frantically ripped the rebreather loop from my mouth whilst my other hand hunted for a regulator that wasn't where it should be. Of course, I'd just used it to blow the second lift bag but hadn't yet stowed it back into the position where, in an emergency, I always knew it to be.

I was on my knees on the seabed at almost 80 m/262 ft, with no air. Not great.

With what could, in hindsight, be classed as a spot of luck, but certainly didn't seem so at the time, one of the amused onlookers pushed his own regulator into my mouth and purged gas through it so violently that the seawater within was forced into my oesophagus causing me to almost drown there and then! "None of this is good," I thought. "Absolutely none of it. Totally dreadful," I thought.

Another diver, in a kind, gentleman-like manner, found my bailout regulator on my behalf, and off I shot along the seabed in the

rough direction of the shot line, apparently faster than a Polaris missile!

Even before I reached the shotline leading to the surface, my small bailout cylinder was half-empty, and I was breathing what was left at a rate of easily three, if not four, times faster than I normally would have.

My sphincter pulsed and I swear the 'turtle's head' was showing. I believe my mind at the time told me to head for the shot line, as it was programmed from British wreck diving and deep expedition diving to think of it as a place of safety, rather than being alone mid-water.

With the deep North Atlantic visibility good, I soon found the shotline, that so sought-after gateway to the surface. My VR3 wrist-mounted computer was a prototype that I was testing with beta software programmed for deep stops. In a kind way it told me "Leigh? A deep stop is required." I can still remember to this day what I said in my head in reply to that VR3, like I was actually talking to a human:

"Not interested. Go FUCK yourself!"

Reaching the shallows, my breathing rate dropped significantly and I settled down, but not without concern over the fact that little, if any, gas remained in my bail out cylinder to breathe - and no friends in sight to purchase any spare gas from.

I recall that I was, at the time, prepared to pay big money for even 10 bar/145 psi! I breathed pretty-much everything that was left and violated most decompression stops up to around 9 m/30 ft.

I could see the surface. Do I make a dash for it? Do I lie on the boat breathing oxygen? "Oxygen….oxygen…" I thought, "Damn, I have oxygen… Leigh you are carrying oxygen!" And with a remarkable piece of luck, I discovered that, in the split second I ripped the loop from my mouth, muscle memory from training had made me close the mouthpiece off.

Thankfully the loop had not flooded; I was able to turn the rebreather into an oxygen

rebreather even if the PO2 was in 1.6+ voodoo territory.

"What the hell, just breathe the damn stuff." Shadows emerged from the depths as my colleagues ascended from their own dives to be with me—colleagues, I must add—who were still somewhat amused. I was now safe, surrounded by spare gas and happy that my built-in survival instincts had saved me from drowning. I cared little if I was the amusement of the dive; I had survived death and was beginning to wonder where I could add that fact into my curriculum vitae.

Ever since that day, I have always filled all my cylinders to the maximum. Often have I heard the words "Are you sure you just want 10 bar/145 psi sir?" Fear has often held me back and kept me cautious; my bailout cylinders are the biggest I can carry and are reserved just for that: bailout. Bailout is bailout, and that's the way it has stayed for the two decades of deep wreck diving that followed that….well, dreadful experience.

In hindsight, there are lots of things I could have done differently, and I'm sure the casual armchair tek diver will be quick to calculate the maths of gas expansion in order to breathe if I had ascended point whatever of a metre.

Armchair facts DO NOT work when you are about to die, and if you think your bailout cylinder is sufficient, take it from me, think again. Unless of course you know for a fact you don't suffer from "Oh FUCK I'm dying" Syndrome!

Sadly, I have one-too-many friends who are unable to contribute to this book, as their own close calls were a little too close and then some.

What would I do if I could turn back the clock? I would certainly fill my diluent cylinder to the maximum. I would have carried enough bailout gas, and that bailout would be bailout, nothing else, certainly not to dump into a monster lift bag.

Oh, and I would perhaps leave that telemotor on the seabed; I'm sure the next generation of divers would have respected that.

I had a somewhat embarrassing diluent dilemma and have now, in published material, confessed this to be one of the stupidest errors of my life. In return, may I ask a favour from you?

Go now and top up ALL your cylinders for that upcoming dive, and please re-think those small bailout cylinders in your garage. Remember: the best and most important thing you will ever bring home from the ocean is yourself.

Leigh Bishop *is a world-renowned shipwreck explorer and pioneer of deep-wreck mixed-gas diving and deep photography. He has been one of the most prolific writers in technical diving over the last two decades inspiring many of today's well-known divers to pick up a camera and write a book themselves.*

He has been a member of most significant deep expeditions as well as scientific projects that have carried the Explorers Club flag. He lectures globally, features on many television documentaries and worked as a deep-water cameraman for National Geographic, the History Channel, and many other global networks.

He has dived an estimated 400 virgin wrecks and his own research has led to the identification of literally hundreds of shipwrecks. Leigh was the man behind the original concept of 'Eurotek', the world's premier Advanced Diving Conference.

Photo by Richie Kohler

LUIGI CASATI

CAVE EXPLORER / CCR CAVE INSTRUCTOR TRAINER
KNIGHT OF THE ITALIAN REPUBLIC

LOCATION(S) OF INCIDENT
VARIOUS LOCATIONS

My life has always been connected with the great outdoors. From mountain climbing to caving, from scuba diving to paragliding, they all have common fundamentals: respect for one's limits, respect for the environment, and deep knowledge regarding equipment and technique. Almost all accidents are caused by an error related to one or more of these elements. Knowing your physical, but also psychological, limits is the basis when dealing with high risk sports.

In all these sports, we find two kinds of people: those who experience the challenge remaining within their limits, and those who try to redefine them. The former have a clear idea of what they want to achieve while the later are unfulfilled, constantly trying to go beyond what has already been conquered. But everyone, sooner or later, will have to accept a personal limit. Physical or mental. Maybe a bad day, or simply because life begins to prevail.

It is not easy to accept that you may be unable to reach a goal, and if this goal involves other people, that acceptance becomes even more difficult for one's ego.

The pressure, even if involuntary, from those who are with us and expecting a positive result, can push us to risky and dangerous decision making. Being able to modify and adapt the limits to the current situation is not easy, but it is necessary; it is better to regret an unfulfilled goal than to realise that you have thrown yourself into a bad situation. Fear is the alarm bell for these limits being reached or exceeded.

Every time we challenge nature, we are in a position of disadvantage. The natural elements we face are often so powerful that they force us to face them only when they are at their weakest. Underestimating that power is a big mistake.

Photo by Davide Corengia

Fortunately, these days we have the ability to predict weather conditions with sufficient precision a few days in advance; serious rainfall or snow melting can lead to rising water levels in a cave, obstructing passages, reducing visibility, or even generating violent flow.

However, it is not just the weather; a cave's morphology also affects our challenge. I remember flooded tunnels particularly rich in clay, bottleneck restrictions with near-zero visibility, and unstable passages with rocks and mud. Equipment keeps evolving, albeit relatively slowly, and most problems related to it have gradually been solved. The need for safety has driven further research.

Regulators have traditionally given us problems for years, particularly when used in cold water or at serious depths. Also, debris falling from the ceiling, mud, or small gravel when crawling through restrictions—all these things have entered second stages and created issues during many explorations. To prevent this, some divers cover their second stages with tights, and I also know cave divers who have mounted grids on them! The downside of this practice is that a mounted grid cannot easily be removed during a dive; if the grid were to become clogged with mud, then it would prevent breathing from the regulator. The tights, in comparison, are usually kept in place with an elastic band, allowing for easy removal underwater. A simple and effective fix, which shows that solutions to equipment problems are not always expensive.

With the arrival of semi-closed and closed rebreather units, the first divers who tried to use them entered an unknown territory. For example, many of the sensors used in the early 2000s would start to become unreliable after around an hour of use. The lime material used to scrub CO_2 had a tendency to become inert and therefore unusable if it was stored at a low temperature. Before this reaction was understood, some divers (myself included) had an unpleasant surprise during a dive, learning the hard way that that carbon dioxide was not being filtered. Today, we are lucky enough to have a simple and somewhat standardised set of procedures and checks that we do with our equipment before a dive, but these were developed over time, through trial, error, and accident analysis of previous users.

Incident #1

In 2004, I was using a passive semi-closed rebreather (PSCR) to reach depths of up to 186 m/610 ft. I was experimenting with it, because back then we would not normally take this type of rebreather deeper than 90-100 m/294-326 ft. Finding reliable partial-pressure readers was not easy, but the simplicity of these PSCRs allowed their use even without one. And then, because of a simple mistake, I got an oxygen hit.

Normally when I was using one or two of these PSCR units (counter-lung ratio 1/14), I would place two cylinders containing the same gas on their sides. However, during one preparation dive, I chose two cylinders containing different fractions of oxygen: one was to be used to reach 70 m/229 ft (28% O2) and the other 140 m/429 ft (18% O2).

Changing the configuration of the cylinders away from my norm, on a demanding dive, was the initial mistake, combined with incorrect management of the fittings that fed the rebreather.

In due course, I found myself at 125 m/410 ft, before descending into the well of the 'White Elephant' cave in Northern Italy, with an annoyingly strong tingling on my lips. As I realised that it was an oxygen issue, I focused on managing the situation, forgetting the (new) configuration of my cylinders. During an emergency, as our mind focuses on the problem, we are often good at following the usual procedures, but we sometimes tend to forget possible new parameters; I connected the cylinder with 28% oxygen, thinking that I had connected the one containing the correct gas for the quota, 18% oxygen.

My 'correct' response, to not change gas in order to avoid a further increase in PPO₂, was wrong.

In the meantime, I scootered across 50 m/164 ft of a tunnel at 120 m/393 ft and started the ascent. The discomfort in my lips was still very intense. When I reached my gas change at 70 m/229 ft, a moment of clarity made me realise what was happening.

For approximately ten minutes, at 120 m/393 ft, I was breathing a PPO₂ of 2.6-2.7 bar! I can still remember how, on my way up, as I was changing the gas in my unit to manage my decompression better, the tingling sensation came back without any sign of moderation.

Managing my ascent without a sensor, and with the threat of oxygen toxicity preventing me from using the correct gases, was not easy but, ultimately, experience and self-control resulted in a safe return.

At the end of the dive, everything went well, although within a few minutes of surfacing, I started having a violent and frequent dry cough that lasted for eight days.

You can learn from mistakes, but sometimes the risk is just too high. Trusting my skills regarding the management of a new configuration for the first time–especially during a demanding work dive—was, without a doubt, not a good idea. Changing habitual procedures can lead to mistakes, as the mind is busy with something else.

Incident #2

When I started using a manual closed circuit rebreather (MCCR) in 2005, I took it easy in the beginning. As with everything new, I had to 'start again', even considering my general level of experience with rebreathers up until then.

Photo by Roberto Rinaldi

The fascinating simplicity of the MCCR unit, with minimal electronics used only for the monitoring of oxygen, was certainly more effective both from a respiratory comfort point of view but also for the freedom of progression that allowed. Among the many dives I used it for, I remember the gallery of 'Vrelo Une' cave at 205m/672ft, in 2009.

I had to stop when I hit 205 m/672 ft, because two of my three oxygen sensors had suddenly turned off; fortunately, by going up just a few meters, I was able to get them to start working again. Explanation: the pressure exerted on the sensors' glass covers was crushing the rudimentary electronic circuits in their metal container and was turning them off.

Little was known back then about rebreathers. Especially how (and if) they would work beyond a depth of 100-120 m/328-393 ft. Many predicted that I would die from hyperoxia, trying to explain it using improbable theories regarding the management of mechanical flow at high pressure. As a result, even today, many still use 'blocked' first stages.

During one of my first dives on the MCCR, while I was testing to see how long I could stay without using that flow, at constant depth, I got into a hypoxic situation. At 12 m/40 ft, I closed the flow of oxygen and waited. After a few minutes spent making knots on a line, I became negative, but with my mind focused on the knots, I automatically added diluent into the unit to compensate for my reduced buoyancy.

I knew very well that at a constant depth with the flow closed, negative buoyancy meant consumption of oxygen and therefore less volume in the counterlung of the rebreather. I should have checked the oxygen sensors, but I was distracted by the knots. After 3-4 injections of diluent, I finally decided to check my PPO$_2$ and saw that I was at 0.12bar!

This lesson made me establish a new personal rule and rigorously stick to it: if I have to close

the oxygen, even if it's only rarely, I always keep my hand on the valve. If I have to do something else, I first open it again and only then manage what I have to do.

Incident #3

During long cave dives, scooters became a standard, but if you rely blindly on them, then problems will occur. It is fairly common practice to leave one or more emergency scooters at strategic points in order to not have to tow them back and forth. Accordingly, on one of my explorations in Vouliagmeni cave in Greece, I left a scooter and an emergency cylinder at around 90 m/294 ft depth and at 700 m/2,296 ft from the entrance. After another 500 m/1640 ft of progression, I was looking around for the best direction in a fascinatingly huge empty space. Unfortunately, in my admiration of the cave, the guideline I had let go of got sucked in by my scooter's propeller and blocked it. I tried in vain to remove it, but to no avail. I had three 20-litre cylinders on my back, and I had already somewhat exceeded my planned progression. For an emergency return on fins, my gas reserves were going to be dangerously tight.

Instinct made me look up and just above my head, I saw a guideline. My thoughts ran faster than the time I was against. I decided to ascend those ten or so meters that separated me from that faint line, and I reached it.

It was a steel cable, covered with white plastic previously placed by us on the right wall, in the first 600 m/1968 ft of the cave. Again by intuition, I decided to follow it, holding on to the wall. The minutes were passing, and my gas was decreasing, as I was still at 70 m/228 ft, when I saw in the distance my safety cylinder attached on the wire. I had chosen the right direction. I was safe.

A bit of luck is necessary in every activity, but it must also come with a dose of good instinct and the courage to follow it.

If I hadn't trusted what I thought I recognised, if I had been discouraged, or if I simply had not been able to fin for such a long time with a lot of gear on, I probably wouldn't have gotten away with it that time. When we have a 50/50 chance, the ability to stay calm and make the correct decision is fundamental.

Incident #4

Knowing how to follow and 'stay on' the line during a cave dive is easy if you understand the technique, and with a rebreather it's even more so. However, my first cave incident happened back in 1986, exactly because I violated those basic rules. Cave diving is conceived by many of us as solo diving, for several reasons.

Mainly because when you are alone with yourself, with your own fears and limits, you are consequently also independent from others.

I was at the 'Source Du Doubs' cave with my friend and mentor, Jean Jacques Bolanz.

I started my dive half an hour after him and crossed him on his way back as I was going down towards 50 m/164 ft. I kept going for about another fifteen meters horizontally, until the end of the line.

A few meters ahead, I saw a restriction never explored before, so I decided to go and check it out. I was aware that, as cave divers, we must never leave the guideline, but unfortunately in that moment the words of an Italian cave diver came to my mind; a few months earlier he had told me, informally, that leaving the line for just a few metres would be ok as it would be easy enough to find it again by simply turning around.

Just like Pinocchio who listened to the cat and the fox, and relying on excellent visibility, I left the line and reached the restriction.

Photos by Andrea Mescalchin

After a brief check to see if it was possible to pass, I turned around to go back to the line and I found myself confronted by a 'wall' of suspended clay that reduced visibility to only a few centimetres. I headed towards where I thought I had come from, but I didn't find the line. My breathing rate started to increase, but I forced myself to keep it under control.

I found a line and followed it, but after just a metre it ended. As I kept looking, I found another one; that too ended just like the first.

They were all pieces of old line that had accumulated there. I tried to ascend hoping that I was at the bottom of the well, but I ended up in a trap full of lines, in which I got badly entangled, before I managed to free myself with my clippers.

Ten minutes had already passed and the gas in my cylinders was getting low, so I decided to go back down and start a lost line procedure. Once on the bottom, I found myself on a line. I was able to see it because the weak current had cleaned the area a bit, improving the visibility to maybe 1 m/3 ft.

I grabbed the line and followed it. It was finally the correct one! I reached the decompression area, stayed there for the necessary time, and surfaced with 10-15 bar/145-220 psi in my cylinders. I ungeared as quietly as ever, exchanged the usual light chat, loaded my car and went home.

After two days, I felt the need to talk about it with Jean Jacques, so I called him and told him what had happened. Jean Jacques, always the great observer, had noticed my strange behaviour and said to me, "Some rules must be always respected as if they were religious dogmas."

This experience, together with many others, was responsible for the change in my approach towards cave diving. A change from a bold, unafraid young man to a more thoughtful, respectful and attentive diver.

However, simple understanding is not always enough to avoid an accident; that moment of overconfidence or too much trust in others is always lurking, in spite of any experience.

Modesty and a healthy dose of self-criticism will help each of us stay alive, help us to save others, and ensure that we don't waste all the amazing experiences that nature has to offer us.

Luigi Casati *has to his credit numerous cave explorations all over the world and different records of depth and / or length, both with open and closed circuit systems.*

Among his main explorations are the caves of Oliero and the Gorgazzo Sorgente in Italy, Vrelo Une (Croatia) and Matka Vrelo (Macedonia). In 2008, he reached the depth of 212 m/695 ft of the Gorgazzo springs at Polcenigo, achieving the record of the deepest exploration of an Italian spring.

He began diving in 1978, cave diving in 1986, and has since explored places never seen by man before, unattainable by technology, and therefore mysterious.

Luigi is a man who has quite literally pushed the doors of the unknown and has explored the true darkness inside our planet. Luigi, during the explorations, has often been forced to improvise technical solutions, modifying his equipment and decompression profiles.

He is a PSS instructor trainer. With the use of trimix mixtures in open circuit (1988), he reached 165 m/541 ft of depth and a penetration of 2635 m/8645 ft. A pioneer of the use of rebreathers in deep diving (2003), he has 15 dives over 200 m/656 ft with a maximum depth of 248 m/813 ft. Luigi has explored more than 50 km/31 miles of flooded caves.

He received several honors: Bronze Medal for Civil Valor, Civic Merit, Silver Medal and Knight of the Republic.

MARISSA ECKERT

CO-OWNER @ HIDDEN WORLDS DIVING
PROFESSIONAL PHOTOGRAPHER
TECHNICAL / REBREATHER / CAVE INSTRUCTOR

LOCATION OF INCIDENT
PEACOCK SPRINGS STATE PARK, FLORIDA, USA

There is a tunnel in Peacock simply called the 'Dark Water Tunnel'. The name itself sounds very appealing, right? Someone had reported that the line in this tunnel was broken. I was full cave certified at the time but not yet an instructor, but I had a great interest in helping with these types of things, so I jumped at the opportunity to do a line repair. However, Peacock is a state park and does not allow solo diving. So, I needed to find a buddy. Not one, but two people volunteered; I was not sure how good an idea it was, three of us going into this tunnel with a potentially broken line, but I was not going to argue.

I was just excited to have found a buddy.

We arrived at Peacock on the day and came up with a general dive plan; we decided to approach the dark water tunnel from the main line, Olsen side.

For anyone unfamiliar with Peacock, there are two main lines in the cavern.

One goes down a tunnel called the Peanut line, the other down a tunnel called the Pothole/Olsen line. The Dark Water Tunnel can be reached from either line. However, to reach it from the Peanut side you need to first jump over to the crossover line.

We gear up, two back mount divers and one side mount diver, and swim into the cave; I am diver number three. As we approach the jump, I am surprised that both of my teammates swim past it. I signal to them that it's back, behind us. Everyone turns around and comes back. It is an unmarked jump that is hidden due to the siltiness of the tunnel. Diver one pulls out a spool and puts in the jump. The jump line is hidden around a corner and is a good distance from the main line.

Photos by Marissa Eckert

Once tied into the jump you can no longer see the main line. We all jumped across and continued. Not long down this line, the cave passage requires you to dip under this extremely low, very silty ledge. Diver number one goes through, and by the time diver number two has also gone through, I am in zero visibility.

My buddies leave me.

I continue to follow the line okaying it. However, it feels loose and very slack in my hand. I know that this line may be broken. As I continue in zero visibility, I think to myself how stupid this is. I turn back and get to the portion of the cave just before the ledge and it is clear there, so I wait.

Our plan was to go in and out the same way, so I knew they'd be back. And hopefully, eventually, they would realise I was not with them. The clock ticked and ticked, and I felt increasingly uneasy, waiting in backmount with no buddy and no additional redundancy. Minutes felt like hours.

All these thoughts started to go through my mind. After almost thirty minutes, I wondered if they had done blind jumps and completed a blind circuit to get out and not come back this way. At the end of the dark water tunnel you can jump across to the crossover tunnel, follow that, and jump back onto the Olsen line. Then you can continue right and get back to the jump we were in.

I decided to start to venture out. At this point I had been by myself for a long time. I wanted to make sure I still had sufficient gas to get myself out. Once I got back to where the jump spool should be, it was not there!

As I rounded the corner looking for the main line, there was diver number one pulling out the jump, leaving me in the cave passage with no line. I flashed my light at them, and they signalled for me to go in the front. I led us out and in the end everyone was fine. They had indeed decided to jump over to the crossover line and then over back onto the mainline completing a circuit that would not require them to come back through zero visibility.

No spools were put in, and this was not part of our dive plan.

Since that day, I have encountered other situations like it, where people leave others due to silt-outs. I have had it happen to me on at least two other occasions. Once a girl actually not only left me in the cave, but left me at the dive site by myself! She must have been so spooked that she left the cave and drove off in a hurry, never even knowing if I, her buddy, was alive.

Flash forward a few years and someone introduced to me the concept of attendance markers as navigational decisions. Some agencies require it, but many do not, and therefore it is also something that is not taught by all instructors. I, however, think it is incredibly useful. I now teach and use this myself, and I think it is an amazing tool. You never know who has been taught this, and who has not, so I tell all my cave students to always cover this information in the predive briefing. That way everyone is on the same page and dropping markers at the correct spots so there is no confusion.

I tell these stories to all my cave students to stress the importance of buddy awareness, having a plan, diving your plan, and keeping your cool in stressful situations.

Team separations can end up with one person dying in a cave while the other person has already left the cave and is waiting on the surface.

Always make sure you have enough gas to get yourself out and reserve enough in case you have an emergency, as well. This is definitely something that taught me an important lesson and changed the way I cave dive on every dive now.

Marissa Eckert *is a passionate, full-time technical diving instructor and dive shop owner specializing in cave, rebreather, sidemount, and photography, with a wealth of experience and knowledge in both open circuit and rebreather diving.*

Marissa is a full-time active instructor in North Central Florida who loves to stay busy. When not teaching, she enjoys travelling all over the world, exploring new places, hiking through the jungle, and doing challenging new dives that help her grow and learn as a diver. What really motivates Marissa is the desire to show people this amazing world, whether that be through caves, wrecks, ocean diving, deep diving, rebreather diving, sidemount diving, or photography. Marissa's major passions are teaching, exploration, and photography.

Marissa is certified on multiple rebreathers and can teach the SM Liberty, the X-CCR, the SF2, the KISS Sidekick, and the KISS sidewinder. She has tons of hours on rebreathers and thousands of cave dives. She loves to teach, whether it is a cavern class or a cave dpv class; she loves helping people get a glimpse into this amazing underwater world.

MARK ELLYATT

OWNER @ INSPIRED TRAINING
PSAI INSTRUCTOR TRAINER / OCEAN GLADIATOR AUTHOR

LOCATION OF INCIDENT
SEVASTOPOL, BLACK SEA

I first noticed a rise in oxygen toxicity incidents among tech divers 12-15 years back, about the same time as internet dive forums were at their peak.

Tech trainers were not so prolific as nowadays, and divers around the world virtually trained themselves by trawling posts and photos. A few years before this, a new dive agency had emerged but they were still facing the uphill battle of recruiting instructors and gaining traction for their standardised equipment and gases doctrine (although eventually their forum hawks changed the status-quo somewhat, and their message took hold).

One of the first issues I had was their mindset of only putting the Maximum Operating Depth (MOD) of gas mixes on cylinders, the mantra of 'less is more' apparently being less confusing

underwater, trumping the common sense approach of 'back-up is better'.

Historically, nitrox and trimix tanks were labelled with both the mixture contents (FO_2) and the MOD of the contents.

Now dive cylinders only displayed the mixes' maximum depth digits alone without either the corresponding symbol for metres or feet, and often there was no indication of the actual percentage of oxygen contained within written anywhere.

When I travelled around the world teaching tech diving, I would often see all the tanks labelled this way, often with permanent large stickers stating one thing with almost always more than one conflicting set of stickers alongside them.

Photos by Mark Ellyatt

The next issue was this agency promoting the carrying of stage / deco / bail-out tanks all clipped on to the left side of the diver, the reasoning being that if you were scootering on mammoth cave dives, then the DPV's propwash would be more efficient. That may be true, but during training, during class ascents, during bailout practice, or gas-switching drills, time and time again divers would be sticking the wrong second stage in their mouths and risking all sorts of dire outcomes. In a group, these issues might be noticed before it was too late, but as soon as the diver flew solo, then the outcomes of this were usually tragic.

Most of the time I just labelled my tanks the way I always did, with both Mix % and MOD, often wrapping tape over the larger permanent markings proudly displaying something the tanks may have once contained in the past - to avoid confusion. Very rarely I would try to clip a couple of deco or bail-out tanks on to my left side to appease the crowd (who are often set in their ways despite having done just a handful of dives like it; more likely they were resistant to common sense, as they had invested in the stickers already, and the divers they wanted to emulate worked this way).

Anyway, fast-forward 15 years. I was teaching a rebreather instructor course to a customer overseas. Our bail-out tanks were already filled and marked with Imperial marking stickers so my nitrox 50 tank was marked 70 (its Maximum Operating Depth (MOD) in feet), the deep bail-out marked with MOD 200' and a third tank marked for 165'.

My rebreather tanks (usually 5 litre steels at home) were S45s borrowed locally, but the valves leaked. We arrived at the dive site to find the diluent tank pressure down to 80 bar. I elected to use the back-up set of S19 tanks (approx. 2.5lts) which were at 150bar/2175psi.

On this particular dive, we were to descend a shot line after a five min submerged shallow swim to do some drills at around 50 m/164 ft depth.

During instructor training, I normally improvise some kind of equipment malfunction to see how the candidate deals with the issue (or even if they notice it). On this day, I had installed an OPV plug on my diluent first stage and had it set loosely so that it vented gas slowly but continuously, getting worse as depth increased.

Down we went. We did the ubiquitous bubble check and my leaky first stage went unnoticed. During the shallow swim, I checked my diluent gauge to see 90 bar/1305 psi. My student looked back from ten to fifteen metres away, gave a cursory 'Okay' signal and swam off fairly quickly towards our destination. Some minutes later, at around ten metres depth, we met up again on the descent line. I signalled for him to slow down; he agreed but still descended much faster than I could, as I was now weighted less than usual due to the last-minute cylinder swap. The distance between us soon increased to the point where I could no longer see him.

Checking my diluent tank pressure, at around 30 m/100 ft, showed 30 bar/435 psi and looking up, I could see the bubble trail heading north. I figured with zero deco obligation I could bail, get my wayward buddy's attention, and abort the dive. Carrying on down to 40 m/131 ft, I noticed an increase in effort to trigger my ADV (diluent addition valve); instinctively I checked my PO₂ on my handset to see it was above 1.8 bar and climbing.

I turned off my oxygen tank valve and simultaneously hit my wing inflator (connected to my oxygen regulator), but the descent continued. Still dropping, I attempted a deep inhale to add diluent, but nothing happened, I bailed to my BOV (bail out reg) and got a mouthful of seawater. I checked my diluent contents gauge, and it was now empty. No Diluent equalled No BOV.

Time to go to my off-board bailout. For some reason, I had decided to wear my three bail-out tanks on my left side this day (mostly

because it was a fairly innocuous dive and the borrowed tanks' rigging clips were luxuriously enormous, allowing me to get even my dry-gloved Homer Simpson fingers into them).

Reaching 50 m/164 ft, I could see the student some distance away, merrily signalling 'Okay' circles with his light-sabre dive light; my own wrist-worn light was useless for illuminating my tank markings, as it was much too bright and being fixed to my left wrist, it didn't give the angle needed for viewing tanks that were firmly strapped to my left side.

So: it was pitch black, I couldn't breathe, and every few seconds a 4000 lumen dive light would shine in my eyes.

Without being able to see my tank markings, and having stage regs that were all borrowed and therefore unfamiliar, I couldn't decide which tank to go for. I unclipped the first tank completely, lungs screaming.

Spinning it round, the label said '21' – this translates to Nitrox 50 (why agency stickering needs translating on the fly is beyond me.

In My Not So Humble Opinion, if an agency was deciding to go against conventional wisdom and only display half of the information needed to make a potentially life-ending decision, you'd think that just maybe they would go for the tank's actual oxygen content, as most divers could then decide if it was appropriate!

But I digress. In my last few seconds before unconsciousness, I decided against the 50% with its likely 3.0 bar pO_2 vs elevated CO_2 and clipped it; the urgency of the situation was screaming loud. I figured my next choice would be a coin toss—either the end of me if wrong vs. working out fine if I chose right.

I dragged another one in front and luckily, it was the 165' tank! Spitting my loop, I grabbed the second stage and stuck it in while purging.

Those few seconds, when the regs fire water before depressurising, are a tech no-man's land, the next breath coming, or not. Instinctively, I spun the tank valve fully on and breathed again.

Normal service resumed in as many seconds, I looked for the student to see him slowly swimming over. I signalled up, and that was that.

Summary: Over the years, I've sorted countless wrong reg mix-ups, turned doubles manifolds back on when a diver had turned them both off, found rebreather divers with O_2 hoses disconnected, counter lungs set-up badly, wrongly-sized, even unrestrained.

Units slowly flooding, wrong diluents, wrong bail-outs, BOVs partially cracked open, mushroom valves unseated or broken, no lime, wet lime, bone-dry lime, flooded handsets—the list is endless, the problems usually stealthily insidious, and all are eventually deadly.

Last minute kit configuration changes, suboptimal light placement, and insufficient sleep are hardly check-list favourites but can definitely piss on anyone's chips in dark, deep water. It is not just the complex dives but also the seemingly routine plunges using complex machines that need a cool head, extensive practice, an eye for detail, plus a healthy aversion to Kool-Aid.

Whilst having solid solo and self-rescue skills is paramount to success when deeper diving, keen observation skills and teammate proximity are equally important when in company.

Bailing out in a timely fashion is often priceless too.

To Quote Hill Street Blues, "Let's be careful out there."

Mark Ellyeatt *has been an instructor for 26 years. He has surfaced safely from over 1000 dives below 60m and more than 250 beyond 100m. Since 1995, Mark has been diving below 150m and in 2003 went to 313m.*

When you receive diver or Instructor training from Mark you get to hear how to do it and how not to from first-hand experience. Mark promises to give you Inspired Training and definitely not simply a recital from a training text.

Mark's Deep Diving adventures have visited wrecks in 180m as far back as 1999 / 2000 / 2001. Read the hair raising accounts of these and others including 21 minutes at 170m in a UK Copper Mine in his book, Ocean Gladiator.

MARK POWELL

TDI/SDI INSTRUCTOR TRAINER EVALUATOR
MEMBER OF THE GLOBAL TRAINING ADVISORY PANEL.

LOCATION OF INCIDENT
SOUND OF MULL, WEST COAST OF SCOTLAND

My closest miss while diving was not due to bad luck or adverse conditions. Nor was it caused by someone else doing something foolish. No, my closest miss was due to me making a very stupid mistake. Luckily, I survived my own stupidity and managed to learn from the experience.

When I started rebreather diving, I started on a KISS classic. This is a fantastic rebreather which definitely works on the KISS principle (Keep It Simple, Stupid). The rebreather has a valve that allows a fixed amount of oxygen into the breathing loop. This amount is tweaked to match your own metabolic rate so it is constantly replacing the oxygen you use and is intended to always keep a breathable mixture in the loop.

In addition, the diver can use a Manual Add Valve (MAV) to top up the oxygen level in order to maintain an exact mixture. It's a very simple system that works extremely well. It also has the advantage of conditioning the diver to monitor their PPO_2 during the dive in order to constantly fine-tune the level.

There is a disadvantage to this system, in that the valve is constantly injecting oxygen whenever the oxygen cylinder is open. So, if you leave the cylinder open for any length of time before or after the dive, it will eventually empty. On a couple of occasions, I forgot to close the oxygen cylinder after a dive and came back for the second dive or the next day only to find it empty. To get around this, I decided I needed to build a habit wherein I would always turn off the cylinder after a dive. I started by making myself turn off the oxygen immediately after getting out of the rebreather. This was a good approach, but on a couple of occasions I got distracted whilst

getting out of the rebreather and still ended up forgetting to turn off the cylinder. What I should have done is been consistent in my approach and developed a habitual muscle memory so that I would do this every time, even if distracted. Instead, what I did was change the process and start a slow-motion car crash incident that would catch up with me several months later.

I was trying to get into the habit of turning off the oxygen before I got out of the rebreather; usually I did this as I was sitting on the bench before getting out of the unit, but at other times I would turn it off whilst walking back to my spot on the bench, or on the lift on the way out of the water. If I was waiting in the water for my buddy to get out, I would sometimes use this time to turn off the oxygen while floating on the surface as I knew I had several minutes of oxygen in the loop.

As I type these words I know it sounds stupid.

I am shaking my head at myself right now. It's obvious where this could end up, but at the time I thought it was okay, as there was still plenty of oxygen in the breathing loop, and I knew I would be back on the boat and off the loop in a minute or two.

The close call came about when I was diving from a boat in the Sound of Mull on the west coast of Scotland. The boat had a hydraulic lift which made it much easier for divers to get out of the water at the end of a dive, especially when wearing multiple cylinders.

My buddy was about to get onto the lift so I turned my oxygen cylinder off. Just as he was reaching out to climb on, he had a minor issue and missed getting a proper grip. The boat drifted away, and rather than getting my buddy to swim for it, the boat captain decided to come back around and pick him up again. I watched the boat steam around in a gentle circle and drift alongside my buddy who was then hoisted back onto the boat by the lift.

He was brought back up to deck level and took a few seconds to clear the lift area in order for it to be dropped back to me. It came back down to the water level and I grabbed hold of it, positioning myself standing on the platform and holding on to the two side rails. Once I was in position, I nodded to the crew man who started to lift me out of the water.

As the lift came up and I emerged from the water, the support of the water disappeared and I tensed my muscles in order to take the weight of the rebreather and bailout cylinders as I came, once again, under the influence of gravity.

As my muscles took the weight of the equipment, I immediately became lightheaded, and I started to experience tunnel vision with blackness coming in from the sides.

It was at this point that I was a split second away from unconsciousness and becoming a statistic. Luckily, I was still conscious enough to understand what was happening; I remember instantly realising what the issue was and that I was in big trouble. It was literally a flash of insight; "F*^£ !! Oxygen off, hypoxia, blacking out, idiot!" I immediately spat out my mouthpiece and took a big gulp of air.

As I did this the blackness in my field of vision cleared and I felt the strength coming back into my muscles. I glanced down at my handset, which of course I should have been doing all along, and saw that the PPO2 in my loop was 0.09. This is not enough to sustain consciousness on the surface and is right on the edge of being able to sustain life.

If I had not reacted at that point, I know that within a second or two I would have become unconscious. I would then have fallen over and potentially ended up back in the water. If my loop had come out it would have flooded, and I would have instantly become very negatively-buoyant and promptly sunk. Even if the loop had stayed in, I would have been breathing a hypoxic mixture and would have been dead very soon after.

Luckily, I managed to spot the symptoms before I blacked out and was able to learn this lesson without becoming a fatality report. This incident taught me how easy it is to make a fatal mistake and how easy it is to fall victim to hypoxia.

It also taught me the importance of monitoring your PPO2 on the surface and not just during the dive.

Mark Powell *had his first experience of diving at the age of 10 when he did a try-dive in a local pool. He was hooked from that point onwards. He learnt to dive in 1987 and has been diving ever since. He has dived all around the world but is most at home in the waters around the UK, where there is some of the best wreck diving in the world. Mark became an instructor in 1994 and has been actively instructing since then; he became a full-time diving instructor in 2002. Mark provides technical training at all levels up to and including CCR Advanced Mixed Gas Instructor Trainer. As well as technical training, Mark also provides instructor training at recreational and technical levels, as well as training instructor trainers. He also provides consultancy services to other parts of the diving industry.*

Mark is a TDI/SDI Instructor Trainer Evaluator and a member of TDI/SDI's Global Training Advisor Panel. He is a regular contributor to a number of diving magazines and a regular speaker at diving conferences around the world.

In 2008, Mark published Deco for Divers, *a widely acclaimed overview of the theory and physiology of decompression. This has quickly become the standard text on the subject and is recommended reading for a number of the technical diving agencies. In 2010,* Deco for Divers *was awarded 'Publication of the Conference' at the EuroTEK 10 technical diving conference, and in 2014, it won the Media Award at TekDive USA. In 2019, Mark followed this up with a new book* Technical Diving – An Introduction, *which introduces the principles behind technical diving to anyone looking to get into this fascinating area.*

MATTEO RATTO

UTRTEK TRIMIX & TECHNICAL CAVE
INSTRUCTOR TRAINER

LOCATION OF INCIDENT
MINE, BERGAMO, ITALY

Back in 2011, I was traveling around Italy with a buddy of mine, searching for unknown caves and mines that could be new places to dive.

After some research, we found information about a particular mine, which we knew had been closed since the 1980s. We got in touch with the mine managers and managed to get permission to enter and carry out some dives, in order to survey a particular area, now flooded with water, and check the mine's stability.

Between 2011 and 2012, we dived different areas of the mine, supported by local caving groups for the transport of equipment. The path to get to the submerged section was complicated; an electric train took us roughly 1 km/0.62 mi into the mine, after which several hundred m/ft of walking were waiting for us among the abandoned paths, where

hundreds of miners had worked, thirty years earlier. On one of the last dives, our plan was to video a particular branch of the mine that was not very clear on the map.

On the day of the dive, we agreed to make a detour from the mainline to the branch we wanted to explore. It was about 200 m/656 ft long, multilevel between 36 m/118 ft and 15 m/49 ft of depth.

After carrying all our equipment, which included rebreathers and bailouts, we started our dive.

Visibility was excellent during the descent, but behind us a mudslide followed as usual. Even without making bubbles, each time we attached the line we created a cloud of light, white-coloured mud, three to four metres all around us.

Photo by Matteo Ratto

All our other dives in the mine had been like this; our return would inevitably be with zero visibility. After connecting the jump, we moved to a new tunnel, about 7 m/22 ft in diameter.

The branch divided in three directions, one went downwards, the other two continued upwards. Once our line was attached, we took one of the upward branches.

The depth rose to 25 m/82 ft, and all around us there were metal pipes, wooden supports, and trolley tracks, all scattered randomly as if the miners had left them in a hurry at the end of their shift. We fixed our line onto a tube. The path started to climb vertically, dividing into two other branches; we took the right-hand fork, but after some metres we ran into excavated rock that obstructed the passage and forced us to return.

At that moment I decided to fix the line to something permanent, but whilst I was cutting the line it slipped from my hand! My buddy, behind me, inadvertently caught it with his fins, and by turning around before I managed to secure it, he took the line away in the cloud of dust which followed us.

Our torches did not help, especially his, as he was already inside the zone of zero visibility. Such a simple thing, but I immediately started thinking about the tragic consequences that could come of it. I could feel anguish and stress building to close to my limit—much more and it could turn into panic.

In front of me was just a white cloud where absolutely nothing could be seen that might help us navigate. I had no idea whether my buddy had found the line, if he was near me or far away, if he was looking for me or if he had even noticed that I was left without a connection.

At that moment the most obvious solution, to fix a spool and start searching for the line, did not seem a good idea. The passage was very rough and uneven in depth, with multiple directions and numerous unstable obstacles to crash into. The main line was more than a 100 m/328 ft away and probably very difficult to find.

The main question was whether the line was still close to me, or been dragged away by my buddy without him noticing. After thirty seconds of blackout that felt like eternity, my survival instinct led me to consider a different strategy.

Perhaps a more dangerous one, but at least it would mean that I no longer had to search for a line that was probably very far away, without having a precise idea of the right direction and with the risk of a collapse wherever I tried to attach my safety spool.

I went up to the ceiling and started to follow the dust cloud below me; I was hoping that by doing this, I would at least be heading in the right direction. Between the rock ceiling and the white cloud there was about 1 m/3.3 ft where visibility was fair. Even if I couldn't see him, I could hear my buddy's breathing nearby. I thought that he was going back, certain that he had the line in his hand. I had somehow managed to calm down.

After a while, the silt cloud completely filled the space to the roof. Without any alternatives, I dropped to the bottom hoping to get closer to the line. I went down a few meters with one hand on the wall and shortly thereafter I felt something, like a cable. Too thin to be metallic, it was the line that I was looking for!

At the same time, I felt a push. It was my buddy, who was trying to understand what had bumped into him. Without wasting any time, we started our return. After just a few meters, the visibility started to improve just a little.

At least I could see the hands and lights of my buddy! We were actually just a few meters from the jump.

By following the silt cloud, I had retraced the entire route, and although the visibility was zero again, I was very happy to have found the line and my buddy. The return was stressful, but without additional problems as there was only one direction to the exit, plus the

permanent main line was there waiting for us. The dive ended with a few minutes of decompression. After surfacing, we talked about the shortcomings and mistakes that had caused this extremely dangerous scenario.

Unfortunately, as is often the case, it only takes a few small errors that, when added up, can have tragic consequences.

Matteo Ratto *is a Technical Cave, Trimix & DPV Instructor Trainer, CCR and P-SCR Diver. He started diving in 2003, and very quickly, through intense training, he started diving caves with trimix and rebreathers. After a long experience as a divemaster, he became an instructor in 2011. Matteo lives in north Italy close to lakes and caves, so cold and dark water are ordinary for him. He likes to dive new spots all around Europe, especially caves and mines. He started to dive CCR and SCR rebreathers in 2005.*

He participates in different projects, including long and deep dives in caves and wrecks. During 2011-12, he participated at the 'Oliero Traverse Project', including the traverse of the two big caves with a 5 km/3.1 mile underwater dive and different dives with runtimes of 6h+ in cold water.

From 2012, Matteo started to collect deep dives, reaching 160 m/525 ft in some research dives in lakes and caves. In 2016, Matteo started participating in international projects that included film and still documentaries. In 2018, he dived in Croatia, participating in the deep exploration and video making of the Re d'Italia wreck. As an active element of the Top2Bottom Filming Team and the World Submarine Exploration Team, he participated in international projects at the TekDive Europe (Belgium), EUDI Show (Italy), Tec-Expo Int (Belgium).

Photo by Nata Kas

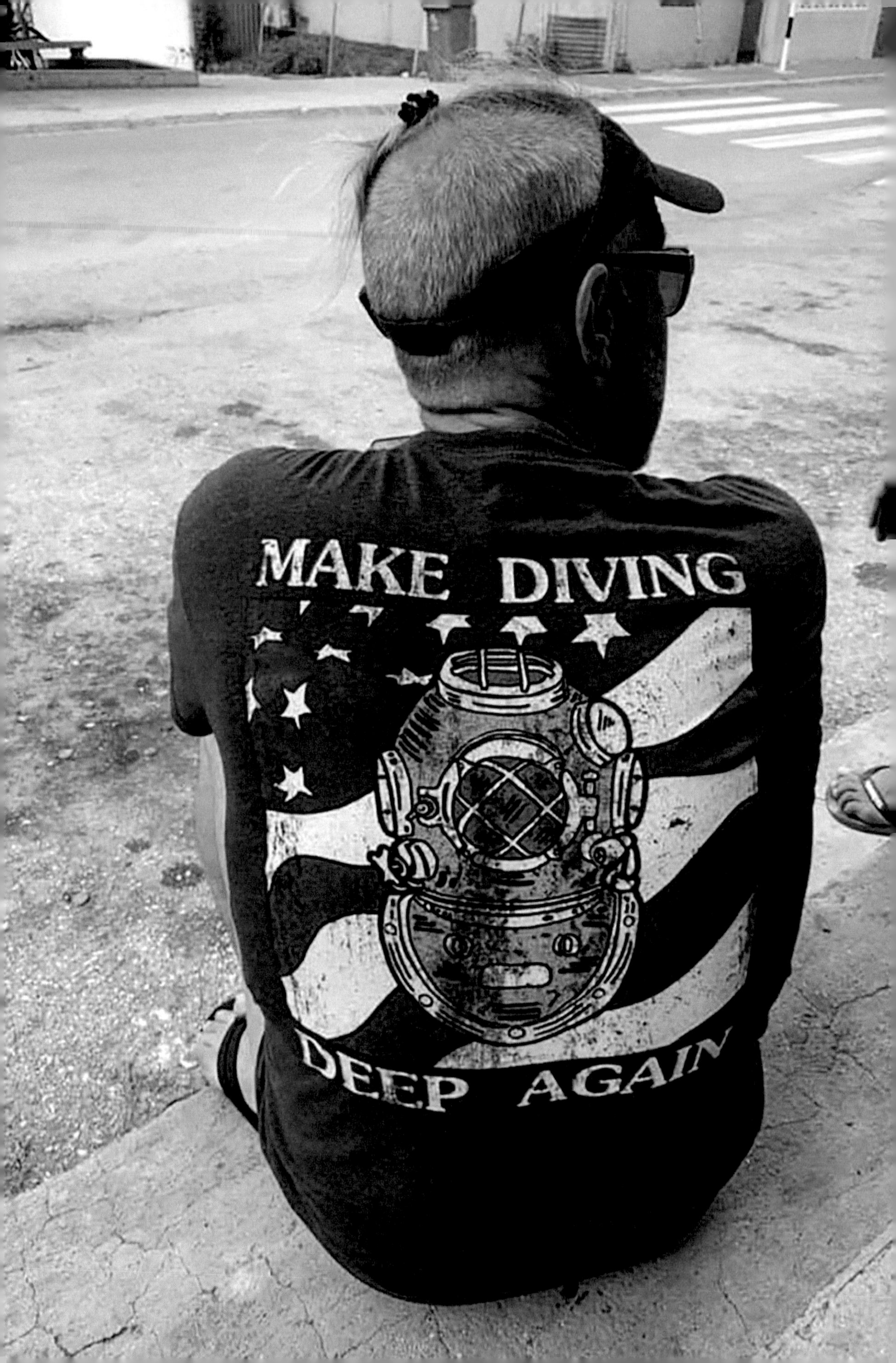
MAKE DIVING
DEEP AGAIN

MICHAEL MENDUNO

JOURNALIST / EDITOR / PRODUCER / TECHNOLOGIST
FOUNDER OF AQUACORPS JOURNAL / THE TEK CONFER-
ENCES & REBREATHER FORUMS 1 & 2

LOCATION OF INCIDENT
KEY LARGO, FL, USA

It was our second 'recreational' dive of the morning. My dive partner, a local open-water instructor, and I had completed our first dive on the bow of USS Spiegel Grove near Key Largo, FL. It was my first time on the wreck; she had been there many times before.

The current was brisk at the surface on that first dive and gradually diminished as we hit the tie-off at 30 meters / 98 feet on the port side of the 155m / 510 ft long wreck, which sits upright in about 43m /150 ft. We hit a max depth of 33m /110 ft while swimming through the upper compartments during the 26-minute dive, and included a three-minute safety stop. We were diving nitrox 32.

The dive boat had moored onto the wreck and there we prepared for a second dive. In addition to ourselves, there was a tech team of four people on the boat who were planning a single, long, open-circuit dive, and a rebreather diver.

There were also a few recreational divers.

My partner was diving a single aluminium 80 (11 litre) and a dive skin. I was just getting back into tech diving after a long hiatus and had come from a week-long full cave re-certification course (I was originally certified in 1990). I had my cave kit rigged for doubles and was wearing my dry suit, despite the 28°C/82°F deg. water.

The dive shop had provided me with double 80s. Argh! I had been diving over-pumped 104 cf/18 l and 120 cf/15 l doubles for the entirety of the previous week and was therefore used to carrying substantial gas.

I was also uncertain how much extra weight I would need; I didn't need any for cave diving. I added 4kg/8 lbs for the first dive, and another 2kg/4 lbs after the dive as the rig felt a little light.

Photo courtesy of Michael Menduno

I started the first dive with a 200 bar / 2950 psi fill and finished it with 99 bar /1450 psi, or about 75 cf of nitrox. I was surprised how quickly my gas gauge fell on the 80s (oh for a set of 120s). My partner finished with 68 bar/1000 psi in her single 80. No doubt, my doubles and dry suit added additional drag in the current. When it came time to get ready for our second dive, I was concerned that my gas was too low. There was no pumping capacity nor an extra stage bottle on the boat.

Should I skip the dive?

My gut said, "Thumb it!" but I had some self-induced peer pressure: it was my first time diving with my friend and I did not want to disappoint. "Hey, it's a recreational dive," I thought. "No biggie. I have roughly the equivalent of an alum 80. I can go down to the wreck, swim around a bit and then just come back up. Leave the wreck with 34 bar/500 psi in my doubles, the equivalent of 68 bar/1000 psi in a single 80."

"What about minimum gas?" you ask. In retrospect, I was complacent and I was not thinking correctly. I decided to take the plunge.

My partner entered the water ahead of me. The divemaster cautioned, "Don't let go of the line.

Pull yourself to the mooring buoy and down the mooring line." I held on and jumped. The current was now ripping. My foot popped out of my left fin when I hit the water. Fortunately, the spring strap held around my ankle. I tried to reach back and fix it, to no avail. My fin was flapping like a flag in a gale and I had all I could do to keep my legs together so it wouldn't slip off. In fact 'flag pole' diving would be the best description; my dive partner (who was 1.5m /5 ft below me) and I were stretched out like flags on the line.

When I turned my head perpendicular to the current, my mask started bouncing on my face.

Just below us the group of tekkies were at their 3m/10 ft stop, crowded around the line. My partner and I literally had to pull ourselves over and around them to grab the line below. There was no letting go. It took nearly six minutes to pull ourselves down to the wreck, where I rebooted my fin. I checked and had about 54-61 bar/800-900 psi in my doubles.

We had originally discussed using a third of our gas to descend and explore, a third to return to the line, and leave the bottom with a third in reserve. At that point, realising my gas was quite low, I figured I would make a loop around the bow deck, call the dive and then ascend. I didn't inform my partner of my gas situation. I also didn't consider what we would do if she had a out-of-gas emergency. We swam towards the superstructure with my partner in the lead.

I suddenly realised that she was headed for the first open door.

I flashed my light at her to no avail. We hadn't briefed on light signals; she wasn't carrying a primary light. She kept on going and disappeared through the doorway. Should I turn the dive and head back alone or should I go after her? We had gone through that door on the first dive and I remembered there was a room with an exit just to the right after a short hallway. I decided to go after her STAT.

In retrospect, that decision likely saved my life. I caught her at the end of the hallway and called the dive. We started heading back to the line with me in the lead. The swim was longer than I wanted. As the buoy line came into view, my regulator started pulling hard and not delivering a full breath.

WTF?!?! I felt a sinking feeling in my stomach. A minute later and I hit the line, sucked on my regulator and got nearly nothing. I pulled out my gauge, which read a little more than 20 bar / 300 psi. Damn, 30m /100 ft down and I can't breathe water. It occurred to me right then that I could actually and easily die.

Fortunately, I felt calm in an existential sort of way and very focussed. Damn! I'm certain that my calmness in the face of reality saved my life.

I grabbed the ascent line, turned around and gave my partner, who was fortunately now within a couple of arm's lengths behind me, the out of gas sign. She looked a bit surprised as I reached for her pink octopus, but then gave a reassuring look—I am not going to leave you. I grabbed her octopus and shoved it in my mouth. She grabbed my harness and we began to work our way up the line, face to face with the line in between us. I was concerned we wouldn't have enough gas to make it to the surface, and worried what would happen in that event. Would I have enough buoyancy to even reach the surface and stay afloat if things came to that? Would she?

The current got stronger as we ascended and it took significant effort just to cling to the line.

I just wanted to make it to the surface; I was not too concerned with a safety stop. Our ascent took six minutes.

My partner remained cool and collected the whole time. We finally hit the mooring buoy just below the surface and I reached around for the tie-in line and surfaced as the current blew me along the side of the boat. I was not going to let go of that line! My partner stayed and made her stop.
"Are you OK?" the divemaster asked. I shook my head, "No!"

I felt embarrassed, with a big dollop of shame. TECH DIVERS DON'T RUN OUT OF GAS!
I made it to the ladder and clung to it whilst I regained my composure. I was grateful when one of the divemasters jumped in and pulled off my fins. I was grateful to be alive. I thanked my partner profusely after she came aboard. No doubt the fact we both remained calm was a key factor in the outcome.

Photo by Tom Boyd

Interestingly, when I surfaced I had 13 bar/200 psi in the tanks and my regulator and inflator were able to access gas. I debriefed with my dive partner and the boat headed back to dock.

Two nights later, I woke up in the middle of the night in a cold sweat, realising that I was in fact extremely lucky to be alive. Gulp! If any one of a few factors had been different, I would likely have drowned on the Spiegel Grove and been carried away by the current, never to be seen again.

Photo by Simon Mitchell

Post-dive analysis: If I had practiced what I had learnt on my cave course, this wouldn't have happened. I made grievous errors.

I had been complacent, I didn't listen to my inner voice and I made the dive with too little gas given the situation. I had not adequately considered minimum gas nor done my math. I didn't call the dive upon reaching the wreck, nor did I do an adequate job of communicating with my partner pre-dive and while diving.

Basically I f***ked up!

The good news? I lived, and learned critical lessons. I will not make those mistakes again! Despite my embarrassment I decided I would write up the incident and share under my byline as an act of personal penance—call it a learning mnemonic—and to support 'Human Factors' aficionado Gareth Lock's notion of 'Just Culture.' I figured if even one other diver learned from my mistakes and survived, then it would be worth a bit of discomfort and cheap at the price. Don't you think?

It's not surprising, given that I am fairly well-known in the diving community, that word of my indiscretion took all of about an hour to reach back to cave country. My primary cave instructor (I was in a group-teaching situation) called me the morning after the dive. "I heard you had a little problem," he began. I explained what had happened. He agreed; a sobering lesson.

Interestingly, in addition to earning my NSS-CDS Full Cave re-certification, I was supposed to receive a full cave certification from another tech agency as well and had completed the requirements. When the card never came, I called the other instructor, "I never received my card."

It turns out that the instructor had also heard about my little embarrassment and had decided to hold the certification. "We think you need to do more work before you're ready." Ouch!

I found myself reflecting again on the dive about a month later. At that point my emotions had calmed, and a couple more lessons occurred to me.

First, I now realise now how quickly things can turn to shit when you hit the accident funnel. Better not to go down the funnel to begin with! I was also reminded how self-judgmental I can be. "Personal penance?" I see now that it may have been a defence mechanism: "Hey if I am hard on myself, then maybe others won't be."

In fact, when he reviewed my incident report,

Mr. Locke suggested to me that there was no need to self-stigmatise; "Everyone makes mistakes," he said. I understand now that I am a human diver and sometimes we do stupid shit.

Please don't make the same mistake I did.

Michael Menduno, *Michael Menduno, aka "M2," is an award-winning reporter and technologist who has written about diving and diving technology for more than thirty years. He coined the term "technical diving."*
Menduno serves as the editor-in-chief of GUE InDepth online magazine, is a contributing editor for DAN Europe's Alert Diver, and X-Ray magazine and is a staff writer for DeeperBlue.com. He is also on the board of directors for the Historical Diving Society.

Michael founded and served as editor-in-chief of 'aquaCORPS: The Journal for Technical Diving' (1990-1996), and its sister publication technicalDIVER, which helped usher tech diving into mainstream sports diving. He also worked with Capt. Billy Deans to set up the first technical diving training centre at Key West Diver, Key West, Florida in the early 1990s, which quickly became a Mecca for tech divers from around the world. In addition, he produced the first Tek, EUROTek and ASIATek conferences, and organised Rebreather Forums 1.0 and 2.0. His work has appeared in numerous diving and adventure sports magazines.

Michael received the OZTEK Media Excellence Award in 2011, the EUROTek Lifetime Achievement Award in 2012 and the TEKDive USA Media Award in 2018. He earned his open-water certification in 1976, is Full Cave certified (1990, 2018), certified on AP Diving rebreathers (2012) and is a member of GUE. In addition to diving, Michael is actively involved in U.S. Masters swimming and has been a performing bass player.

MIKE YOUNG

OWNER @ KISS REBREATHERS / CAVE EXPLORER

LOCATION OF INCIDENT
YUCATAN, MEXICO

We were pushing a cave system in the Yucatán. Dives were getting longer and longer. My dive buddy and I were using semi-closed rebreathers on nitrox 32. We had a custom scooter that would run off our video light batteries.

We started our dive and ran our scooter for about 45 minutes, to the point we were planning to 'drop' it. Two of us were being pulled by one scooter. We swam another 20-25 minutes and came to an air bell we had found the day before during an eight-hour dive. We were prepared for this and brought with us food and Gatorade. I was starting to get queasy, so I didn't eat all my snacks. After another 20-minute swim we started laying line.

Brendan laid line as I surveyed. After about 137 m/450 ft I felt worse and called the dive.

Brendan didn't question it and just turned.

We got back to the air bell. I was in a pretty bad shape. Really queasy, barely holding my food down. I was very weak.

We stayed there for about 30 minutes until I started feeling better.

As we were swimming back I felt pretty good, but I was so happy to see our scooter. On our way back I bailed out a few different times. Each time I felt bad instantly, so I would go back on the loop. I was feeling horrible, weak, lethargic and on the verge of throwing up.

"Not in the loop," I repeated in my head over and over.

The exit was so far away it was disheartening. I started picking out attainable goals.

Photos by Exploration Team

Just make it to that corner. Make it to intersection five. Make it to intersection four.

Soon I was starting to go from knot to knot on the line. About 77 m/250 feet from the exit my peripheral vision started getting fuzzy and I was seeing black. Then our scooter died. I kicked and bam! My vision closed-in to just small holes. There was a stalagmite about 1 m/3 ft from me. I reached for it and kicked. Everything went black.

My hand hit the stalagmite. I grabbed it and held on for a few breaths until my vision started clearing again. I motioned for Brendan to come next to me. I grabbed his arm and yelled "swim!". He couldn't figure out what was wrong and said "what?"

I yelled again "swim!", as loud as I could, and so he did.

I held onto him and ran the scooter with my other hand. It had just enough power to keep me straight. We came around the corner and finally I saw daylight. I was going to make it!

I got to the entrance, crawled up on my knees and filled my BC. Adam, who was there as our surface support, said. "What's wrong with you? You look like crap!" I said, "Get this stuff off me, I can't move!"

He jumped in the water and stripped my equipment off. I was able to crawl out on the grass on my hands and knees and then lay down. They brought me some water. About an hour later I was finally able to stand up.

Later that year I was talking with Curt Bowen and Brent Hemphill about it. We concluded that it was a case of 'bad gas'.

Carbon monoxide. Brendan saved my life.

A few years later, Brendan traded dives with me. He took my tank, and at about 18 minutes into his dive he died from carbon monoxide poisoning. Saving my life, again.

Mike Young *grew up in the mountains of Colorado. At a young age, he became an extreme skier, an avid hunter, mountaineer, and extreme motorcyclist. No adventure was too big.*

His parents owned an alligator farm and he and his brother, Jay, were the only ones available to play with the saurian beasts.

Mike first learned to scuba dive in the early 90's and made his first open water dives in a sinkhole on the edge of the Kalahari desert, Africa. This, combined with his passion for extreme sports made it natural for him to gravitate toward technical diving. He was soon performing deep cave dives and his interest for sump diving grew.

Today, Mike is a member of the Advance Diver Magazine Exploration team as well as the US Deep Caving Team.

Recently, while exploring and mapping cenotes in the Yucatan Peninsula, Mike discovered a Mayan vase that dates back 1300 year. In 2010, Mike was on the J2 expedition, exploring a system in southern Mexico that is 1200m/3937ft deep and took 2 days of caving just to reach the water.

In 2011, Mike and the deep caving team mapped an underground river system in Puerto Rico that totaled over 23 km/14.2 miles in length, making it the world's longest underground river. Some of the area surveyed had never been seen by human eyes before.

Mike's desire for diving and reaching areas unseen has led him to custom build many of his own products. Together with Hollis, he has been influential in designing several products.

Mike is also responsible for the development of the KISS GEM gas extender rebreather.

MIKKO PAASI

OWNER AT KOH TAO DIVERS
CCR / TECH INSTRUCTOR TRAINER
INTERNATIONAL MEMBER OF THE EXPLORERS CLUB

LOCATION OF INCIDENT
OJAMO MINE, FINLAND

I started diving in the early 90s in Turkey, where I was thrown in the water three times out of four with an empty tank, without any theory whatsoever.

But the real bug for diving and overhead environments kicked in 1998 when I got onto a year-long diving instructor program conducted at the Ojamo mine, Lohja, Finland. Three-hundred dives later, I earned my instructor status and was ready to follow my passion. That passion led me to Asia where I established my first dive centre, which I still run today.

Even though most of my diving career has taken place in warm water wrecks and caves, I'd like to consider myself an all-terrain diver. There is some unique and brutal beauty in the Baltic Sea wrecks and in the ever-cold mines that tunnel kilometres into the Finnish bedrock.

Part of the fascination toward diving in extreme cold environments comes from the elevated technicality of it. Executing a hypoxic trimix stage dive in a cave is complicated enough as it is, but adding ice cold water to it changes everything.

The simple fact that you have to change pretty much all your thermal exposure gear means that you need to change not only all your snaps and bolts, but also the whole set of skills that you have been fine-tuning throughout the years.

Diving all terrain means that you also have to be able to constantly keep up with the skills and different tools that you need to survive the unforgiving and so-very-different demands of the various surroundings. All of that, combined with complex dive planning and relying on a ridiculous amount of added dive gear, makes it one of the most technical,

Photo by Jukka Repo

but also one of the most rewarding types of diving for me. I am proud to have some friends in Finland who dive these Godforsaken rusty mines throughout the year like 'a walk in the park'. I rank them as some of the most solid divers on the planet. They are their own very special breed.

I was going to dive the Ojamo's infamous Hell's Gate for the first time in my life, with these tough men and women. Even though I had dived the mine hundreds of times, I had never been to the Gate. At the end of 90s, we had neither the training nor the equipment to go any further than the first chambers.

Ojamo lime mine is a complex labyrinth of shafts and tunnels with its deepest point believed to be at 250 m/820 ft.

The first level starts at 28 m/91 ft, the second at 38 m/124 ft, then levels at 44 m/144 ft, 58 m/190 ft, 88 m/288 ft and 138 m/452 ft. The mine goes deeper still, with plenty of unexplored tunnels. The combination of rust, artifacts, and long tunnels makes mine diving a mix between wreck and cave diving, and therefore incredibly interesting. On the day in question, we were a team of five experienced divers, and our plan was to take some photos of one of the narrow side passages at the 58 m/190 ft level, and then shoot the Hell's Gate at around 52 m/170 ft and return through the 44 m/144 ft level. We were all on scooters and rebreathers with hypoxic gases.

I had a brand new drysuit, and as with any piece of new equipment, I tested it before the dive by jumping in to check for leaks and proper fit.

All checks done, we headed towards the 38 m/124 ft entry point. The plan was to start the dive in two groups and reunite at the 58 m/190 ft passage so that Laura, as the model and guide, and I as the back-light and camera man, would come through the narrow tunnel and meet the others taking the images from the other side of the deep passage.

Once that was completed, we would then head on to the 'Gate, where it would be my turn to capture some images.

On my first descent attempt I noticed some water entering my suit and signalled my buddy to ascend. On the surface I tried to fix the inlet valve and it seemed that the leak had stopped. We plunged back in after the rest of the team.

Whilst staging our deco cylinders and squeezing through the bars at the 38 m/124 ft 2x2 m/6.5x6.5 ft entry point, we both knew that we had fallen back a few minutes from our schedule to meet the others for the photo shoot. Luckily, we had powerful scooters, so we triggered in as fast as we could. The water temperature is always around 4 C/39.2 F or less and a leaky drysuit in this temperature can lead to some serious issues. Not just the cold itself but the fact that you are much more likely to get decompression sickness if you add it as a factor.

After about 20 minutes, and 500 m/1640 ft in, I started to realise that, each time I added gas to my drysuit, the valve was leaking freezing water in. At that point,I was still relatively comfortable, feeling the cold water only on my fingertips. I considered my options.

The rest of the way, via Hell's Gate, would be shallower and fairly level, as mines tend to be, without too many ups and downs; I wouldn't have to use my suit inflation much. Since we were just about to take the first photos, I got busy with my lights and scootered into the passage after Laura. This distraction was clouding my judgement; I was taking a leap of faith by trusting that the leak wouldn't get any worse. If we'd turned around at that point, we would have been out in about an hour or so including deco. Continuing and going back via the "Gate" would add only half an hour extra.

I decided to proceed with the original plan. Cruising through the huge chambers with a group of five, all having a massive amount

of light, was as spectacular as it comes. The visibility in the labyrinth of the tunnels is infinite, and we could make out the sheer size of the chambers reaching out from the depth tens of metres below and all around us. By the time we got to Hell's Gate, I regretted not having turned around earlier.

The 4 C/39.2 F water found its way to both my arms and legs. I felt it dripping in from the inlet valve. My hands were numb, and I was struggling to take any photos. After a minute or two, I signalled that we should call it, because my suit was broken. The nearest exit from the mine was only 500 m/1640 ft away, but my computer was giving me fifty minutes of deco; meanwhile my hands and feet were both starting to become numb. Where's a heated vest when you need one!? Although if I HAD had one, it would probably have electrocuted me by then, with all the water in the suit!

I tried to add as much air as I could to my drysuit on the way out, but once we got to the exit point the numbness turned into a burning sensation.

I still had forty minutes of TTS (Time to Surface); I would feel pretty helpless if I had to assist my team (or myself) if some kind of emergency occurred. Clipping stages, manoeuvring valves or even fin kicks are super difficult when your hands and legs have no feeling at all.

The thought of cutting my deco short, ascending to the surface and bolting for the comfort of the warm dressing room had never been so tempting! Instead of cutting it short, I knew that I had to do the exact opposite; I would have to stay under even longer to somehow get the inert gasses through the constricted blood vessels in my limbs and out of my body.

I was slowly climbing up my deco, every step just a bit warmer than the previous one.

Photo by Mikko Paasi

It is amazing how much difference there is between 4 C/39.2 F and 14 C/57.2 F while struggling to stay warm.

Ojamo has one unique safety feature that I was very thankful for at that moment: a habitat at the 6 m/20 ft level. Climbing into the barrel and getting my upper body out of the water made a huge difference. Suddenly there was much more light at the end of the tunnel. Exhausted and with mixed feelings about the dive, I finished my deco (with an extension to it). I exited the habitat and headed back to the parking lot where I had started the dive a couple of hours before.

This was one of the most beautiful, but also one of the most unpleasant, dives in my books. I can only blame myself for what happened, and I will never again enter an overhead environment with even the tiniest leak; if something similar were to happen to me again, I would turn the dive immediately, not only for my sake but also for my team's. Unfortunately, the struggle wasn't over for me just yet.

Three days later, I took a plane to Northern Finland to give a presentation about the Thai Cave Rescue in Oulu University and to the local dive club. I flew back that same evening and noticed my left arm was swollen and becoming numb again. The next day, I took a train to Turku and went through table six - twice - in the hyperbaric chamber to be sure that all residual gas was out. Due the dramatic change in the blood circulation from being warm at the beginning of the dive to the extreme cold during the decompression part of the dive, it is most likely that some gas left in the capillaries near my skin caused a mild decompression disease that escalated during my flights to Oulu and back.

This incident took place in 2019; I have no real excuse except that we all do make mistakes and poor decisions, no matter how experienced we might be. I hope that by reading the stories in this book we can all learn something new, change our ways and habits, and bypass what used to be sort of a taboo amongst us divers, on all levels. These real-life close calls by experienced divers offer an unparalleled learn-by-mistake experience in the safest way possible.

Fortunately for us, this experience had a good outcome, but it was certainly a lesson to learn from.

Mikko Paasi *is an International Member of The Explorers Club and a member of the Suratthani Rescue Team. After becoming a certified dive instructor, he decided to move to Thailand. He is the owner of Koh Tao Divers and has expanded his diving business to Malta. He organises technical dive expeditions, and his passion is to explore and document the undiscovered underwater realm through the lens of his camera to inspire others to get involved.*

For the past 10 years, in addition to training technical/ccr divers and photographing the underwater world, he has been mapping World War II and other deep-sea wrecks around the South China Sea and exploring new overhead environments around the world. Over the years, his team has found dozens of Japanese war ships and other vessels lost in the seas. In August 2018, he received the 1st class Knight Grand Cross of the most admirable order of the Direkgunabhorn from the King of Thailand for his efforts in the Thai cave rescue.

In November 2018, he received an accolade from Finnish Association of Fire Officers given by the Minister of the Interior in Finland. In April 2019 at ADEX (Asian Dive Expo) he received the award for 'Inspirational Excellence.' In May 2019, he received the Lifesaving Medal from the President of Finland granted for his efforts in the Thai cave rescue.

Photo by Mikko Paasi

MOE ALMEHAIRBI

ADVANCED TRIMIX CCR INSTRUCTOR

LOCATION OF INCIDENT
TIRAN ISLAND, EGYPT

Growing up on an island meant I grew up partially underwater. Abu Dhabi, my hometown in the UAE, was rather dull and boring in the 1980s compared to today, but my dad would take us freediving and spearfishing in the Arabian gulf on school holidays. Cooling down from the heat of the sun with a pair of fins and a mask felt so refreshing. My grandfather was a pearl diver, and my father loved spearfishing.

So, with all of that said, it's no surprise that I find myself working underwater, too. As an Advanced Trimix CCR Instructor working in Sharm El Sheikh, Northern Red Sea, my career has offered many wonderful moments that I could never forget, from unbelievable encounters with marine life to discovering deep, unknown wrecks. Above all else, though, the most unforgettable moments are the ones that offer us a second chance.

A wake-up call, if you will.

During the aftermath of the Russian flight incident in Sharm El Sheikh, business was very low, and we had loads of free time to dive and explore the unknown dive sites around. Boats were cheap and the weather was excellent.

Sharm is a great place to dive with abundant coral reefs and perfect conditions. Most exciting for me personally, though, are the caves. A few of us diving professionals decided to organize an exploration dive into one of the deeper caves in the area.

White Angel is a cave that we had dived many times before, but being bound by the routines of daily diving boats makes it difficult to do any long decompression dives, so we were never able to enjoy it entirely because of the accumulated deco time at such depths.

Photos by Karim Massoud

It was decided that we would hire a private boat for the day and invite a professional photographer to take some photos. Needless to say, all four divers were on closed circuit rebreathers; a dive such as this is almost impossible in open circuit.

The morning of the dive, after loading the boat, we were on our way to Tiran Island, where the cave is located. The sun was shining and the sea was calm as the divers prepared their CCR units. I chose to dive on a side mount CCR unit as it makes passing small restrictions much easier. Whilst setting up, I remember noticing a tiny leak in my diluent side; I didn't pay it much attention as I never use much diluent anyway, and I really didn't want to delay the dive. In hindsight, I now know that this was a mistake, but hindsight is 20/20.

The dive began as any other: clear blue water, S-drills and bubble checks completed during descent, and we soon arrived at the entrance. The cave is a beauty to behold with delicate formations and a surreal, flat, almost man-made wall on one side. As we descended deeper and farther in, I felt mesmerised by the formations emerging from the darkness.

Passing restrictions and all-of-a-sudden being in huge chambers was just awe-inspiring. We staged bailout bottles at various locations as it was impossible to pass the restrictions with them attached. It wasn't immediately apparent that I was using more diluent than usual, since the cave forced us to ascend and descend a few times as we pushed forward.

A little while after passing 100 m/328 ft, it was decided to turn around, as the decompression time was getting longer by the minute. Following the line back out and still utterly fascinated by the environment, I was suddenly shocked to find out, at about 80 m/262 ft, that I had run out of diluent.

At this point, we were in a narrow tunnel, and the nearest bailout was still a long way ahead. As my loop volume decreased, the only option was to top off the loop with O_2. Watching the partial pressure of O_2 in my breathing loop rise higher and higher, I was feeling more and more anxious and nervous.

Trying to remain calm and just following the line was getting more difficult by the second. I could feel panic rearing its ugly head.

Symptoms of oxygen toxicity started to kick in shortly afterwards, and that's when I began to realise how bad the situation really was. At first, visual disturbances occurred: blurry vision, inability to read my handset clearly, and then tunnel vision. I tried my best to remain calm and just follow the line; the thought of passing out now was absolutely terrifying, as it would mean trapping the rest of the divers behind me in the cave.

A loud ringing noise in my ears soon followed, accompanied by a feeling of twitching, and pins and needles in my lips and fingers. The feeling of impending doom couldn't have gotten worse as we inched our way out through the tight restrictions and narrow passages. Then, just as suddenly, I bumped into one of our stage bottles staged on the line!

I remember feeling elated as I fumbled around trying to connect it to the loop to flush down the PPO₂. Ears ringing and vision out-the-window, it wasn't as easy as it was during training or in a non-emergency scenario! I started feeling slightly better. Then, like a divine vision, through my completely blurred sight I could make out the blue light of the open water! The relief that light offered was so strong I couldn't stop myself from darting towards the blue. We still had loads of decompression time ahead, but at least now I could see the exit. After making a beeline to the open blue water, I started feeling a bit of relief. If the worst came to worst now, there would be no risk of entrapment for anybody. Decompressing on the vibrant reef nearby was quite a sombre experience.

I was so glad we had all made it out of the cave safely but couldn't get over how bad this could have turned out. It would have been an incredibly sad–and completely avoidable–disaster. A couple of hours later we were back onboard and on our way back to port. Such an experience shakes us to the core and forces us to reconsider our safety procedures and pre-dive preparations.

Never give in to peer pressure and excitement for a big dive! Always remember that if something feels wrong, then it definitely is.

Looking back at the dive, I feel lucky that we made it out; it could have been a disaster for the entire team. My ignorance and complacency put us all at risk of death.

This incident would have been avoided had I stopped and found the source of the leak; it turned out to have been a small piece of sorb stuck in the auto-diluent valve. It would have taken less than 5 minutes to sort out. Complacency, peer pressure, and excitement for a big dive had caused us to turn a blind eye to issues that I deemed minor, but which could have led to serious issues underwater. I learnt a lesson that day that could have cost more lives than just mine, but, as they say, "What doesn't kill you makes you stronger."

Moe Almehairbi *learned freediving from his father during his childhood. He started scuba diving in 2003. After years of travelling and diving around the globe, Moe decided to settle down in Sharm El Sheikh, Egypt.*

In 2015, Moe and his partners founded Infinite CCR, the premier CCR and Tech diving facility in the Middle East.

Moe teaches CCR diving at all levels on multiple CCR units, but his unit of choice is the Defender CCR. When he's not teaching, Moe's passion is exploring unknown caves and deep wrecks of the Red Sea.

Photo by Svetlana Yanyushkina

NATALIE L. GIBB

CAVE DIVING INSTRUCTOR & EXPLORER
PHOTOGRAPHER / UNDER THE JUNGLE DIVE SHOP

LOCATION OF INCIDENT
AKUMAL, MEXICO

Most good cave-diving stories start the same way, with a hole. This particular hole was a fifteen-minute walk behind my house in Akumal, Mexico, just on the side of the road, and it already had a name: Cenote X.

I found it while walking my dog one afternoon, did some research, and discovered some information about it in a dishevelled folder of cave notes a former explorer had given to me when he left the region. It was on an unpunched loose sheet of white paper, GPS coordinates matching: "Cenote X, cave does not continue." We'll see about that, I thought.

In 2010, my exploration partner Vincent Rouquette-Cathala and I were just starting to explore caves in the region, and we were desperate for new projects. We were young, ballsy, and stupid. After years of dreaming, we were finally exploring caves.

Nothing would stop us.

So, one summer morning we grabbed our third buddy, Anders Knudsen, and headed out to Cenote X with a full reel of line. We scrambled down a muddy path to the cenote and were greeted by a murky, mosquito-infested hellhole. There was already a cave line just faintly visible in the turbid water, and attached to it was a blank white arrow with no name. Might as well dive anyhow, we decided; we were already there.

As we started the dive, two things were immediately apparent: first, this was a crumbly cave. Small pieces of rock showered down on us as our bubbles hit the ceiling. Second, this was a treasure trove. We collected strings of arrows, a spool, pencils, and other small bits of dive gear abandoned by people who had dived the cave before us.

They just left stuff in the cave and never came back. Amateurs.

Fifteen minutes later we reached the end of line at about 24 m/78 ft. There was a small hole in the wall in front of us, and I was thrilled! I immediately invoked our "ten-minute rule." The ten-minute rule is an idiotic idea we came up with when exploring a tight cave in a team of three.

Whoever sees a restriction first gets to call "ten minutes" by signalling the team and holding up ten fingers. The rest of the team then has to hold back, and the lucky diver gets to go investigate the restriction and see if the cave continues without having a traffic jam of two other divers stuck behind him in the event he has to back out. He gets ten minutes total before the team must either launch a rescue mission or abandon the dive: three minutes to explore, three minutes to get out, and an additional three minutes to survey any line

he leaves. Vince and Anders sighed, signalled that they would hold, and off I went on a little solo jaunt through the restriction.

Turning sideways, I could just barely fit through the crack. I grabbed the wall to pull myself through, and noticed it was possible to press my fingers into the rock. It was soft. Just on the other side of this crack was a huge chamber. It had sparkling white limestone and brilliant blue salt water.

Screw it. I tossed my reel through the crack in front of me and went on in.

I had two minutes to go. Passing the restriction, I grabbed the reel and ran a single, 60-meter shot of euphoric line through the chamber. I cut the line right on time, in front of another small crack in the far wall. It was time to go get the guys, the cave continued. When I turned to survey out, there was a rock the size of a Volkswagen Beetle on top of my newly laid line, with wisps of silt wafting out from under it where it had hit the floor. The cave was so unstable that just my bubbles had caused a massive collapse.

Given sufficient motivation, anyone can become an excellent freediver. I held my breath through the chamber, through the restriction, and out into the room where Vince and Anders waited patiently. The whole incident had taken maybe five minutes.

I swam up to them and shoved my thumb in their faces, the universal cave sign for "end the dive." Out we swam, over abandoned pieces of dive gear from other divers, gravel still raining down on us from the ceiling.

On the surface, Vince and Anders excitedly asked me if the cave continued. Yes, I said, but it's not safe. There's some rather large percolation. We should not go back there.

Perhaps I was not as emphatic as I could have been, but I was still processing my experience. If that boulder had fallen a few meters closer to the restriction, I would have been trapped in the cave.

You can imagine how this story ends.

The next day I had to work, but Vince and Anders decided to go back to Cenote X– without telling me and against my warnings– to check out what had frightened me so much. They showed up at my house that afternoon, their eyes the size of saucers.

"The cave is really unstable," they said. I was shocked.

"You went back?" Of course they had.

We all learned a few valuable lessons, and the experience of the collapse in Cenote X has probably saved me on subsequent explorations. In cave exploration, excitement is as dangerous as fear and can lead an explorer to make poor decisions in the adrenaline-rush of the moment.

Now, if I become too excited on an exploration dive and cannot maintain a cold, emotionless mindset, I turn the dive. Safety is dependent upon the decisions a diver makes underwater. No one forced me to go through that soft restriction in the crumbly cave; that was a choice I made.

Finally, I carefully consider stability whenever I am diving in a new cave. As a team, Vince and I call each other's attention if the cave has "heavy percolation" behind the lead diver. If the cave seems questionable, we leave immediately and discuss our plans out of the water.

An unstable cave is just not worth it, and I never want to have an experience like that again.

Natalie L. Gibb's *passion in life is underwater cave exploration and conservation.*

With her exploration partner Vincent Rouquette-Cathala, she has led her team to discover over 20 previously unknown cave systems in Mexico's Yucatan Peninsula, mapping more than 80 kilometres of cave passageways.

She is a public speaker, author, photographer, and videographer, and a member of the Woman Diver's Hall of Fame.

Natalie is co-owner of Under the Jungle, a cave diver-training center in Mexico, and a TDI Full Cave Instructor.

NATHALIE LASSELIN

UNDERWATER CINEMATOGRAPHER
EXPEDITION LEADER / SPEAKER / TECH INSTRUCTOR

LOCATION OF INCIDENT
ST LAWRENCE RIVER, MONTREAL

From the very first day of my technical diving experience, I always told myself I would do everything I could to not end up as a statistic. The idea of getting out of air, drowning trapped somewhere in a cave or a wreck was something I feared.

To be honest, I loved my fears. They made me stronger, wiser, safer and have helped me to stay alive. Along the way, they put me in a position where I questioned my goals, my means, and my team. But also my mental, physical, technical, and logistical state of mind. As a fresh tech diver, I took all the training I could with various instructors from Europe and North America. I tried to always be on the very thin edge of my comfort zone in order to expand it regularly and constantly.

I have numerous deep dives in zero vis, cold water, caves, wrecks, arctic with cameras—you name it. Despite all of this experience, I nearly died not so long ago. So here it goes: I had dreamed for years to do a 70 km /44 mile dive from one end of the island of Montréal to the other one, raising awareness about our source of drinking water.

One of the many challenges was to be able to do the dive despite having seven bridges to cross, deadly rapids, shoals, commercial marine traffic, and low visibility. To give you an idea of the planning obstacles, when you look at the nautical chart, about a third of the path is blank, without any information. We ended up being a team of twenty-five people and five boats. No single boat could do the whole traverse due to the rapids in the middle of the way.

At specific boat ramps, each team would be replaced by a new, fresh one. Each team had a supervisor, safety divers, and a boat captain. I wrote a bible with everything that needed to be done and how. During the sessions where we practiced changing my equipment underwater, explaining the logistics, I told my teams, "I am the weakest point.

You can't trust yourself, either, and everything needs to be double-checked by someone else."

Friday, September 14, 2018.
The sun rose, the thermos flasks were full of coffee for my team. I finally hit the water for my big dive. I put on my CCR, my KM48 with a communication system. I had DPV number 1. My buoy (actually a goose decoy) was attached to me, so my safety surface team would know where I was at all times, all good. I was good to go.

During all the preparation, I kept asking myself, "What is the detail I didn't–we didn't– think about?"

Once underwater, the visibility at its best was a little under 2 m/5 ft. The first couple of hours went really well, everything was as expected until outside conditions intervened. The trouble was that the weather forecast had predicted a really, unusually hot day: 28 C/82.4 F. So guess what–it's a Friday, the end of the boating season, what do you do? You go on the river. The thing is that the river in Montreal is not deep, not at all. So in order to navigate safely, I was supposed to follow the seaway or a channel.

But very quickly the volume of pleasure traffic meant that option wasn't safe anymore, so I had to take refuge in the shoals, where aquatic plants grew.

Basically, in order to make my way through, I was mowing the lawn with my DPV, greatly overusing the batteries and slowing me down so much that I couldn't reach the rapids before night. The rapids were just too unsafe to dive at nighttime; even for a small boat equipped with a turbine, the danger would have been too much. So for safety's sake, we had to call it a day and keep on going the next morning.

On Saturday, I kept on going, diving the rapids and the bridges. I didn't reach the end before night. With heavy boat traffic and other challenges, everything took more time.

We changed gear again for night set-up, but we were getting close to the end, finally. We were just 3-4 km/1.8-2.4 m from the end. In the pitch-black night of Montréal, in the pitch-black waters of the river, I was scootering my way, looking at my compass when I heard Anne Marie screaming: "Nath, come up, come up now!"

Her tone of voice did not leave room for question. I tried not to come up too fast, and when I reached the surface, something hit me directly at the bottom of my CCR tek frame, and it pushed me fast. I was under a boat; if I slid, I would have my legs directly in the props. I tried to free myself, but I couldn't. I was trapped!

"Nath are you OK?" I couldn't understand. Was I OK?! I was stuck under the boat!

The seconds passed in slow motion. I realised this was my own boat pushing me. I recognized the sound of the hull of the pontoon against the CCRframe. I didn't want to slide and reach the props. I asked myself: "Why don't they stop? Don't they know I can't free myself?"

Suddenly the engine slowed down, the props stopped. I could see the surface and the fear in the eyes of my teammates.

"Nath, are you OK?"
"Yes, yes, but ..."

What happened? In the darkness of the night, everyone was looking at what was supposed to be the weakest point or at least the most concerning one: me and my buoy with the flashing light. Three boats, fifteen people, all eyes on me. But a tug was coming with minimum lights until it was so close to my boat and me that the tug captain spotted us and switched on his big, bright, front light.

If nothing had been done, the tug was going to hit not only me but also my first chase boat, with the potential of eight people killed or badly injured.

When they saw the danger, they urged me to come up; my boat captain deliberately pushed me out of the way of the tug that, of course, couldn't stop on a dime. At the same time, one of my team members, Neal, thought fast and tried to grab me by my tek frame, but he couldn't hold on with the pressure of the flow. As he was losing me, another team member, Simon, jumped on top of him and caught me before I disappeared underneath the boat. I wasn't trapped, in fact. They were holding me safely. Eventually, my boat stopped.

"Are you OK?"
"Yes, I am."
"OK, let's keep going."

Around 10:30, I completed the traverse. It might not have been at all the way it was planned, but everyone was there for the project until the finish line, no matter what it took to finish it. So what happened? A mistake of communication and human factors in a complicated logistic involving many people in an extreme environment—diving in an urban area where normally divers are nowhere to be seen.

My team had a mission: to be there for me. It is what they did. Near the end of the dive, of course, everyone wants to be there. At the same time, the more people are involved, the more difficult communication becomes. They were looking at me and for a fraction of the time, the surroundings didn't exist anymore.

In the team, we were all technical divers with enough experience to understand the importance of self, global, and situational awareness: the three awarenesses. But in that fraction of time, the situation was out of our diving knowledge. It was about surroundings that were pitch-black; not an empty pitch-black, but a black just as full of dangers as a wreck penetration in low visibility can be, where you could be trapped in wires.

We all made mistakes during that dive. Maybe I did emphasise too much that I was the weakest point.

We were certainly pushing the limits of our ability to focus in a noisy, busy environment. We are not warriors. We do train for many situations; I'm used to harsh environments, camping, and filming in the arctic, fighting to understand nature, but our training will never be completed. Each time we push our limits, no matter which ones, or at which level we are, we expose ourselves and our teammates to hazards that can be underestimated.

By talking about our misses, our mistakes, our lack of knowledge, or communication, we will become better divers, better explorers, and will be able to achieve dreams bigger than us. For a moment, we all look in the same direction, the same way. However, it is only because of experience, diversity, and commitment that my teammate reacted so fast that, today, we are all alive with a story to learn from.

Nathalie Lasselin *is an award-winning filmmaker and producer. She trained at the National Film Board of Canada and is an arctic dive expedition leader, CCR, cave and wreck explorer and instructor.*

As an international speaker, a writer, and on-camera talent/technical dive specialist for TV shows, she shares her passion for discovery in a challenging environment. For the past years with her project, Urban Water Odyssey, diving the 70 km/43 mile long shore of Montréal, she brings people together to raise awareness and better action towards the preservation of fresh water. She is also a WDHOF inductee, RCGS fellow.

Photo by Bénédicte Lasselin

NUNO GOMES

CIVIL ENGINEER

LOCATION OF INCIDENT
DAHAB, EGYPT

My Red Sea depth-record dive was nothing more than an attempt at being the deepest scuba diver. I could have described my record attempt as 'finding my inner-self', 'exploring the limits of human endurance' or 'pushing the envelope', which it may well have been, but I did not; we engineers like to call a spade a spade. In the end, it was nothing more than a contest for the deepest scuba dive in the sea.

The dive was to be done in the middle of the Red Sea, in the Gulf of Aqaba, between Egypt and Saudi Arabia and far from any land.

I would not be able to get to, or see, the bottom of the sea; I would not even get halfway to the bottom of the sea. It was what is called "a big blue" dive. There would be nothing there, or at least that is what I was hoping.

I did not particularly want to find an elusive giant squid or giant oarfish, nor even a deep-water shark looking for a snack.

There are two kinds of sports: bare basics and technical. Scuba diving is technical and needs tons of equipment. Some of us find this sport enjoyable.

Regarding equipment, there is one thing you can say for certain: at some point in time, it will fail. I cannot even count how many dive computers have failed during my deep-diving career. The most critical factor was my decompression schedule, worked out prior to the dive on my laptop. To determine the depth, I use a descent rope with depth markers, and to determine the time, I use my reliable Casio watches. It is a simple system, and it has worked well.

Photo by Theo van Eeden

"Why not Sharm el Sheikh?" asked Dr. Adel Taher. The purpose of his question was to indicate to me that there was no decompression chamber in Dahab in 2004. For the rest, it was the perfect spot.

Dahab lies in the Gulf of Aqaba, an inlet protected from underwater currents, strong winds, and big waves; that was the theory at the time, anyway. The water is warm and crystal clear; the sea near the shore is deep, a hundred meters-plus; the abyss is almost at your doorstep. What makes Dahab unique is the atmosphere of an unchanged fishing village with a touch of European hippie culture.

In 2004, there was only one boat available in Dahab that was capable of taking divers a few miles offshore; she was the Ganet Sinai. We began with build-up dives, mostly deep descents on air down to 100 m/326 ft. These were followed by dives on trimix to depths of around 150 m/489 ft. Needless to say, my team and I certainly became acquainted with both nitrogen and helium!

We were a focused team with a common aim. Personal issues, if any, were set aside. We were strict in terms of being punctual, sober, and competent, but if someone did not conform then we would replace that person with a more willing diver without much fuss. In Dahab, a Tuesday is not much different from a Saturday. We all had a job to do, and I knew very well that when my alarm went off at 5 a.m. on July 23, 2004, the other clocks would also buzz. It was time to dive.

My descent that day was like an elevator ride to the ground floor of the Empire State building from the 102nd floor. Instead of watching the number of the floors passing by, I was checking the depth numbers on my computers, constantly equalizing and adjusting my buoyancy. If a whale had passed by, I would not have noticed it. My surroundings were the ocean void and the descent rope. A great nothingness with at least 50 m/164 ft of visibility.

A descent to 300 m/979 ft could take around 15 minutes, quite a bit longer than the world's longest wingsuit free-fall performed by Adrian Nicholas in 1999, lasting four minutes and 55 seconds. Unlike Nicholas, who descended with an average speed of 140 km/h (87 ml/h), I was much slower at about 40-20 m/min (131-66 ft/min).

At 60 m/196 ft, I clipped off my 10 L/70 cf air cylinder to the ring on the line and switched over from air to my trimix travel gas, one of the three independent travel gas cylinders. The three side-mounted, trimix cylinders of travel gas each had a capacity of 14 L/110 cf.

My four back-mounted cylinders had a volume of 18 L/140 cf each. The seven cylinders were in fact the only cylinders that I had on me during the descent (a total weight of 150 kg/331 lbs) excluding regulators and the back plate).

The total weight of all the equipment around my body was closer to 200 kg/441 lbs. Besides the cylinders on me, I would also be using another 23 cylinders for decompression.

My first staged decompression cylinder was at 160 m/522 ft. It was there to be used instead of the travel mixture I was carrying with me, in case of an emergency. At 20 m/66 ft, it would have lasted almost forever, at 160 m/522 ft, only about six minutes. At the start of my dive, obviously, I did not expect anything to go wrong. As I approached the depth of 271.6 m/886 ft, the regulator started sputtering with intermittent loud bangs, and then it stopped working altogether.

The regulator had gone past the 200 m/652 ft mark, as claimed by the manufacturer, but it would go no further. It fell very short of my expected performance requirements. More to the point, I now had big problems.

The contents of the three 18 L/140 cf cylinders on my back, filled with bottom trimix, immediately became unavailable to me.

I had only one 18 L/140 cf cylinder available, the bailout cylinder on my back, with my old regulator. My life hung in the balance; would this regulator work?

I inhaled cautiously and to my relief, it worked.

There was hope.

The prospect of reaching my first stage cylinder at 160 m/522 ft was slim to non-existent. My record for dynamic apnoea with fins is more than 100 m/326 ft; my best time for breath hold static apnoea, after breathing pure oxygen, is 11 minutes and 45 seconds.

These were both performed in the controlled environment of a swimming pool, not at 271.6 m/886 ft below the surface with over 150 kg/331 lbs of equipment on my back.

My Equivalent Narcotic depth (END) was 47 m/153 ft, and Total Narcotic depth (TND) was 80.5 m/263 ft, but I had to make some very quick decisions.

I couldn't use my travel mixes; at this depth, their content would be hyperoxic and highly narcotic. The bailout cylinder reserved for this type of situation would last only five minutes. Normally, ascending 111 m/362 ft should take at least 11 minutes; I had to make it in five. The dilemma was either to drown trying to reach my stage cylinder at 160 m/522 ft or to die from deep water blackout using one of my travel gas cylinders. I chose to try the first option.

I had the best probability of survival due to my breath-hold capabilities. People can be resuscitated even after one hour of being submerged in cold water, not as warm as the Red Sea. I was hoping for the best. The literature didn't mention any successful rescue operations after diving close to 300 m/979 ft; that was a small detail that I did not have time to think about at that moment.

For most people that I know, a 100 m/326 ft dive is the pinnacle of their diving career; an emergency ascent from the kind of depth

Photo by Nuno Gomes

was pure science fiction. I would have to do much more than hold a few breaths, and even if I succeeded, I would still be at someone's record depth. The reality could have been far more brutal; at least it was not an emergency ascent to the surface (which would have killed me in the blink of an eye because of the difference in pressure).

Whichever way you look at it, I still had 111 m/362 ft to ascend. In the few minutes that followed, all my spearfishing vacations and underwater hockey matches paid off to such an extent that, when I reached the 200 m/653 ft mark where my travel mix would not be hyperoxic, I chose not to use it and kept going for 160 m/522 ft, on my bailout.

I had, however, missed my 190 m/620 ft, 180 m/587 ft, and 170 m/555 ft decompression stops. The travel mixture would have its role to play later, and I did not want to exhaust it just yet. When I saw the stage cylinder, at 160 m/522 ft, I knew that I would probably live to dive another day.

My immediate problems were not over; the cylinder at 160 m/525 ft, which was meant to be used from that depth up to 120 m/392 ft, had its carabiner nut locked so tight that I did not have the strength to undo it. I would have to leave the cylinder where it was.

Because my ascent had been too quick, I would have to spend an additional five minutes at 160 m/522 ft plus at least one additional minute of mandatory decompression.

The memories of my five-minute ascent were over, and my next stage was 40 m/131 ft above me. With the carabiner on the 160 m/522 ft stage still refusing to cooperate, I could not move the tank up the line, so I had to start using my travel gas. Good thing that I had not used it before, as it was my last resort! I made it to 120 m/392 ft, and luckily the nut of the carabiner on that stage cylinder was not locked tight. For now only one 'little' question was left unanswered: would I get bent or not during my ascent and decompression pauses, on my way to the surface?

Photo by Theo van Eeden

The answer to that question would not be known for ten or more hours. Doing the full decompression schedule that had originally been planned for the 300 m/979 ft plus dive would certainly improve my chances. After all the misadventures at depth, I decided to do just that. It was not long before a welcome silhouette defined itself from above; it was Pieter Venter's face, at 120 m/392 ft. He was the only deep diver on the team who was filling the role of deep support diver, although I was working with other divers who were also capable of diving to 120 m/392 ft.

"Nuno honestly said at the beginning that deep support is for Pieter; support down to 60 m/196 ft is for the other support divers," remembers Krzysztof Hryczyszyn.

It would emerge later that I had led a diving team of future stars back in 2004. All of them were now shallower; at 120 m/392 ft only Pieter was present at my decompression stop, as per the plan. I indicated to him that the regulator had failed and showed him my "Parkway" computer with a depth of 280 m/914 ft; he indicated "too bad" but was glad to see me still alive. He deployed his signal buoy, which would be the first communication with the surface, to alert the team and crew on the boat that I had begun my ascent.

"The buoy popped up with only an "OK" tag. We knew something had happened but that at least Nuno was still alive," recalls Theo van Eeden. For the ideal outcome there would have been two tags: "'OK'" and "World Record." A tag with "Not OK" would have meant that I was missing.

Down below I still had at least 10 hours to go.

Although the dive was shallower than calculated, I had decided to stick to my original run-time.

The next five stops went uneventfully. I was alone contemplating my narrow escape and my newly gained experience. I was also wondering what had happened to the regulator that had served me so well on the record dive with Leszek the year before.

There was a deliberate gap in support divers below 60 m/196 ft; this was the result of years of experience, not only mine, but also from the divers before me like Sheck and Jochen. We had learnt that every diver in the water and on trimix is an additional potential risk.

Approaching 60 m/196 ft, I was certain that at least I would not be dying alone. Gareth Lowndes was supposed to be the first in the line of support divers who would take turns in assisting me on my way up to the surface. The plan required me to decompress on air from 60 m/196 ft to 40 m/131 ft, and it would take 40 minutes; the narcosis would be manageable, at least for me. I made the depth on time, but Gareth was not there. I thought maybe something had stopped him from descending, equalization or trim problems maybe. Nobody could see me from the surface: I was on my own. I couldn't do much about Gareth's problems; I had my own now.

After 15 minutes, I became nervous. The partially used 10 L/70 cf cylinder that I had left on the line, at 60 m/196 ft, on my way down would not last long.

With a normal breathing rate of about 20 L/min (0.7 cf/min), what was left in the cylinder could last me about 11 minutes until totally empty, not the planned 40 minutes. The only way to make these decompression stops was to simply lower my breathing rate. It is nearly impossible to use only 6 L/min (0.2 cf/min), at this depth. It is very close to actually holding one's breath—the biggest problem being the carbon dioxide buildup, which can lead to unconsciousness or deep water blackout. It also tremendously increases narcosis.

First, I had to oxygenate my blood and the deep tissues by doing slow, deliberate, deep breaths and exhaling very slowly. I had to concentrate with my eyes closed and make sure that all my muscles were relaxed. I needed to keep my heart rate low.

It surprises some people that, just as one can tell one's body to move, we can also slow it down. Miguel Indurain, the Spanish cyclist and five-time Tour de France winner, has a resting heart rate of only 28 beats per minute– one of the lowest ever recorded in a healthy human. In my case, a lower heart rate would equal lower air consumption.

Lower air consumption meant that I might survive the dive. With this sort of relaxation comes the mind check and body check. It begins with the toes and ends with the neck making sure that the parts of the body are functioning.

The brain, when active, accounts for approximately 40 percent of our oxygen consumption, and there is no doubt that constantly thinking about how much air was in this cylinder would not help. I usually let my mind drift, not focusing on anything intensely,

and I let my brain go blank. Any disturbance of vision or confusion would indicate that it was time to breathe. Failing to notice this would end up in a blackout. Blackout without Gareth and my air decompression cylinder would mean certain death.

Gareth arrived just a couple of minutes before my decompression stop at 40 m/131 ft was due to end; as it turns out, I still had just under 50 bar/735 psi left in the cylinder. He would have been there earlier had Pieter Venter, who was decompressing from his deep support dive, not stopped him on his way down to me and asked him to go back up and bring something down for him, from the surface.

Later on, furious, I found out that the dive marshal had misread the run-time schedule. Instead of Gareth arriving at the start of my air decompression stop, he had arrived just before the end. I kept my anger confined.

It was no use, especially in the water. I promised myself, however, to discuss and rehearse every descent with the team more thoroughly on future dives. After Gareth came Lenné, then Artur and Zbyszek, followed by Craig, Boguslaw, and Krzysztof. Then Craig again and Gareth at 12 m/40 ft. Then Ryszard and Stewart, the Canadian cameraman, at 9 m/30 ft. At some point all the support divers were too exhausted to dive, and Stewart, the National Geographic cameraman, took over some of the final shifts. Hovering in oblivion, I did not know about it.

The continuous stream of support divers, however, was breaking the monotony of breathing, sipping fluids, changing regulators and staring at the endless blue void.

Without any reference point, it was hard to estimate how big the surface whitecapped waves were up above. The swell had turned violent and from 21 m/70 ft all the way up, I felt like an invisible monster was bouncing me on a huge swing. Every metre up, I was pushed further and faster than before. Soon nausea engulfed me, and I started to vomit the liquid meals that I ingested before along with some seawater. With each swell came the noise of several decompression cylinders clanging, and knocking against each other. Eventually, Krzysztof dived down and tied them together to muffle the clatter.

I thought that everything would change when I moved from the vertical shot line to the deco bar, constructed by Theo while we were in Egypt. But the move did not help much. The whole oxygen tree was dancing effortlessly to the rhythm of the waves up above. I knew the surface was tantalizingly close, but despite being at 9 m/30 ft, I still had nearly half of the dive before me.

My arms grew weaker and weaker with every hour of gripping the oxygen tree's deco bar. Besides the support divers, my only other companions were some blue jellyfish and a few little zebra fish with black and blue stripes that tended to flock around my cylinder

valves. When, after 10 hours and 45 minutes, I surfaced and said to Theo van Eeden. "I have reached my limit. I won't be doing this again." I knew that it had been a very close call and that I was lucky to be alive. I had been able to survive four major incidents during the record dive. If I had died, no one would have ever known what had caused my death, and it probably would have been attributed to diver error.

Dr. Hermie Britz decided to rehydrate me with a saline drip. I did not feel cold but was utterly drained of energy. The only thing that I needed now was a good night's sleep.

Nuno Gomes *was born in Lisbon and now lives in New York. Growing up on the Portuguese coast, he practically lived in the sea and learned to swim and spearfish in the temperamental Portuguese Atlantic.*

His father relocated his family to South Africa when Nuno was 14 years old. They settled in the Pretoria / Johannesburg area, landlocked. Cave diving was a natural progression. Nuno joined and pioneered many cave dive expeditions. He dived in all the known water-filled caves in Southern Africa.

On August 23, 1996, the deepest cave dive was carried out by Nuno Gomes, when he dived to a depth of 282.6 m/927 ft, at Bushmansgat in the Northern Cape, South Africa. This water-filled cave dive, at an altitude of 1550 m/5086 ft above sea level, required a decompression schedule for a dive equivalent to a depth of 337 m/1106 ft at sea level.

Nuno was subsequently also awarded a Guinness World Record for Deepest Sea Dive. Along with his team, Nuno achieved a record dive to a corrected (with rope stretch) depth of 321.81 m/1056 ft, in the Red Sea (Dahab) in June 2005..

Photo by Shareen Anderson

PASCAL BERNABE

CONSULTANT & INSTRUCTOR TRAINER
CAVE / TRIMIX / CCR / DPV

LOCATION OF INCIDENT
PROPRIANO, CORSICA

I was in Croatia exploring an undersea spring. I had heard about cave explorations of this sort in Croatia and had set off there on my own expedition.

Earlier, during a first visit, I had been surprised to learn of a virtually unexplored cave just 40 minutes drive from my hotel. It was reported to be 300 m/984 ft long, sinking to a depth of 46 m/150 ft—a golden opportunity, and an invitation to explore.

By the time of the incident, I had twice explored the magnificent underwater cave of Zecica, unrolling 380 m/1246 ft of cord to enable me to retrace my route at depths of between 40-50 m/131-164 ft. I was using a mixture of trimix and nitrox 50%, with oxygen during decompression stops, as well as a rather capricious underwater scooter. The cave extended to 780 m/2559 ft of galleries, which were up to 18 m/60 ft wide and around 10 m/33 ft high, punctuated by enormous stalagmites and stalactites.

I fell completely in love with this strange undersea saltwater river with its eels, mussels, and other marine fauna, which opened so mysteriously at a depth of 9 m/30 ft some 50 m/164 ft from the shore of a little bay. From there, this big underwater river extends north into the limestone hills that sweep down to the coast.

During one dive, something unbelievable happened. First, my main computer fell victim to a bug. It failed to start at the outset, and the stops it ordered made no sense. So, I fell back on my emergency computer. I quickly realised that it too was not working, probably because of a battery problem. I now had two failed computers!

Photos by François Brun

I got out my wetnote and studied the rough dive plan I had drawn up the previous day, and then counted the minutes and seconds in my head, as if I was doing cardiac massage. I had read Sheck Exley's autobiography, *Caverns Measureless to Man*, in which he described having a problem of this sort during one of his exploration dives in the Nacimiento del Río Mante at a depth below 200 m/656 ft. Although I hadn't planned for this kind of incident, I adopted the same strategy.

And then something else happened. Something which could have had dire consequences—during a manoeuvre, I lost my wetnote. Two things saved my life: one was knowing how to calculate decompression on the fly using the Deco ratio; the other was a rope installed for the dive between the depths of 6-30 m/20-100 ft, graduated every 3 m/10 ft, which was nearly vertical.

The moral of this story is simple but vitally important: everything we read, every technique we learn, every moment we spend absorbing knowledge about the sport which we love so dearly can save our lives.

The psychology of fear of the unknown during a dive to 330 m/1082 ft.

During my world record dive to 330 m/1082 ft in the Bay of Valinco, Corsica, in July 2005, I again experienced a situation where only the habits acquired during thousands of dives of all sorts, from caving and deep dives to professional diving, saved my life.

I was well prepared, and with an excellent team, yet that morning I was very anxious in the face of the unknown; above all about how High-Pressure Nervous Syndrome (HPNS) would affect me at a depth of more than 300 m/984 ft.

One can view this fear as an emotional adaptation that helps us to avoid needless risks. My fear centred upon the things that were hard to predict; I had huge quantities of gas and an excellent decompression procedure, but what was going to happen at depth? Although I was psychologically well-prepared, I remained anxious throughout the descent, which helped me to stay alert. The psychology studies which I am currently pursuing would suggest that excessive dramatisation of the event is similar to that which occurs in other fields—that it arises from perceptions of powerlessness in the face of the unknown; from giving undue importance to the situation and from ruminating on negative thoughts and dysfunctional mental representations, often because one is insufficiently focussed on the present, on the action of the moment.

But, after 13 minutes of rapid descent, as I arrived at a depth of 330 m/1082 ft, my body started to be shaken by a strong HPNS event, with visual disturbance. I saw hundreds of concentric circles when one of the lamps on my helmet exploded, bursting my eardrum. I felt great pain, but I also felt my stress disappear completely, to be replaced by an intense focus on the very real problem as I adopted reflex actions acquired through conditioning and training over many years.

I was now in real danger of dying, but fear had disappeared. Here again, a lot of psychological research shows that stress adaptation strategies are more effective if they are focused upon the problem that needs to be resolved, rather than the emotions we are feeling. The final element was that, knowing my dive plan by heart, I followed it rigorously, despite the sharp pain that increased steadily as I rose toward the surface. I was able to endure the eight hours and 57 minutes of the dive, the strong swell, with 2-3 m/6-10 ft between crest and trough, and the nausea this caused. I no longer had any doubt about the successful outcome of the dive.

Studies unanimously concur that feelings of personal effectiveness, going beyond personal self-esteem, increase the probability of success. I emerged worn out by pain, the swell, seasickness, and the sleepless night that preceded my record dive. Nevertheless, I was safe and well, saved by the versatility and multiplicity of my diving experiences, my high level of fitness that had enabled me to endure, thorough mental preparation, and a team who were not only highly efficient, but also emotionally very close in terms of our social bond. All of these factors are essential to effective adaptation to extreme situations and environments. The only ill effect (other than my ear) was a feeling of nausea because I had swallowed too much food during the dive! Two days later, I ran for an hour in the mountains of Corsica.

Pascal Bernabe *is above all an explorer. He began, 20 years ago, by exploring French underwater caves. He has used caving techniques, futuristic diving suits, rebreathers, helium-based gas mixes, scooters, and decompression chambers. He has explored several kilometres of unvisited galleries, of which some were between 70-250 m/229-820 ft deep. This has included a dozen dives to depths of 200-330 m/656-1082 ft. He has explored deep-water wrecks and has been a safety diver and cameraman for the freedivers Pippin and Audrey Ferreras to a depth of 170 m/557 ft. Pascal has taken part in film shoots like the Imax film, Oceanmen, in the Bahamas and with James Cameron in Mexico.*

After spending time as a coral gatherer in Tunisia, he became a consultant and instructor trainer in cave diving, deep diving, mixed gas, rebreathers, and DPV for TDI and CMAS. From 2005 to 2014 he held the world depth record for scuba diving: 330 m/1082 ft on the 5th of July 2005 at Propriano, Corsica.

He co-authored the Guide de la plongée TEK and Guide de la plongée recycleur (CCR) with François Brun, has contributed numerous articles for French and foreign magazines and helped draw up new diving tables and develop new gases for deep water diving. As a rescue diver, he has been called on to help with rescues such as that of a rescue diver trapped in a spring in the Jura Mountains, or the case of an exploration robot trapped 174 m/570 ft down in the Fontaine de Vaucluse.

PATRICK WIDMANN

CAVE EXPLORER / EDUCATOR / EQUIPMENT DESIGNER
EXPEDITION LEADER & PUBLIC SPEAKER

LOCATION OF INCIDENT
REMOTE REGINA SECTION OF OX BEL HA CAVE SYSTEM

It has taken me quite some consideration and thought to write this piece for the simple reason that 'close calls' in my experience only happen when someone violates the rules of safe cave diving practices. Hence I am sharing here my blatant disregard for one of said rules, which ended up with me almost losing my life; admitting to it, as you can imagine, isn't easy to do.

I tossed the idea back and forth of maybe writing about CO_2 hits I had sustained as well as other CCR related emergencies and also having been in a cave during an earthquake. But all of that just didn't feel like a 'close call', and I wanted the reader as well to benefit from a lesson I had learned the hard way from making a very bad decision.

Our team was exploring a section of cave that was quite unusual for Mexico, as the average depth was 30 m/100 ft, and you would have to pass several major restrictions (divers couldn't fit in using back mount configurations) to get there.

Once there, the cave is a crazy spectacular salt water tunnel full of decoration. At the end of this line one comes again to a tricky-to-navigate collapsed area, which is quite silty but has some very cool bear bones with canine teeth and some sloth remains.

We (two person team) documented the bones and then made our way to the end of line to continue exploration. My exploration partner that day was Jaime, who was in charge of the reel while I was behind him surveying with the MNemo (digital surveying device). Both of us were very excited about the cave seemingly continuing and also about the size and coolness of the passage.

Photo by Kim Davidsson

As the 'Number Two', another job of mine besides surveying is to look left and right and see if I can spot any potential leads and mark them with arrows. This means that sometimes I am swimming a little bit off the line to have a look if the black hole I see is actually a hole or just a shadow.

The next question then is if it's actually worthwhile to further investigate it with a reel. As this happens quite frequently and I don't want to get separated too much from the lead diver, these little side tours are usually done while trying not to waste too much time, hence no line-laying.

I guess you can already picture where this is going. The more often you do this, the more comfortable you get with it, which is not a good thing. In this particular situation, we were on top of a boulder collapse, and my experience has taught me that very often on the bottom of these collapses there is a way to bypass it as you stay in the original tunnel before the ceiling collapses.

I left the MNemo on the line and swam to the edge of the collapse some 6 m/20 ft to the right of the line. From there I could clearly see a hole at the bottom, which was very intriguing. As this is a rather big room, zero viz wasn't going to be an issue as I could have just ascended straight up from that hole coming out of the cloud and I would see the tunnel and line right in front of me. So with that thought in mind I made my way down towards the hole at the bottom of the collapse. When I say "hole" I mean a gap in between the massive boulders.

We were on KISS Sidewinder closed circuit rebreathers, which meant that the visibility generally stayed very good, as we produced hardly any percolation (sediments raining down on you after getting dislodged from the ceiling by diver's bubbles). Arriving at the gap, I could see right away that there was a tunnel on the other side of it, and so I went closer and closer to try and make out if the tunnel

continued behind the corner I could see in front of me.

By that time, I was basically hip-deep into that new passage and could clearly see a space to turn around and a possible continuation of the tunnel. That was when I made the first terrible decision.

With one fin stroke, I passed the entrance restriction, and as I was just about to initiate a gentle helicopter turn I could hear the sound of very jagged rock rolling down a slope. You might think it's weird how sure I was about the shape, but heavily-eroded saltwater rocks that aren't round just have their own sound to them. It was in that instant that I knew I was in trouble—big time!

As I finished my helicopter turn, I could see the hole again in front of me just seconds before I got engulfed in a white zero-visibility cloud. I made a swift kick and headed into that restriction. By the time I was halfway in, I got a weird feeling, as I felt it to be smaller with both of my sidemount tanks touching the walls.

As I lifted my head up, I emerged out of the zero visibility and realised that I was in a dead end inside a 'Mikado Maze' of massive boulders. Before I could fully grasp the exact situation, I got swallowed by the zero visibility again and was pretty much stuck in a 45° angle, facing upwards.

Rebreathers are not really built to be breathed whilst vertical, as the hydrostatic pressure forces the gas up towards your mouth, which makes breathing less than ideal–especially if you are also already quite scared and unhappy.

Bailing out to open circuit came to mind, not only to reduce my stress level caused by the work of breathing, but also due to the fact that visibility was too bad to see my handset. It was all about balancing risks at that moment; if I went open circuit, then breathing would be easier, but percolation would turn the place into an absolute shit show with zero chance of being able to see again.

Thank God I had over ten years of experience teaching people how to dive their CCRs temporarily in bad visibility! It was that very knowledge and experience that allowed me to stay on the loop while remaining (relatively) calm.

I closed my eyes and focused on my breathing noise, reminding myself of an old credo: "Dum Spiro Spes;" as long as you breathe there is hope.

I also reminded myself that I had a fresh 6.2 lbs of scrubber with hours to go before I would pass out due to hypercapnia.

In moments like these, my mind plays heavy tricks on me. I remembered images from body recovery dives I had done in the past, wondering if this was what they had felt before they drowned, and if I too was going to remove my mask in a last desperate attempt to inhale through my nose.

I could see my mother standing upset in front of my grave; I was yelling at myself for having made this unbelievable stupid decision, and so the circus show in my head kept spinning in circles.

When I was a kid, my dad used to tell me that I shouldn't feel bad for being scared; that it was a good thing, something that would sharpen my senses and keep me alert, just so long as it didn't make me freeze. After a few minutes of trying to suppress the fear of dying, I decided to open my eyes again and, yes, I could see a little.

It became instantly apparent to me that I had taken the wrong hole out of the tunnel; one that didn't lead into the main chamber but ran parallel to it, into a dead end at the bottom of the boulder collapse, which meant that I was now buried under tons and tons of rocks.

I could see gaps between the boulders right on top of me, one of them big enough to squeeze through in no mount, yet the space I was in was so small that removing the tanks would have not only been challenging, but would also have reduced the visibility to zero again. Even if I made it through, I was still not sure if I would be in the main chamber, or yet again in just another little void inside the collapse. I determined this to be my last option.

I was quite sure that the visibility would go to shit again once I moved, and so I made the decision to take my backup lights out, turn them on and push through the cracks on top of me, in the hope that when Jaime came back after either having realised that I wasn't behind him anymore or having emptied the reel, he would see the light rays and locate me at the bottom of the collapse (later he told me that he first saw the MNemo on the line, and it was only due to that that he could see the fine rays of light emerging from the bottom of the breakdown).

I was sure that even when he came back, he wouldn't be able to navigate through both restrictions in zero visibility only to find me in this little chamber, facing away from him and then sort of pull me out from my fins. So, after placing the backup lights, I took my safety spool out and searched with my hands in the zero visibility below me for tie offs. It was a pretty small void, and I had very little room to move. Unfortunately, all the commotion meant I was back to pretty much zero visibility; I could barely see my Shearwater controller when I pressed it against my mask.

The next step was to try to back up out of the restriction feet-first, which led to instant proper zero visibility again. Once I made it out, I tried to turn around to face the direction of travel again, only to find that I was in a seriously confined space. I was literally wedged with fins against the wall pointing to the ceiling while my DSV (rebreather mouthpiece) was grinding against the wall in front of me as I tried to turn.

I shat my pants, abandoned that plan, and returned through the restriction back into the void following my safety spool line. I was pretty scared at that point.

It became clear that I would somehow have to turn around in that void, enabling me to come out of the restriction face first. This seemed to be an impossible task at that point, so I went back to just closing my eyes and waiting to see if the visibility would get a bit better so I could at least see my PO₂ again.

I let some five minutes pass I reckon, which felt like half an hour, and really just focussed on my breathing.

Any type of positive thoughts had left me by that point and, to be 100% honest, the thought passed through my head that if I couldn't make any progress, then I would rather close my oxygen and go hypoxic than to wait for hypercapnia (which comes accompanied by heavy anxiety) to take me out.

As I opened my eyes, I could see the space above me again, which was a relief. It meant that, given enough time, the visibility did improve somewhat.

It also allowed me to chart the void I was in a bit better, and just as I was thinking about trying to turn again I could see a ray of light from above me with the mumbling voice of Jaime yelling my name into his DSV!

Due to the gas volume of a rebreather, we can actually semi-talk, it's just quite a bit "mumbly" as you obviously cannot close your lips.

Photo by Kim Davidsson

I tried to yell up to him that I was stuck and explain my situation, but it became quickly evident that he couldn't understand me and I wasn't able to make out what he was saying; just as suddenly, his light disappeared again.

I was quite worried that he was going to swim into the zero visibility, potentially getting stuck in the entrance restriction, as he wouldn't be able to see and properly evaluate it. Yet his mere presence rekindled the hope that I might make it out alive, and so I took a last look at my handset and started to go more vertical in order to turn around inside the void.

Again I found myself wedged between these tight walls, but with my new-found confidence, I wrestled through it, trying not to entangle myself in my own safety spool line.

But I did it!!!

Coming out face first from the restriction, I felt like the hard part was over, and just as I turned to the left, I could see the faint glow of Jaime's light shining through white silt out from the other side of the hole where all my nightmares began.

As I came out of the restriction and out of the zero visibility, I could see his face in front of me. Never have I been so happy to see him! I grabbed his head with both my hands and exhaled deeply with relief.

Now that the layout of the location was clear to me, it wasn't a problem to tie off the safety spool and go back to get my back up lights. Once back at the main line, I finished the survey of his line, which wasn't too long, as he had quickly run out of cave (thank God for that!) and therefore returned. It was normal for us to dive independently within a team while exploring, with each member having a specific task while usually still being connected through the guideline.

After that, we went back to another lead and finished the reel due east which ultimately led to a very important connection of two cave systems (one being the second largest submerged cave system in the world, called Ox Bel Ha).

The lesson is quite simple: a short moment of overconfidence can turn the best dive of your life into your worst nightmare!

Stick to the rules! Cave diving for a trained cave diver with proper equipment is quite safe, unless you choose to make it dangerous.

Patrick Widmann, *born in Austria, has spent the last thirteen years living in Mexico exploring caves and teaching cave diving. He is one of the owners as well as the training director at ProTec Dive Centers.*

Patrick is an explorer, educator, public speaker, and a key member of the product design and development department of XDEEP. He is on the board of advisors of PSAI and an Instructor Trainer Evaluator who also helped to develop their CCR Cave Class.

Patrick has explored and dived caves in fourteen different countries on this planet. Since 2014, he has led annual expeditions to Madagascar where his team has discovered and explored several stunning and vast underwater cave systems. The team has been credited with discovery and analysis of important paleontological remains which were covered by 78 news outlets around the world including CNN, NBC, Washington Post, and National Geographic, amongst others.

The team is also credited with discovering and exploring 'Anjanamba', currently the longest submerged cave system of Africa with 10+ km/6.2 miles of surveyed cave passage and a single entrance.

Photo by Phillip Lehman

PAUL TOOMER

OWNER @ DIVING MATRIX
PRESIDENT @ DIVE RAID INTERNATIONAL

LOCATION OF INCIDENT
MALTA

I would love to enthrall you with stories of how I have escaped the clutches of the Grim Reaper, but I'm afraid this is not the case. My father and grandfather have always said that it is better to be born lucky than rich. And I am lucky. That being said, luck rests firmly on hard work. And I have been blessed to have been mentored and taught by the best underwater instructors and explorers on this planet. All of the issues I have had while diving have been dealt relatively simply because of this training.

You're now scratching your head wondering "why am I reading this?"

My close call happened while teaching a Hypoxic Trimix 100-metre course. I was teaching a very good friend of mine who is a highly skilled and knowledgeable diver. The diver had completed many courses with me and was very familiar with how I work. I was not expecting any issues and had relaxed, perhaps a little too much, and had become overconfident in the ability of my diver to be able to overcome any hardships.

The dive in question was the final dive of the course, and we had planned to dive a beautiful wreck in 100 metres of water. We had completed all the skills and deep dives up to this point, incrementally increasing our depth so as to not be overwhelmed. Diving to 100 m/328 ft is not something that anyone should take lightly.

We arrived at the boat fully prepared, planned, and full of excitement, since all the previous dives had gone as perfectly as possible. The course only had one student on it, and I had brought two safety divers plus surface support for the planned dive.

Photo by Lisa Toomer

The skipper was slightly stressed, as he was running another dive later in the day and wanted to get us on the dive as quickly as possible—this was the first sign that I foolishly ignored as a significant stressor to my diver.

The weather was extremely warm, but because the water was temperate, we were wearing drysuits. My diver started to overheat, and although we cooled the diver down by flushing cool water over their suit and head, this was stressor number two. Again, it went relatively unnoticed.

Upon arriving at the dive site, my diver had some issues fitting some of the stage bottles, and when they finally hit the water, the stress had elevated yet again. We performed our surface checks, then an S-drill at around 6 m/20 ft, where I gave the thumb down descend sign. I received a return descend signal and an OK, and the four of us began our descent. During the descent I noticed how slow my diver was moving and how they constantly kept checking in, but each time I checked, I got the OK signal back.

Once near the bottom, I noticed that the wreck was about 10-15 m/33-49 ft away from the descent line, and I also noticed that we had eaten up a significant amount of our planned bottom time. I decided to lay a sacrificial line in from the shot to the wreck so we could jump the wreck, have a little look around, and then easily find our ascent line within a few minutes.

I tied my line into the shot, signalled that we would swim to the wreck, received my OKs, and I started to lead us to the wreck. After swimming for about 5 m/16 ft, I felt something wrap around my leg, then both legs. I turned, and my diver had managed to tangle us both in my jump line and was trying to head to the surface. I turned, and with every bit of movement I had left I grabbed my diver's fin tips to prevent the fast ascent.

I managed to arrest the ascent and held fast to my diver. I reached my Z-knife and within seconds had us untangled from the line.

I dragged us back to the ascent line and started tapping on my student's mask to get their attention. Nothing. But thankfully, the desire to flee had abated and the diver simply stared at me while following my basic instructions.

Photo by Danny Barber

We began our ascent and, thank the stars, we had not broken our planned bottom time, so the plan would not change and we could simply head home. My two safety divers had taken up station and were prepared to immediately respond.

We made our way to our first decompression stop and planned gas switch. Again, things started to get better, and my diver, although still in a semi-catatonic state, accepted the new mix and allowed me to direct the dive.

We successfully completed all of our decompression, and on the final gas switch at 12 m/39 ft, my diver's eyes focused and they suddenly became aware of their surroundings.

For the final decompression, there were a few tears but mostly just four divers floating in the water thanking the heavens for giving us the skills to get through what could have been a life-changing moment for all of us.

We all spent the rest of the day speaking openly about what had happened, and I am pleased to say that my friend came back for some more training, faced their demons, and went on to become a great trimix diver. Since we had actually executed the decompression plan perfectly, and since my diver had become aware during the final deco, I was able to pad it a little bit, just in case.

That was the final time I ever took open circuit to 100 meters. Since then I have always worn a rebreather. I do this because if the rebreather is working, all my bailout gas could be used by a diver in trouble. When we got to the surface, I checked how much gas I had in my twinset and I can tell you, it was not good. I was too scared to look at how much my diver had left for many hours.

What did I learn? I learned never to be complacent or become overconfident, in either myself or any diver I teach or dive with. This is called 'respect'. And I have a healthy amount of that now.

Paul Toomer *is the President of training agency RAID, he is a working instructor trainer and expedition diver.*

After living in South Africa for 23 years, it's odd that Paul discovered diving in the cold waters of Southern England. It is this kind of behavior that defines Paul and his passion for doing things differently. Within months of learning to dive, he had his own center in London and rapidly progressed to course director before finding his passion for technical diving in 2002. Paul is an avid wreck, cave, sidemount, and rebreather diver.

In 2002, Paul began pursuing his technical diving interests, and rebreather diving became his main focus. In 2007, he decided to concentrate purely on technical diver training and expeditions, and Diving Matrix Tec Lab was born. Tec Lab was innovative in its design and philosophy and set the benchmark for advanced diver training.

In 2011, Paul was offered the position as Director of Technical Training for SSI (Scuba Schools International) and was responsible for writing diver and instructor manuals and training standards as well as training future technical instructors and trainers. In 2014, Paul became a co-owner of RAID International. Initially he held the position of Training Director, but in 2019, he accepted the position as President of the company.

He has participated in multiple expeditions including the HMS Hampshire, Vanguard, and Royal Oak in Scapa Flow. He has participated in exploratory dives on Italian and Phoenician wrecks and other exciting projects including WWI and WWII submarines, destroyers, and planes.

Paul regularly contributes to various dive magazines and has worked with film and TV companies as a diver, supplier, and advisor. A little boy called Sebastian, motorcycles, tattoos, and playing drums are the other major influences in Paul's life.

PETE MESLEY

OWNER LUST4RUST DIVING EXCURSIONS
& WRECK EXPEDITION LEADER

LOCATION OF INCIDENT
RMS NIAGARA, NEW ZEALAND

Planning a deep wreck expedition and only having one week to get out there is always a bit of a gamble. The ever-changing New Zealand weather always makes for a challenge when trying to predict a suitable time to execute a dive of this magnitude.

Our objective for this trip was to dive RMS *Niagara*, sitting in 125 m/410 ft of water. We wanted to learn a little more about the wreck, find out which areas had collapsed, and then get into the bullion room. The team was nice and intimate, with only two bottom divers— Simon Mitchell and me—and three support team members.

We sat around the weather channel on the VHF, waiting like expectant mothers, but the weather conditions did not look rosy. On the plus side, the forecast for the next few days looked a bit better, so we steamed out for the

Hen & Chicken Islands (the closest islands to the Niagara site) to be prepared when a break in the weather occurred. All we had to do now was wait. Quite often a six-to-eight-hour weather window appears in between the wind and the rain. An opportunity opened and we took it. It was all go.

RMS *Niagara*, a stately ship, known as "Titanic of the Pacific" was a 13,415 ton, 165 m/541 ft long, triple screw vessel, with a top speed of 17 knots. Built by John Brown & Co in Glasgow, she was launched on August 17, 1912. On June 19, 1940, while on voyage from Auckland to Vancouver, she struck a mine laid by the German Black Raider Orion in New Zealand's Hauraki Gulf and sank in 125 m/410 ft of water. She was carrying eight tons of gold bullion on board, most of which was salvaged the following year.

Photos by Pete Mesley

We held onto the shotline just below the surface for a few minutes, rechecking gear and getting ourselves nice and relaxed for the descent. The signal was given, and Simon and I made for the bottom. Both of us were diving closed circuit rebreathers; Simon had his Mk 15.5 and I had an AP Diving Inspiration. On earlier trips to *Niagara*, I used my homebuilt, fully manual CCR dubbed "The Widowmaker." I don't know what the hell I was thinking!

This time I was using a more dependable, robust, tried-and-tested unit! Doing such a dive on open circuit would be dramatically restrictive and would mean that we would have to carry over 12,000 litres of gas on the dive. That's a fair few cylinders to carry around!

It is hard to explain to someone the feeling you get as you are descending. Looking down along the shot line disappearing beneath you, knowing that on the other end is a world-class ocean liner waiting patiently for you. At about 70 m/229 ft, the wreck came into view. The shot was sitting perfectly in position. Our support team had done a superb job in placing the descent line exactly where we wanted. It lay over the hull opposite where the front chimneystack used to be.

There was not a breath of current, and the visibility–well Simon just looked at me with those eyes that said, "This is unbelievable!" The conditions were near perfect. On the surface, things were a little different, but down here the rain had stopped, the sun came out and there were two kids raring to go and play! One of the first things I noticed was the abundance of aquatic life.

The same huge school of Kingfish that had kept an eye on us the first time anyone had dived the wreck in 2000 were there. They spiralled around Simon and me only inches away, just out of reach. Another fantastic experience. Huge schools of golden snapper abounded too as we waded through the mass of fish life.

We swam over the hull toward the bow until we found the infamous hole that was blasted open all those years ago when Johnson and Williams made history in recovering the gold. Armed with only a viewing chamber, a radio, and a grab lowered from the surface, they successfully recovered just under eight tonnes of gold. There is always the thought of, "What if we come across one of the five bars of gold that were kindly left by the team?" But alas, the prospects of finding a 25 x 9 cm/10 x 3.5 inches bar amongst 14 thousand tonnes of shipwreck were a little slim, to say the least. Just being there, swimming around the wreck, was our 'bar of gold'.

The hole blasted into the bullion room was huge. By now, all the walls had fallen in, and there were few recognisable features to indicate that there had ever been any rooms in that area. Huge steel plates, metal girders, and debris hampered penetration opportunities, so we headed round in between the two stacks. Before the dive, we had both looked at the ship's deck plans and some photos that I had acquired from a museum, copies of pictures of the internals of the magnificent ship. They were not wrong when RMS Niagara was labelled "Titanic of the Pacific". So luxurious and stately!

A huge, oval, stained glass skylight that started in the first class smoking room drew our attention. This magnificent structure assisted in the natural lighting of the 1st class accommodation block vestibule and the 1st class Dining room. We looked at this structure and tried to imagine its beauty and elegance in the *Niagara's* heyday.

Not only had the promenade deck (B deck) disintegrated, but the Shelter deck (C deck) was gone too. This was where the 1st class accommodations had been. Simon and I swam into the 1st class Dining room through the oval hole that had once been the top deck; I could recognise the sculptured columns and the moulded ceiling patterns.

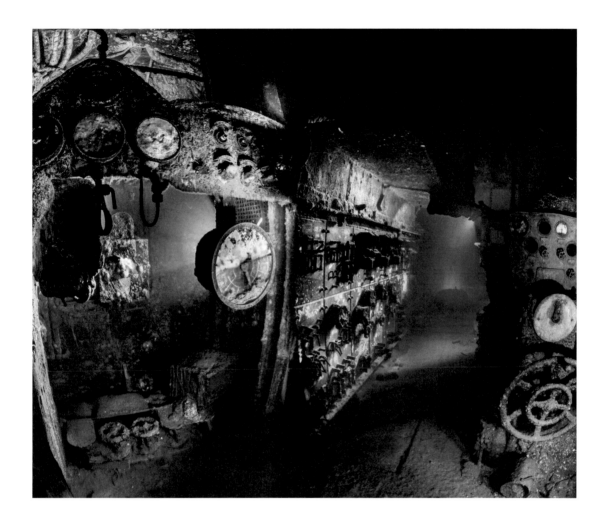

The tabletops in the dining room had long since disintegrated, leaving only the main table legs bolted to the floors. A ceiling fan hung by a cord. The once beautifully polished floorboards, which would have been modestly covered with well-made rugs, now lay at a 90-degree angle with a thin layer of silt covering them. All the handmade chairs, table fittings, cutlery, and crockery predictably lay in a huge pile of rubble on the ocean floor, covered with nearly 60 years of silt and broken down wreckage.

We exited the wreck and made our way back over the hull and towards the shot line. I still could not believe the amazing conditions. As we ascended the shot line I looked down and had the most fantastic view of the wreck; at 80 m/262 ft I could see how far the two decks had collapsed. Almost three quarters back towards the stern. Incredible.

At our scheduled 50 m/164 ft stop I popped my deco marker buoy and our drifting shot with bailout gas was deployed by our surface support.

We arrived at the 9 m/30 ft decompression stop. The decompression so far had been uneventful and we both relaxed, going over every aspect of the amazing dive we had just experienced. About two minutes into the stop, I felt something wasn't right. My attention turned inwards.

I looked at my dive computer. Woohhhhhh….

I started to feel extreme dizziness and (in my mind) I started to spin uncontrollably – or at least it bloody well felt like it. I grabbed onto the line to give me some sort of orientation. I immediately thought it was my rebreather and switched to bailout. No change. That ruled out problems with the breather. I was still spinning! I switched back to CCR.

Signalling to Simon "Mate, something is not right!" I tried to control the increasing nausea by keeping my eyes shut but, after about 10 minutes, the urge to vomit became overpowering.

I had to switch to my open circuit offboard bailout regulator, and was sick. Within a few minutes, I had completely emptied the contents of my stomach. Once things had eased, I returned to my CCR. This happened frequently throughout our three and a half-hour deco. The only saving grace was that I could feel it coming and so had a few seconds to switch to my bailout regulator. This was before I bought a BOV (Bailout Valve). I won't be diving without one ever again. Over the next few hours, Simon stayed beside me in support, doing all he could.

He communicated with the surface support team, making preparations for when we were on the surface. During this time, I had worked out the best thing to alleviate the discomfort, by keeping my eyes closed and making a 'V' with my fins with the shot line in between them.

I had to check my deco status regularly, so I would open one eye very slightly to see my computer deco time remaining. As soon as I opened my eye, the spinning increased 100-fold. At one point I thought I was upside down and proceeded to push my legs down (they were of course still in their original position).

Massive cramping occurred in both my legs from straining my muscles for so long.

That was the worst part. It felt like ten million daggers being plunged deep into my tissues. Those were probably the longest three hours of my life.

The most essential component of any expedition of this type is the support team; without skilled people acting immediately to resolve problems, fatalities can occur. There is no room for error. Willy, Geoff, and Rex were amazing in their support efforts.

Thankfully, with 10-15 minutes of deco left at my last stop, things started to clear. I could open my eyes for longer now and I wasn't so dizzy anymore. My legs were still really sore though. Once I had cleared all my deco, we surfaced and got back onto the boat.

My first steps onboard the vessel brought all that lactic acid in my legs to life again and it felt like I was walking on glass!

On the way back to shore, we tried to piece together what happened to me.

Having one of the world's leading hyperbaric physicians on the dive had its advantages; Simon had my diagnosis figured out well before we surfaced.

I had suffered a case of inner ear decompression illness (DCI); pure inner ear DCI to be exact, meaning that the inner ear was the only organ affected. I had none of the other more common symptoms of DCI such as pain, tingling, or weakness.

Simon explains: "Pure inner ear DCI is a rare condition that is almost unheard of in air diving. It is well recognised in mixed gas diving, particularly when gas switches are made from mixes containing helium to mixes containing nitrogen and no helium (such as air or nitrox) during the ascent. Both Peter and I changed the diluent gas in our rebreathers from helium-rich trimix to air at the 30 m/100 ft mark during the ascent. This practice can shorten the decompression from a deep dive quite substantially (this practice is not used at all anymore, for obvious reasons, and the same diluent is used for entire dives).

No one knows for sure why the helium-to-nitrogen gas switch precipitates inner ear DCI, but there are two prevalent theories: the first focuses on the possibility that tiny helium bubbles form in the fluids of the inner ear during the ascent.

The theory suggests that these bubbles are not big enough to cause any problems on their own, but that when the change to a nitrogen-rich mix takes place, the higher number of nitrogen molecules that suddenly appear on the scene diffuse into the bubble faster than the helium molecules can diffuse out, with the net effect that the bubbles grow.

The second theory focuses on the possibility that there are no initial bubbles, but that the helium molecules diffusing out of the tissue and the nitrogen molecules diffusing in have to 'pass each other' on their journey (for want of a better way of putting it). This potentially causes a transient local gas supersaturation in the area, particularly if the passage of the molecules in each direction is impeded by a natural diffusion barrier (for which there are several membrane candidates in the inner ear).

Pure inner ear DCI in mixed gas diving appears to be a fundamentally random event, and the frightening thing is that almost all cases occur in divers who have completed (or are completing) uncomplicated dives where there has been no breach of ascent rates or table/computer decompression prescriptions.

In Pete's case, he was lucky because it was only the balance organ of his ear that was affected. In some cases the hearing mechanism can also be affected. Pete was treated at the Auckland Navy Hospital, and made a complete recovery."

This experience demonstrates that you can plan an expedition, be methodical in your planning, factor-in foreseeable contingencies, have backup plans and emergency procedures in place, execute the dive with precision, and still have problems.

This is the nature of this extreme sport. Hence, a dive of two halves. The first half was the biggest blast a technical diver could ever wish to experience.

The second was a blast of a less pleasant sort, but one that we will just have to chalk up to experience. Next expedition we will be doing more exploration and uncover more data on the ship's state.

Pete Mesley has been full time in the diving industry since 1993. His main passion is in deep wreck exploration and he is one of the Southern Hemisphere's most experienced Technical Instructor Trainers and divers, holding the highest levels of Instructor ratings in PADI and TDI.

He has led countless deep wreck expeditions, finding, diving, photographing, and documenting them. He has been on numerous expeditions to HMHS Britannic. Pete owns and operates Lust4Rust and ShocknAwe Big Animal Diving Excursions, leading trips to over 28 different countries and specialising in remote location technical diving.

Pete is a Member of the coveted Explorers Club and has assisted on numerous scientific papers, which have been published in noted medical journals.

His award winning underwater imagery is globally recognised.

PHIL SHORT

FRGS
DIVE INDUSTRY CONSULTANT
DARK WATER EXPLORATION LTD DIRECTOR

LOCATION OF INCIDENT
SOMERSET – UK

On the Mendip Hills in Somerset beneath a country village named Priddy lies a labyrinth of subterranean passages known as Swildon's Hole. In a field just outside of the village a small stream enters a strange-looking stone folly and disappears, not to be seen again before emerging at the birthplace of cave diving: Wookey Hole.

On October 4, 1936, Jack Sheppard, using a 'homemade' diving apparatus, passed the first flooded section of Swildon's labyrinth, Sump 1, reaching the stream of Swildon's 2. From there over the next 29 years teams of cavers and cave divers, he explored the cave, passing Sumps 2-11 and eventually arrived at Sump 12.

First dived in 1965 by Drew, Savage, and Wooding, Sump 12 is a remote 2.8 km/1.7 mi. in through the twisting maze of passages. Believed to be the final sump blocking progress to Wookey Hole, this forbidding pool of brown water taking the entire Swildon's stream has remained the end of the cave to-date. This is the story of one dive in one team's attempts to pass Sump 12.

Sitting in the warm common room of the Wessex Caving Club one winter evening, I was talking to some of the old legends of Mendip caving; I wanted to start up a project to dive and attempt to pass Sump 12. After much scoffing and some rather rum comments the conversation turned more productive, and late into the night a plan was hatched.

This would be a long-haul project to try to reduce the unknown distance between the end of Swildon's Hole, Sump 12, and the known end of Wookey Hole, Chamber 25. My regular caving and sump-diving friends at the time, Greg Brock and Andy Stewart, agreed to join me.

Photos by Gavin Newman

There was of course a reason why no progress had been made in Sump 12 for nearly 30 years; the sump was blocked with river debris washed into the pool over thousands of years, blocked with gravel, sand, mud and rocks, all of which the Swildon stream flowed through on its journey to Wookey. Now, in cave exploration, two of the more extreme methods of 'finding the way on' are of course firstly, cave diving, and secondly excavation (digging). The concept of doing both at the same time—digging during a cave dive—was thought by many to be bordering on insanity.

With that said, digging is fairly popular among the community of caving clubs in the Mendip Hills; there are tens of digs all over the region, some of which have, over time, broken through to some of the longest, largest, and most decorated cave passages in the region. The process is to follow natural, small, blocked cave passage to the cave beyond, normally by following the water flow or the draught of air. On Mendip, teams compete for the longest section of new cave found in a dig each year, the prize being a barrel of local beer, most likely as a pain killer for the process of digging.

So in late 2000, Andy, Greg, and I took our first trip down to sump 12 with lightweight kit as a recon to test the water, so to speak. The journey involved dry caving, which can be crawling, squeezing, climbing up and down, sometimes swimming, and cave diving, or more accurately in this type of cave, sump diving. Sump diving is better described as caving underwater rather than diving in a cave and is built on a long-earned background of caving rather than diving. Mostly it's very unpleasant with limited or no visibility or space.

With a couple of 3L cylinders on a belt, wetsuit, mask, hood, and welly boots, it took us around two hours to cave and dive our way to Sump 12. Once there I made a recon dive in the terminal sump to confirm the dive reports of previous explorers, descending a low, sloping passage where the ceiling met the gravel floor and blocked our way forward. We knew that to progress any further we would have to dig underwater to remove this gravel, so we spent the rest of our time in the dry passages of Swildon's 12 looking for a suitable place to dispose of the spoil and then set off for home with a plan.

The next three years saw us visiting Swildon's 12 most weekends to work as a three-man team, one member diving and using an old frying pan to scoop gravel into a plastic drum until full, then pulling three times on an attached loop of line, the second teammate hauling the full drum to the surface and replacing the full with an empty and the third member of the team emptying the full drums into a 1000 kilogram heavy duty plastic sand bag on a ledge above the stream.

On average, each trip allowed us to move nine drums of debris from the sump. Eventually, this slow, painful and cold progress allowed us to reach a low arch with space beyond, too small to pass but seemingly the elbow of the sump with the passage appearing to ascend on the other side.

A few weeks later, neither Greg nor Andy were free, so I and a friend, Mike Thomas, took a walk across the fields. He helped to carry my gear, and I bid him farewell at the blockhouse and took a nice solo trip down to Sump 12 to check out the condition of the Squeeze.

Once I entered Sump 12, I moved fast and alone, hoping to beat the disturbed water and have some visibility as I neared the elbow. The plan worked! For the first time ever I was able to follow the guide-line by sight to the lowest point of the sump and saw an open black space between the rock ceiling and the gravel floor.

I rolled onto my back and with one arm forward I pushed my way through the opening. All visibility was lost, my chest was tight to the roof, my back and both sides were tight to the gravel but my upper body was now past the restriction!

I was in open new cave passage that was heading up!

My heart raced a moment before I calmed it at the thought that just maybe above and ahead of me lay that elusive Swildon's 13.

Then boom! My body was like a cork that had stopped the water flow through the hole - and that water flow was the only thing holding back a huge debris pile of gravel and rocks beyond the elbow. With no flow, the pile promptly collapsed onto and around me, I was buried, and worse my next breath was water!

I managed to roll over in the loose, collapsed gravel, locate my backup regulator, and take a breath of part air, part water, and some small stones. I blew out hard to clear it all, and the next breath fed my burning lungs.

I tried to back out, but the rocks were locked around me. The only remaining option was to push forward away from home and into loose gravel, then try to turn when I could, and finally dig my way back like a mole through the elbow, in the dark, in zero visibility, with one functioning regulator. To cap it all off, I had also managed to lose my mask somewhere in the fight.

Eventually, I pushed through the gravel-filled squeeze and ascended to the surface of Swildon's 12. Once I had calmed down a bit, I realised that my lost mask was pulled from my face but luckily was still hanging by its strap from my helmet.

Less fortunately, I also discovered that the failed primary regulator had in fact been sheared off at the first stage by the rock fall, thus draining all that cylinder's gas.

The next two hours saw a cautious journey out with a single working cylinder, through some dives, some free dives, and some bypasses to reach the exit, then a walk across the fields in the dark, and finally arriving back very shaken at the Caving Club hut to tell my close call tale to Mike over a large whisky.

After talking with a local digging and caving legend, Tony Jarratt, and others in the community, it was decided the safest way to proceed would be to place an explosive charge in the roof of the elbow to enlarge the hole; this would of course block the passage with 'Bang Debris' again, but once cleared it would leave a safer, roomier way to pass the elbow to what lay tantalizingly beyond!

So Greg, Andy, and I, along with Cave Diving photographer Gavin Newman, set off with all the required equipment to proceed with this plan.

We carefully placed the detonator into the charge, and then I carried it down to the squeeze with the detonation cord being spooled out behind me, base-fed by Greg.

Once there, I wedged the charge into the roof and filled a sand bag with gravel to tamp it in place. I carefully followed the detonation cord back to the surface, and once we were all clear of the water, we set off the charge to a thunderous explosion, a spout of water from the sump, and ultimately a cloud of rising fumes, which prompted a quick retreat to the surface.

Over the next few months, we cleared the debris formed by the charge, enabling us to pass the 'Squeeze' and elbow and ascend the far side, sadly just to link into an even smaller and more remote pool—Sump 12 A—in October 2004.

Our three years of work had gleaned new knowledge of the complex Hydrogeology of the Swildon's 12 area but had not provided the elusive way into the hoped for Swildon's 13 and the route to Wookey Hole.

Phil Short *started diving in 1990 from a background of dry caving and climbing and at first only completed an Open Water Diver course in order to use SCUBA to pass short flooded sections of dry caves in Mendip and South Wales. At this time, Phil became a member of the British Cave Diving Group and has remained so ever since. In 1993, he was involved in forming one of the first Trimix wreck-diving teams in the UK. He is now one of the world's foremost IANTD IT Trainers, in addition to being a member of the IANTD HQ Board of Advisors. He was appointed the Training director of IANTD UK by Tom Mount in 2011.*

Over the years, Phil has been involved in film projects for ITV, BBC, Discovery, Nova, and Channel 4, covering the M1 submarine, the shipwrecks from the battle of Jutland and cave diving projects in Northern Spain (The Road to Certain Death) and the UK (Secret Underground), the BBC series "Oceans", the Movie "Sanctum", a Discovery "Curiosity" series documentary on the J2 Cave Project, and a documentary on the location and recovery of a WWII pilot from a downed B-24 Bomber off Vis in Croatia. As an educator, Phil has trained divers from groups such as the HSE, BBC, police dive teams, DSTL, NOAA, the US National Parks Service, Woods Hole Oceanographic Institute, and the archaeological team from the National Museum of China.

Phil completed a three-month expedition with Bill Stone to the mountains of Southern Mexico where he spent 45 days underground in three exploratory trips of 19, 5, and 21 days caving and diving to extend the J2/Last Bash cave system to over 8 km/4.9 mi. in length and 1.2 km/0.7 mi. of depth passing sump 4 at 500 m/1650 ft of length in 2013. Phil has logged over 6000 dives in caves and open water, with over 4000 dive hours on rebreather. He is currently the owner of Dark Water Exploration Ltd. and Diving Operations Manager/Diving Safety Officer for Lund University. He is a Fellow of the Royal Geographical Society (FRGS) and a Fellow of the Explorers Club, holds the NSS-CDS Sheck Exley 1000 safe cave dives award, and was Diver of the Conference at Tek Dive USA 2016.

RANDY THORNTON

CAVE DIVER/INSTRUCTOR TRAINER/EXPLORER/
DIVE EQUIPMENT DESIGNER

LOCATION OF INCIDENT
PEACOCK SPRINGS, FLORIDA, U.S.A.

In keeping with my philosophy that all divers (including manufacturers and instructor trainers) should be willing to admit when they screwed up, I share the following event which happened to me last year, while teaching a CCR Cave course at Peacock Springs.

My hope is that the consequences of the lack of maintenance on my personal CCR unit can somehow be a motivation for others to not follow suit.

As is my usual practice, I had prepped my unit the night before, including scrubber fill, cylinder top offs, battery charging, leak tests, flapper valve tests, checked my calibration, etc. Everything looked 100% good to go. Upon arriving at the dive site the next morning, I placed my CCR on the tailgate of my truck and proceeded to go through my secondary checklist prior to dressing for the dive—checking my O_2 cells, checking O_2 and dil pressures, pulling a negative and a positive, etc. As part of my secondary checklist, I turned on my O_2 gas. Strangely, I could hear what sounded like a small leak escaping from somewhere in the vicinity of the O_2 first stage. I put my fingers down there to see if I could feel precisely where the leak was coming from; I thought I could feel it, but couldn't identify the exact location.

At that point, I decided that I needed to remove the reg from the tank valve so I could inspect it more closely. In order to do so, I needed to depressurise the lines, so I pushed the O_2 manual add valve to relieve the pressure.

That's when it happened! Kaboom!

The noise was incredible and at first I wasn't sure if all of my body parts were still intact.

After I got my wits about me, I sprinted away from my unit in fear that perhaps the tank was going to blow or even worse, perhaps my truck might go up in flames! After a quick inventory of my body parts, I seemed to be no worse for wear, other than a burned finger that was now black and had Delrin embedded in its skin!

After several minutes of dealing with the shock of an explosion in my proximity, I started to investigate what had happened.

Upon closer examination of my unit, I discovered that the O_2 MAV had exploded, the button was missing, and it had melted both inside and (partially) outside.

The hoses on that side of my unit were also melted, including braided hoses, which surprised me greatly. Pieces of metal hose fittings were exploded and missing.

My entire unit was covered in soot. It basically looked like someone had briefly tossed it into a campfire!

The O_2 SPG was burned up, the T-piece was destroyed.

On consideration, one of the first things I noticed was that my O_2 first stage did not have an OPV attached; I'm guessing that, sometime during the past year, it must have started leaking at a dive site, so I had removed and plugged it.

I honestly don't remember when this would have happened, but a quick inventory of five other CCR instructors who were in the vicinity showed that none of them had an OPV currently attached to their O_2 first stage either, for exactly the same reason.

Go figure!

Also, when checking my positive pressure on the unit, I had filled my counter-lungs with O_2. In hindsight, this was really dumb, as it undoubtedly contributed to the volume of O_2 in my loop, which most certainly was above ambient pressure due to the suspected IP creep on my first stage.

Speaking of IP creep, the brand of first stage on my unit had a history of faulty seats throughout the previous year, and we had seen numerous regs fail with IP creep. Of course, this should not be catastrophic, provided that there is an OPV on the line somewhere.

Lastly, perhaps most importantly, and quite honestly most embarrassingly. I had not serviced my MAV in two or three years. The SubGravity owner's manual states specifically that the MAVs should be cleaned and serviced a minimum of once per year or more often as needed.

Apparently, I don't listen very well!

Fortunately, the only serious injury was to my unit and to my pride. It's always fun to have an explosion with half the cave diving world in the immediate vicinity and have them come running to see if you are still alive.

Since my head was on the backside of the canister and away from my MAV, it was protected from the blast. I had a finger which was burned and stained black from Delrin in my skin, but other than the ringing in my ears, there was no serious injury to me personally.

Fortunately, as per my pre-dive protocols, I was not wearing my unit at the time I turned it on! I am grateful that it was not more serious; it very easily could have been.

So, in keeping with my personal philosophy of sharing my screw-ups so that others might learn from them, please be diligent about the following points:

1. *Service and maintain your equipment on a regular basis according to the manufacturers' recommendations.*

2. *Replace all broken or missing parts immediately, without fail.*

3. *Don't over inflate your counter-lungs with O_2.*

4. *Turn on your gas before donning your CCR.*

5. *Treat O_2 with extreme caution! It can and will create quite a mess.*

Please feel free to chastise me, although I guarantee that you cannot possibly do so more stringently than I have already done to myself.

Randy Thornton *is an SDI/TDI Instructor Trainer Evaluator and a member of the TDI Training Advisory Panel.*

As a CCR Advanced Trimix IT as well as a CCR Cave IT, Randy has trained divers and instructors in numerous locations around the world. His real passion is cave and wreck diving, and he can be found on various expeditions and projects throughout the year.

Randy is a co-owner of SubGravity, a manufacturer of high-quality, technical diving equipment. He is also owner of Dive Addicts, a retail dive shop and training center in Utah, and is a partner in TEKDiveUSA, the premier technical diving conference in the USA.

RICHARD HARRIS

UNDERWATER CINEMATOGRAPHER
CAVE EXPLORER / SPEAKER / DIVING PHYSICIAN

LOCATION OF INCIDENT:
PEARSE RESURGENCE, NEW ZEALAND

I have lost count of the close calls, the near misses, the "oh shit" moments whilst diving, and yet here I am to tell the tale.

I sometimes wonder why I have survived thus far when friends have not; it is hard to spend a lifetime underwater without mishaps.

Maybe the same applies to everyone who has been diving for many years, or maybe I am just accident prone! Either way, the ability to problem-solve is key to survival in this environment.

Sometimes an issue arises and you have an hour to resolve it, but equally sometimes the prospect of breathing water is only moments away. The important thing is that every mishap is an opportunity to learn and develop as a diver. Make mistakes, but never make the same mistake twice.

Most importantly, become more resilient to the greatest hazard any diver will face: panic. I am convinced 100% of divers will panic in those final moments when they realise there is no escape, but panic in-and-of itself can prove fatal. The ability to hold panic at bay and continue rational thought is a strong defense against a lethal accident; so long as you are working to find a solution, there may still be a chance. To be fair, everyone has a different threshold for when that panic will inevitably arise, but it is by building experience and gradually pushing your limits that you will help yourself most when your test comes.

Despite these wise words, it can all come unstuck in a very short period of time. In 2012, I was diving in the Pearse Resurgence. The Pearse is a formidable cave, currently 245 m/803 ft deep and just 6 C/42.8 F. The hard marble walls are very dark, absorbing much

of your light and making the place rather intimidating when first dived.

Our team uses four separate habitats staged at increasing depths, so that we can get out of the water to decompress as early as possible. The first week of any trip is occupied by installing the habitats, communications, heater cables, and other paraphernalia to support the very long dives.

Setting up the habitats has become pretty routine. The deepest one goes in first at 40 m/131 ft. We use intermediate bulk containers (IBCs) for these, inflated with air and with seats in the corners for the diver to sit on. These dives serve as excellent refreshers to reaccustom ourselves to the very bulky undersuits and dry gloves that severely restrict mobility and dexterity.

On the dive in question, my buddy and I floated the habitat down to 40 m/131 ft and clipped the corner ropes to the pre-installed climbing bolts and hangers. From there, the plan was to release a small amount of air into the IBC to get it off the ground, so that we could start to level it prior to full inflation.

I was diving my rEVO CCR with a single 11L aluminum bailout tank on this occasion. Normally we would use a separate cylinder without a regulator to inflate the habitat, but because I was only planning on putting a very small amount of gas into it, I decided to give it a quick squirt from my bailout regulator.

My bailout cylinder was configured to supply my BOV through a quick disconnect. The ADV on the rEVO had been playing up a little and needed some adjustment to get right. That would become a factor very shortly. I swam around to the opening of the habitat which was lying on its side with the mouth against the cave wall.

I had to squeeze between it and the cave to get into position, with me lying on my right-hand side. I pulled the reg off the cylinder and purged some gas into the habitat. It had the desired effect and the IBC started to lift.

However, in the 6 C/42.8 F water, the second stage immediately froze on and my gas continued to flow uncontrollably out of the cylinder, pulling the habitat up and destroying the visibility in the immediate area.

Photo by Simon Mitchell

Unconcerned, I reached to the cylinder valve and shut it down. I must have sunk down to some degree because my loop had bottomed out and I didn't have enough gas in the unit to inhale sufficiently. The ADV decided not to work at all at that point, so I reached to my right shoulder to use my manual (diluent) add valve (MAV).

The block on the rEVO is a fantastic bit of kit; large and it's easy to discriminate the O₂ and diluent add buttons. If you can find it, that is. In my haste to set up my unit and get diving, I had failed to secure the MAV to my right shoulder, and it had fallen to the side whilst I was lying next to the IBC. My need to breathe was starting to become a priority at this stage, so I flipped my BOV to open circuit, still sinking down the steep shaft and further from the help of my buddy.

A single bailout cylinder supplying the BOV is not helpful when it is shut off. Getting close to desperation now, I suddenly realised I was in genuine trouble and had about 20 second before I'd be breathing water. Panic was only moments away. In a heartbeat, I had gone from fun to terror. I was 45 m/147 ft under water, and nearly 100 m/328 ft from the entrance.

I launched myself up the wall hand-over-hand towards my buddy seeking a second stage. I remember flipping back to the loop hoping the ascent would be enough to expand the loop and give me another partial breath. As I reached him, I recalled in horror that he was going through his "no second stage phase", preferring the simplicity of QDs and relying on his BOV. I gave him the out of air signal knowing full well there was nothing he could do to help me.

I will never forget that feeling of thinking, "What a stupid way to die." I actually cannot remember exactly how I resolved this, to be here to tell the tale. I think I tried the cylinder again but it still free flowed. I must have gotten a partial breath from the loop to give me another moment's grace. I remember my buddy passing me the MAV after I signaled to

it, and then sitting quietly for a few minutes regaining my composure. I don't think he ever realised how bad the situation had been.

It was pretty clear to me how the issue arose: pure complacency on my part.

A shallow working dive compared to the exploration dives ahead had promoted a casual attitude. A harness not yet set up properly for the thick undersuits, and the position of the MAV unsecured. Straying from my plan to use the extra cylinder for IBC inflation. No shutoff on the second stage for cold water diving, and no second bailout. I can't blame my buddy for not having a second stage. I should have been self-sufficient.

Dr Richard "Harry" Harris *is an Australian technical diver and underwater image maker. He started diving in 1979 and became serious about technical diving in 2000.*

A rebreather enthusiast, he has owned and dived a variety of backmount, side mount, front mount, manual and electronic units including some very dodgy homemade ones.

Harry has a particular interest in deep exploration and primarily enjoys exploring caves, although he can be tempted out for 'special' wreck dives. The wreck of the SS Ventnor (150 m/492 ft), Song Hong Cave, Thailand (196 m/643 ft), Daxing Spring, China (213 m/698 ft) and the Pearse Resurgence, NZ (245 m/803 ft) have been recent projects. Harry works as an anaesthetist and has experience in diving, pre-hospital and remote area medicine. He is notable for his involvement in the 2018 Thai cave rescue.

RICHARD STEVENSON

WRECK / CAVE DIVER
UNDERWATER CAMERA OPERATOR

LOCATION OF INCIDENT
RMS CARPATHIA, NORTH ATLANTIC

I've only ever had one true close call, but it was close enough to make me sure I never wanted another one.

My close call takes me back to 2007, when a group of us were exploring the wreck of the Carpathia alongside Comex, who were carrying out artefact recoveries on the shipwreck. RMS *Carpathia* was the rescue ship to the Titanic but was sunk by U-55 later on in its life, and now lies in 158 m/518 ft depth, some 321 km/200 miles offshore in the North Atlantic.

Four of us had first dived the wreck in 2001; the object of the 2007 expedition was to work with Comex and try to get some videography of the shipwreck itself. Not many camera housings would take such depth back then, and most of ours failed on the dives.

With that said, we were there primarily to explore the shipwreck; she was largely intact and sitting upright but with her main decks collapsing down into the bowels of the ship itself. Jumping in one morning saw me descending through clear blue water, making my way to the bottom of the shot line which was fixed just in front of the bridge area. Today I was diving on my own, and my plan was to scooter around the length of the wreck, as I'd never seen the stern.

Deco soon racks up at 150 m/492 ft, and when I reached the stern, a quick glance at my tables showed I was behind schedule and racking up quite some deco. I decided to start the journey back but ascended some 10 m/33 ft above the wreck to try and save some deco time, not that it made a huge difference!

I set off in the direction of the shot, keeping an eye on the wreck below and glancing ahead of me to try and spot the line and strobes.

I was using a Silent Submersion UV18 DPV, as they could take the depth, and mine had a locking throttle screw which meant I didn't have to depress the trigger for the whole duration. Anyone who has dived in cold water knows how this makes a huge difference to not getting cold fingers!

I settled in behind the DPV and started my journey back; locking the throttle trigger would soon prove to be my undoing. Halfway along the wreck, I strained my neck upwards to look for the shotline; as I looked upwards the loop caught the onward rush of water and was ripped straight out of my mouth, ending-up behind my head. Instant confusion was quickly replaced with an understanding of the situation, but as my natural instinct was to reach behind and grab the loop I forgot the DPV was still towing me along at full speed some 10 m/33 ft above the wreck.

As I fumbled around to grab the loop I let go of the DPV, which promptly started to head downwards towards the seabed some 10 m below me. I decided breathing was better than hitting the seabed, so as I plummeted towards the sand, I continued to grab for the loop.

As this was unfolding, I realised I still had the mouthpiece between my teeth; it quickly became apparent that the zip-tie had given way, and the whole loop had pulled out, leaving the rubber grip still in my mouth. It would have been quite a comical sight and one that we all might have laughed about afterwards, but it didn't seem quite so funny at that moment. Hitting the sand, I simultaneously hit the boss on the DPV prop which de-pitched the propeller and stopped the forward motion of the DPV; thanks to Rodney Nairn for explaining that feature many years ago!

I then closed the mouthpiece on the loop and took a few breaths from my bailout cylinder. I felt I was getting back in control then. I undid the trigger on the DPV and regained some composure.

All I had to do was refit the silicon mouthpiece onto the loop and clear the water from the front-mounted counterlungs; fortunately the CCR I was diving had a water purge valve which made this possible. I gingerly scootered back to the shotline at 1) a much lower speed and 2) holding the loop firmly in place with my hand.

After quite some deco, I was very happy to be back on board the boat! As you'd imagine, the next day there was much activity on deck with the team carefully checking their mouthpiece cable ties.

Richard Stevenson *has been diving professionally and managing marine operations since 1997, during which he experienced all aspects of underwater TV and film production; it's this experience that he prides himself on bringing to a shoot, however large or small.*

Rich is an IANTD Rebreather Instructor and Instructor trainer, IANTD Rebreather Cave diving instructor (also valid for wreck and ice-diving environments), MCA commercially-endorsed boat skipper – 32 km/20 miles offshore for vessels up to 24 m/78 ft in length, CAA UAV (drone) pilot – owner/operator–used for flying and operating from boats, HSE First-Aid at Work certified with remote location add-on training.

He also runs a small bespoke company called Waterproof Media Ltd, which focuses on dry hire of underwater equipment. Waterproof Media Limited is named on the BBC and ITV approved diving contractor's list, and has been independently vetted by 1st Option Safety services in London, details of which can be provided.

The company operates as a dry hire business for underwater filmmaking and provides the insurances and liabilities required by production when filming on or under the water.

RICHIE KOHLER

PROFESSIONAL SHIPWRECK EXPLORER / DOCUMENTARY
FILM MAKER & AUTHOR

LOCATION OF INCIDENT
NORTH ATLANTIC OCEAN / WRECK OF THE ANDREA DORIA

In 1985, I received Captain Steve Bielenda's call inviting me on his next Doria expedition.

How could I say no?

Every dive I had made before paled in comparison, and the only way to get on this expedition was to be personally invited. I thanked Steve for the opportunity but knew that the person responsible was Pete Guglierie, the unofficial leader (or "Emperor for Life") of the 'Atlantic Wreck Divers'. I was the youngest member, and Pete had taken the 'greenhorn' under his wing, teaching me the ropes about deep wreck diving. Pete had called Bielenda and told him I was ready to dive the Doria.

When the Wahoo finally headed out of Fire Island inlet for the all night journey to the wreck, the enormity of the dive really sank in, and the pre-dive jitters in my head turned to a palpable fear.

I was painfully aware that in the handful of Doria expeditions to-date, two men had died inside the wreck. During the long motor out, a few of the divers stayed up late huddled over deck plans, studying the interior of the Andrea Doria and planning their dives. Pete made it clear that, on my first dive, I was not to go inside the wreck nor deeper than 60 m/200 ft. I went to bed nervous, and sleep did not come easily that night; the following morning, when it was time to dive, I could barely muster enough spit to clear my mask.

The current tugged at me the whole of the way down, and soon I could see strobes flashing below me in the darkness.

Photos by Richie Kohler

I was almost on top of the wreck before dark shapes came into view, macabre shadows dancing in the strobes' stabbing lights.

Once my eyes adjusted, I saw that the grapple was secured to a stanchion on the promenade deck. All the upper decks were to my right, like layers of a cake, but the view to my left was flat and featureless; with the occasional anemone or starfish, it looked more like the seafloor than the side of a ship. Only by looking carefully could one see the outlines of closed portholes, aligned in rows and disappearing into the murk. I smiled as my hand touched the hull, "I made it!"

Dropping into the promenade to get out of the current, I noticed the wood grain on the teak-lined deck, now a wall, as green ambient light filtered down through the open window frames. After a few minutes exploring here, I headed back up and noticed another diver's penetration line leading forward.

Following the white line into the current, porthole after closed porthole appeared in my light when suddenly the line disappeared into the wreck. I grabbed onto the edge of Gimbel's Hole, held myself steady and peered down into the Doria. The blackness was complete and soaked up my light like sponge. I turned around and headed back up to do my deco.

On my second dive, Pete would take me inside, but first he detailed the dive plan step-by-step. Dropping into Gimbel's Hole, we would face aft and swim at an angle to 65 m/210 ft, keeping our buoyancy trimmed. Pete reminded me to stay close to what had been the ship's floor (now the right wall) and watch out for cables hanging down on the left, (near to what was originally the ceiling).

When we got to the china cabinets, we would turn around and face the exit. My left hand was to stay on the wall at all times and my right hand on his harness – "and do not let go!"

Once Pete started digging, the visibility would be gone. My hand on the wall would prevent us getting turned around and swimming through the swirling murk headlong into the cables or the wrong way into the cavernous expanse of the dining room further aft. My head was full as we quickly descended the anchor line for my first dive inside the Andrea Doria.

My pulse quickened as Pete's dive plan played out in real time. Down we went, through Gimbel's Hole and headed aft, the long snaking cables seeming to stare back at me, almost moving in our lights. They'd killed a man, ensnaring and holding him trapped here until he ran out of air.

Continuing slowly into the wreck, side by side, we soon came across the disturbed area where divers had previously found china. The easy pickings were gone; now you had to root through broken shards, silt and junk to find anything. Pete turned around; then I followed suit before settling down to work. Hooking my right hand under his harness, I gave a tug to say "I got you." Soon, swirling mud and silt filled the water as Pete probed through the mélange of mud and debris.

With little to do or see, narcosis slowly ebbed into my brain, so I focused on keeping one hand on Pete and the other on the wall.

Soon the rhythmic sound of our exhaust bubbles was interrupted by the unmistakable clink of china being stuffed into the bag and Pete giggling through his regulator.

Hearing him laugh put my rising anxiety at ease.

My light was switched on and secured to my chest harness, but almost useless in the swirling maelstrom of silt. In the few inches of visibility below me, my light reflected off something and as I dropped closer, I could see a plate and read the 'Italia' signature on the rim. Pete kept crabbing along, and we would soon move past this dish.

Without thinking about it, I let go of the wall and grabbed it.

I tugged hard on Pete and waved the dish where his head should be in the mud-stained water. I thought he would take it and put it in the bag, but instead I felt him tense up and stop cold. Through the darkness he yelled "the wall, the wall?" through his regulator and the urgency in his voice jarred me.

Alarmed, I dropped the dish like a hot coal and swung my hand back into the wall.

Edging closer and swinging his arm in the near zero viz, he asked again for the wall, so letting go of his harness, I brought his hand on top of mine, patting it and assuring him I did have the wall.

His head was now so close I could see his eyes large in his mask. Pete was scared.

Grabbing me hard by the arm, he said, "let's get out of here". He counted on me, and I screwed it up, and now we were aborting the dive. Swimming out of the huge silt cloud we created, we searched for the pale green light filtered down through Gimbel's Hole and followed it out.

During the ascent, the few seconds where we made eye contact spoke volumes. He wasn't angry, but disappointed. The decompression seemed much longer than it was. Once aboard the Wahoo, other divers congratulated me on my first dive inside and took pictures with the dishes Pete had bagged. Pete didn't say a word about what happened.

After dinner he pulled me aside on the back of the boat and asked. "What were you thinking man…Don't you realize what could've happened?" His eyes looked at me with the same sense of fear and urgency as they had in the wreck.

I didn't answer right away, but held his gaze. "Yeah, I lost my focus down there and could've gotten us both killed for a dish.

It won't happen again," I replied.

Pete turned, stared out at the darkening sky for a moment and without looking back said, "You learned your lesson, and I know you'll do better tomorrow—you just went to school."

Richie Kohler *is an author and shipwreck explorer whose 40 years of underwater research and shipwreck exploration have taken him to all corners of the globe.*

Detailed in documentary films and in the NY Times best-selling book Divers, by Robert Kurson, Kohler's diving adventures have inspired new generations of divers to explore the underwater world.

Working both in front of and behind the camera, Richie Kohler has reached an international audience, having hosted fifty-six episodes of "Deep Sea Detectives" for the History Channel, and numerous other documentary films on networks such as National Geographic, Discovery, Animal Planet, the BBC, Smithsonian and NOVA/PBS.

These educational and entertaining programs have detailed his exploits and discoveries on some of the most famous shipwrecks in the world, including the Andrea Doria, RMS Titanic, and the HMHS Britannic.

Working alongside some of the most talented filmmakers and screenwriters of our time, Kohler has consulted with major film studios such as Twentieth Century Fox, Paramount and Universal Studies on major motion picture projects and scripts, helping to promote recreational scuba diving and the world of underwater exploration.

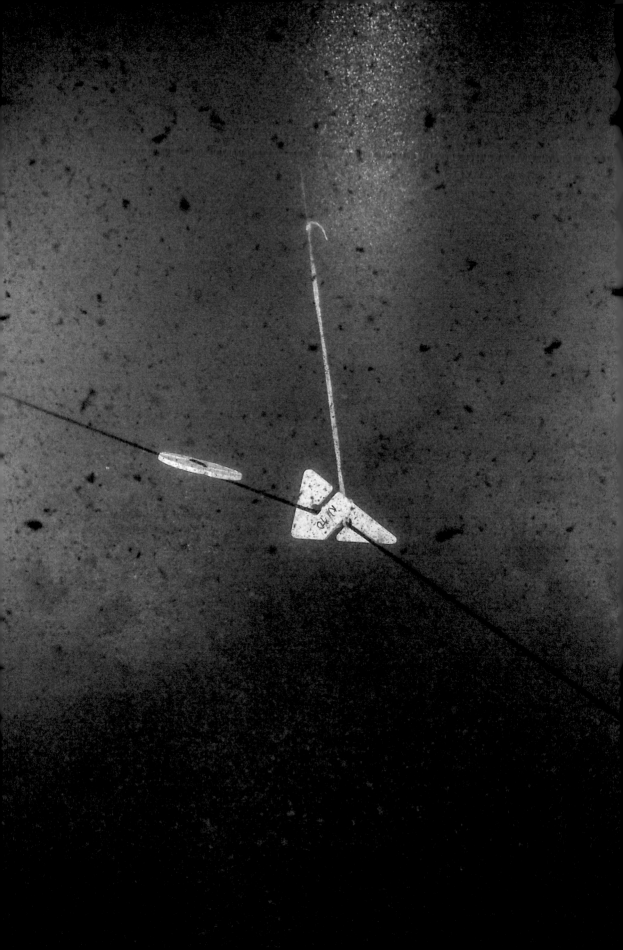

ROB NETO

UNDERWATER CAVE EXPLORER

LOCATION(S) OF INCIDENT
HOLE IN THE WALL, MARIANNA, FL, USA
CUEVA QUEBRADA, COZUMEL, MEXICO

As I swam along the line, I came across a T. The options were to continue straight or turn left. I decided to turn left. My training had taught me to mark my exit at the T but the arrow at the T pointed toward my exit, and I was alone, so what was the point? I slowly made my way past the T to the left and continued swimming along the passage, admiring the beauty of its walls and ceiling.

A few minutes later, I came across another T. The line there continued straight, with another line heading off to the right. I pictured the map of this area in my mind and decided to head right. Again, the arrow was pointing toward my exit, so I neglected to leave a personal marker. This went on for another couple of Ts before I finally came to a T with the arrow pointing away from the way I had come. This made me pause for a moment.

The passage looked familiar.

I thought it might be the first T I had come across several minutes earlier. But what if I was wrong? Should I continue and hope for the best or turn around and retrace my path?

Of course I decided to turn at that point, but before turning, I placed a clothes-pin on the arrow so that, if I did come back across it, I could confirm where I had been. As I swam back, I began scolding myself for not leaving personal markers.

I approached the last T I had passed and found myself questioning if the arrow was pointing the way I had come or if I had made a mistake in navigation or even missed a T along the way. I decided to follow the arrow and continue down the passage.

Photos by Laurent Miroult

With every fin-stroke, the doubt continued to grow. Why hadn't I marked the Ts on the way in? My training had taught me to do that.

Why did I think it was okay to ignore that training? The next T brought even more doubt and concern with it. I was no longer admiring the passage and enjoying the dive. Looking at the passage only caused more doubt, because it didn't look familiar. I reminded myself of my training and being told that referencing behind you as you progress is important because the passage looks different exiting than it does entering. That was another mistake. I continued to push on, hoping I had not screwed up even more.

As I came around another corner, I saw another T in the distance. This one looked like it had a clothes-pin on it. It could be the T I had turned the dive on, or it could just be an old clothes-pin left behind by another diver. I would have to wait to get closer to verify that. Even if it was my clothes-pin, all it would prove was that I had been at that T before, not that it was the way I had come from. Sure enough, it was my clothes-pin. If this was the first T I had come across, then I had about ten minutes of swimming before coming to my jump spool and DPV.

At least I had deployed a jump spool. Those ten minutes were the longest ten minutes I had ever experienced on a dive. Mounting fears that I had really screwed up were difficult to push back. I focused on maintaining an easy, steady breathing rate.

If this route didn't lead back to my scooter, then if I could at least follow these arrows and get to the main line, which fortunately in this Florida cave was gold, I would be able to swim out. I still had one stage cylinder with me and had sufficient gas to swim out, though it would be close. I finally came to the end of the line and saw my jump spool. At the other end, clipped onto the main line was my DPV. I had averted what could have been a really bad situation.

It would have been so easy to get lost in that cave, in an area that is a maze of interconnecting passages with arrows that point in all directions, all pointing toward the exit, but not always your exit or the best exit route, and definitely not a continuous guideline to the way out.

If I had not been able to remain calm and keep my breathing controlled, it could have turned into a very bad situation.

There were a few times during the return that I noticed my breathing rate increasing. Each time, I had to take a moment to focus on it and keep it under control. The more gas I had, the more time I would have to deal with the possibility that I might be lost.

After that dive, I never again went past a T or jump without leaving a personal, non-directional marker indicating my exit route. Better to carry 20-30 markers than to risk making a navigational decision in a maze of passages. I've also made sure to either visually confirm every centimetre of line in passages I've never been in before, or to okay the line to make sure I don't pass any hidden Ts.

There are hidden Ts like that, and I've witnessed dive buddies swim right past them without seeing them. There is one such T in a cave that I have spent a substantial amount of time in, which is not only hidden behind a formation but also positioned at the halocline, making it twice as difficult to see.

On exploration dives the convention is for each diver to leave personal markers at every navigation decision since there is always the possibility of exiting separately. After one particular dive, my buddy told us he had come to a T with none of his markers on it.

The arrow was pointing the way he was swimming. Rather than turn around, he took a chance that this route would get him out. He swam a couple of minutes and came to a second T without any personal markers. Again, rather than turn around, he continued on, following the arrow. Another couple of minutes brought him to a third T. Fortunately this T also had three personal markers on it: his, mine, and one belonging to the third person on our team.

He had missed a T both on the way in and on the way out. On the way in, he was simply following me and, whilst I had placed a marker at the suspect T, it was in a halocline so he didn't see it because of the disturbance of visibility from our movement.

On the way out, the line we had come from was hidden behind a formation, so he just followed the line heading straight without noticing the T. The third person on our team did the same thing on the way out, but I was there to catch him and correct him.

He swam right past the T without noticing it. When I approached it, I saw that I was the only one who had placed a marker at this T on the way in. So the lessons that come from this are not only to always place personal markers at navigational decision points, but to also make sure to learn the line well on the way in—and be vigilant about checking areas of the line where there are formations or disturbances in the visibility.

Rob Neto *is an experienced cave diver, explorer, and surveyor. He has been diving and exploring caves for more than 15 years and was a dive instructor for over ten years.*

His current focus in diving is cave exploration and mapping, as well as travelling around the world to experience caves everywhere. When not exploring, Rob focuses on documenting underwater caves with video and as a photograph model. He has been cave diving in several countries and has ongoing exploration projects in the US, Mexico, and France, as well as assisting with a project in Italy.

He primarily dives sidemount configurations, due to the nature of his dives, but also dives SCRs and CCRs when appropriate. Rob currently lives in Greenwood, Florida, with his wife, three dogs, and three cats.

ROBERTS CULBERT &
BILL HOGARTH MAIN

CAVE CCR/TRIMIX/DPV/SIDEMOUNT
NSS-CDS GUIDE FOR ALACHUA SINK (MILL CREEK SINK)
FORT WHITE DIVE CLUB (FWDC)
KARST UNDERWATER RESEARCH (KUR) DIVERS

LOCATION OF INCIDENT
CAMP INDIAN SPRINGS, WAKULLA, FL, USA

The Dive:
Three of us prepared for a recreational dive at Camp Indian Springs cave system: myself, Bill Main and a third diver (Diver 3) from out of state. I had done numerous dives at Indian with Bill, one of our favorite sites, and he told me that several years prior, he and Diver 3 had done a few uneventful dives at the same location. The plan was to go upstream on scooters with one extra stage of bottom gas to drop along the planned route.

The third diver arrived in an older van and, as he geared up, I noticed his gear was also a few decades old with some corrosion on the outside of his back-mounted doubles. His scooter (diver propulsion vehicle) was a ride-on missile style in bright orange, reminding me of Cold-War era Soviet devices. However, he seemed confident setting up his equipment

and I was not otherwise concerned about his abilities in the water. Bill later told me that Diver 3 had quietly asked if I was "Okay to dive with." This is of course understandable for a serious cave dive with a stranger. Bill assured him I would be reliable and that we had many dives together.

The first section of the cave leading to the upstream/downstream junction had unusually low visibility from tannic rainwater intrusion. The reduced visibility made it difficult to maintain contact with each other, so we stayed close during the first moments of the dive. After dropping our oxygen and 50% decompression gas at 6 m/20 ft and 21 m/70 ft depths, we continued on scooters into the wide murky passage toward the clear water connection. By the time Bill and I had reached the three-way junction, we had lost contact with the third diver behind us in the tea-colored mud tunnel. We waited for a few minutes, assuming he would not be far behind us. Just as we were about to double back, the third diver appeared above us in the passage and broke into clear water as he continued to push forward without looking down or noticing us.

The third diver ran his scooter directly into a section of an opposing rock-wall near the ceiling, without slowing down. Bill looked at me with wide eyes and I returned the expression, somewhat delighted at the dramatic error this diver had made. We attempted to signal him with our lights, as he abandoned his scooter and grabbed onto the guideline nearby, slowly descending. He was clearly shaken, pulling the line down with him and looking dazed. He had immediately abandoned the customary horizontal swimming position that trained divers adhere to and was coming down fins-first with the line in one hand. Simultaneously, his stage began to free-flow wildly in front of him, and I looked at Bill again in shock, a mix of amusement, curiosity and concern swirling in my mind.

Bill was shaking his head, and I could see that the third diver was not attempting to stop the gas erupting in front of him. He was staring straight ahead while pulling the line down and drifting haplessly toward the floor. Bill reacted with the alertness that those fortunate enough to dive with him can verify. I had still not transitioned from enjoyment to distress, as he bolted toward the third diver's stage and stopped the free-flow by sticking his thumb into the mouthpiece. Diver 3 was looking ahead and began swimming into the clear water downstream, where a large mountain of broken limestone leads further into the cave.

Bill attempted to signal and slow him, and I could see Diver 3 was returning the same hand signals but was apparently not concerned that he had abandoned his scooter and was swimming further into the cave.

I guessed that he was embarrassed, or perhaps confused about our plan. Bill tried again to communicate, but I could see that Diver 3 was simply looking at him without understanding. I clipped off my scooter to the line and swam down to look him in the eyes. My signals to turn and exit were acknowledged in the same way, his eyes wide and staring past me. "The lights are on, but no one is home," I thought. Was he having a medical issue? He seemed out of his mind.

Diver 3 was gradually pulling up and along the pile of breakdown and heading further into the downstream section on his own personal mission. Bill and I each took another turn pulling against him, signaling to turn and exit as he stared blankly at us with no indication of understanding. We could see his increasing agitation and a continued determination to go further up the breakdown and into the cave. As the minutes passed we became deeply concerned. We were both breathing faster from the exertion and had already switched from our stages to now dwindling back gas reserves.

Bill began to pull on him again with a signal to turn around but was met by firm resistance. Again, we tried to communicate with desperation, but it had been too long at depth. We were getting light on gas. It was time to exit soon. What can we do? Bill had a desperate look in his eyes that I had never seen before. He signaled me to exit, and I went to get my scooter and turned to leave. The usual joy of diving was gone and a dark feeling was coming over me. This diver was going to die here and we couldn't help him. I had to wait for Bill. He was trying to pull on Diver 3's harness again and I could see how hard he was working.

I scootered over and grabbed the third diver's manifold, pulling hard, but he was firmly holding the limestone and pushing forward and further into the cave. I grabbed his manifold firmly again and drove my scooter in the opposite direction, reaching full power with three quick twists at the handle.

Photo by Martin Hartley

The scooter pulled as strongly as expected, but the diver wouldn't budge as my arms spread wide, his tanks in one hand and my scooter in the other. Another hard yank at his tanks, and the third diver's grip broke loose, but I was making no progress with the significant amount of drag. It is relatively easy to tow a cooperating diver, but this was a scenario for which I was entirely unprepared.

After a short distance, I was able to rotate him more in line with my body by holding him upside down behind me. Improving our positioning, I began to make slow progress toward the dark water tunnel. I pulled him sharply down to clear the ceiling at the junction and then up the other side towards the tannic water of the connecting tunnel.

The biggest challenge now was to hold on and not crash in the dark. I couldn't easily hold my light in the direction of travel with both arms locked up and I couldn't see the line. Already on his scooter, Bill quickly saw what was happening, and got in front of us with his light on the guideline. We rode close together with diver three behind us and locked in my grip. I was breathing hard and could feel my strength fade as we approached the exit.

When we got to the first set of deco bottles my burst of energy was gone, and I dropped Diver 3 behind me to catch my breath and check my gauges. I hoped he still had a regulator in his mouth, and a few minutes later, I could confirm he was still breathing. He had switched to breathing his nearby deco gas and seemed to have fully recovered his senses. Now the blank stare was gone and the remaining stops passed by as if nothing had happened. At the surface Diver 3 asked, "Where is my scooter?" He seemed to have limited memory of what had happened.

Later, as we ate our lunch quietly, we casually asked Diver 3 what he had been thinking, and were surprised when he said, "I thought I was at the entrance." He had somehow become lost in his mind, unaware that he had scootered back nearly a thousand feet into the cave. He thought we were trying to stop him near the exit. This disconnect couldn't be explained by simple confusion; he surely must have had contaminated gas in those old tanks.

He confirmed that it had been many years since they had been filled, but we did not ask further questions, sensing that he was just happy to be out and alive. Whether he had some bad gas, suffered a minor stroke or had a mental break of some kind, we were just happy it ended well and didn't feel the need to push him for further details. Always ready to joke, Bill had one more question for Diver 3 before we left: "Well, did you think this guy was okay to dive with?"

Later Bill and I discussed what we thought had happened and came to the conclusion that Diver 3 had bad gas that left him catatonic at depth. What could we have done differently? Analyse gas for hydrocarbons or other contaminants?

We are not sure how we could have foreseen the problem or better prepared ourselves. When a fellow diver becomes disorientated, panics or has a medical issue, you need some idea of how far into your reserve gas you can go without compromising your own safety. I've heard Bill say a few times "You need to know your point-of-no-return before you get there."

Roberts Culbert *is a recreational cave and ocean diver and guides experienced cave divers at Alachua Sink (Mill Creek Sink) an NSSCDS property. He is an active member of several cave diving organizations including the Fort White Dive Club (FWDC) and Karst Underwater Research (KUR) He has been cave and ocean diving since early 2001, and has been involved in numerous cave adventures, rescues and survey-mapping projects.*

His current focus is underwater adventures in the North Florida region and guiding at local caves. He currently lives in Gainesville, Florida, with his girlfriend and three dogs and also enjoys, travel, motorcycling, freediving and surfing.

William (Bill) Hogarth Main *is a cave diving pioneer and explorer, who co-founded and developed the minimalist hogarthian gear configuration and was also a co-founder of the Woodville Karst Plain Project (WKPP).*

Bill has been cave diving since 1969, and has explored many areas of popular Florida caves and has been a crucial contributor in several well-known cave rescues. He currently lives in High Springs, Florida, with his wife Jane and continues to dive new and familiar caves, and mentor new cave divers on a regular basis.

SABINE KERKAU

CCR CAVE & WRECK DIVER / WOMEN DIVERS HALL OF
FAME MEMBER / CO-FOUNDER OF THE BALTIC SEA
HERITAGE RESCUE PROJECT

LOCATION OF INCIDENT
LAKE STARNBERGERSEE, GERMANY

Is there a dive worth losing your life for?
Risk? - To what degree? Adventure? -

At all cost? The decision is in our hands...

Ask yourself if you are ready to die for a dive—on every dive—then you will understand what it is about. Our sport takes place in a very hostile environment for humans, and we should respect it. We get a second chance for (almost) every dive, but not for life. Common sense and a realistic self-assessment of their own abilities are the most important characteristics that technical divers should possess. With proper training and a good team, almost everything is possible.

My first dives were in 1986, in the Maldives. I have been a technical diver since 2001. In all these years I have experienced and learned a lot.

Maybe I got lucky, or just had the right instincts, but I never had a serious problem where I was facing a fatal situation.

The story I am about to tell dates back to the beginning of the millennium, when I discovered a fascination with technical diving and the possibilities it presented. After 15 years of being very happy watching colourful fish in warm water, I met Mario Weidner in early 2001. Mario was one of Germany's best and most successful technical divers at the time. His fascinating stories excited me and made me decide that I wanted to do things differently. So I did a nitrox course.

At the time, nitrox courses were only offered by the few technical diving associations. This was the first time that I met active and ambitious technical divers.

Photos by Sabine Kerkau

Their world was so different from what I knew from my 'Club' diving trips to Egypt. I was dreaming; I wanted to dive the Andrea Doria, dive the Britannic and I wanted to do it all as soon as possible!

I did my training and became an Open Circuit Full Trimix diver in six months. I would have loved to put a cave course on top of it as well; I felt invincible!

Then came the day that brought me back to earth: One of my instructors whom I admired very much had been involved in many important international wreck expeditions. I therefore felt very honoured when he asked me if I wanted to go diving with him on Lake Starnberg on a Saturday afternoon. Without really thinking about it, I said, "Yes." Making this decision like that, on the spur of the moment, was to prove very nearly fatal.

That Saturday I had to work until 1 p.m. Once I got away, I made my way around Lake Starnberg to the place where I had arranged to meet my diving buddy at 3 p.m. Under normal circumstances, it takes me about an hour and a half to drive there, but that day it felt like everything was against me. This caused me enormous stress, as I definitely did not want to be late. During the drive, my buddy called me several times to inquire about where I was staying, which didn't really help to lower my stress level. I reached the dive site on time, at 2:50 p.m.

My buddy stood there, fully dressed. He didn't have to say anything, I saw that he was annoyed. I didn't want to keep him waiting any longer, so I didn't take the time to look around first, check the conditions and try to relax a bit. I started getting my scuba gear ready. I had just started when my buddy said that he would go into the water.

My stress level rose even more. Today, I would have stopped at this point and simply wished him a nice dive, but on that day I didn't. On the contrary, I hurried even more because I didn't want to keep him waiting for me.

As I rushed to the water, my equipment was not as it should be. Somehow, I didn't notice the weather conditions until I was already in the water; they were not ideal at all. It was very windy and there were waves. My buddy saw me coming and said that he would dive down and wait for me at a depth of 3 m/10 ft. I was carrying a big camera with me and was having problems with the surf, which was pulling at my fins. My brain was completely switched off. When I finally managed to get myself into my fins, I dived as quickly as possible. The same story continued under water. As soon as my buddy saw me coming, he turned around and continued to swim at high speed. I was still looking for the carabiner of my camera to attach it to my equipment, but it wasn't there! I had forgotten it because I was in such a hurry at the car.

I usually become very calm and relaxed when I get my head under water. It was not the case that day. The hustle continued under water. I was having to hold onto my camera when I realised that I had also forgotten to connect my inflator hose to the jacket. The hose was jammed between my cylinder and my back. I couldn't get it free, not with just one hand. We were heading down a steep embankment. I was adding more and more gas to my drysuit. At a depth of about 20 m/65 ft, my buddy turned around again and asked for my OK. I gave it back to him although nothing was OK!

I just wanted him to look away as quickly as possible. My only thought was: "He will never dive with me again if he realises the problems that I have!" On top of all the mistakes I had made up to that point, that was the biggest. My buddy did me a favour and turned away. Suddenly everything went terribly wrong, terribly quickly. The big and heavy camera that I was holding with one hand, pulled me head-downwards; I began to sink faster. I tried to counter that momentum by adding even more gas into my drysuit but the gas naturally went straight to the highest point - my feet. When I was rushing to put on my fins, my hectic pace meant that I hadn't pulled the straps properly over my heels; this meant that

when the gas reached my feet, it shot both my fins off. They were gone. I reached the water surface feet-first without being able to do a damn thing about it. It happened so quickly, there was nothing I could do.

The situation didn't improve for me on the surface. My feet were out of the water and the rest of my body was underwater.

I had no idea where I was, nor in which direction the shore lay. I still couldn't get to my inflator hose and I couldn't turn as I was still holding on to my camera.

Through a combination of waves and wind, I must have slowly drifted towards the shore without realising it, because suddenly I thought I could see the steeply sloping lake bottom beneath me. I started paddling towards the shore with one hand. When I was absolutely sure that I was moving in the right direction, I finally let go of the camera, which made my swimming somewhat faster.

The waves had gotten stronger and instead of getting out of the water somewhere on the beach, I arrived directly in front of a high stone wall. I was completely exhausted and couldn't get up. I ended up crawling on my knees in the surf around the wall; luckily two bystanders saw me and got into the water to help me ashore. My diving buddy arrived about an hour later. He had found my camera on one of his decompression stops and brought it out with him. Needless to say, I will never forget that dive.

But what were the reasons for this close call? On the one hand, I subjected myself to a lot of peer pressure; I wanted to be part of 'it' and never fail. In addition, I only knew my buddy as an instructor and trusted him blindly in that role.

What have I learned? I learned that I am responsible for myself, and today I can say, "NO" at any time during a dive—and my diving partners know that. It's part of each dive and expedition planning to include this possibility.

I plan my expedition dives as if they were solo dives; that's not to say that I don't trust my diving partners. I have a really good team now, and my trust in these people is great, but I want to feel that I am able to deal on my own in case of an emergency.

I'm definitely not a hero, and it would be presumptuous to put myself on a par with the big names in this book! Diving is one of the most important things in life for me, but much of what I have experienced was only possible with the help of a good team. Never take yourself too seriously and don't believe the illusion that you are perfect. In the water we are all just laymen and we never stop learning!

Sabine Kerkau *is a technical wreck and mine diver, a photographer and videographer. She is a member of the Women Divers Hall of Fame Class of 2019. She has dived hundreds of shipwrecks to depths of 150 m/492 ft, including virgin wrecks that have had successful identifications. Among others she has been on expeditions to the HMHS Britannic and the HMS Victoria in Lebanon. Sabine is part of the founding team of the 'Baltic Sea Heritage Rescue Project' in Lithuania. This project is committed to wreck protection, wreck search, wreck identification, and ghost net salvage. She was an expedition member of the MINEQUEST 2 project in Newfoundland, an Explorers Club 'Flag Expedition'. With her team, she is currently researching the flooded part of the Gonzen visitor mine in Switzerland to a depth of 180 m/590 ft..*

Sabine regularly writes on the topics of her projects in various magazines such as Wetnotes, Divemaster, Unterwasserwelt. de, Unterwasser, Xray online free Magazine and Tauchen. She has also been involved in several TV Productions and specific international conferences.

SIMONE VILLOTTI

FOUNDER @ 4FREEWORLD / CAVER & CAVE DIVER
SIDEMOUNT & CCR DIVER / SIDEMOUNT TECHNICAL TRIMIX
INSTRUCTOR / OUTDOOR SPORTS ADDICT

LOCATION OF INCIDENT
BUS DEL DIAOL, TRENTINO, ITALY

There are moments in life when we choose to take challenges lightly that hide potentially life-ending dangers, dangers hidden behind the complacency which grows whenever more extreme experiences become habit; the complacency which makes us lower our guard. Years when air diving in caves at depths of 70 m/229 ft or more in a wetsuit was almost normal.

Moments when a sump - just a few arm lengths of silt and sand, something that would normally be considered about as challenging as jumping over a water puddle, can suddenly make you realise that you may just have drawn your last breath.

In moments like that, your mind relies on your survival insticts to (hopefully) bring you home while you think, "I promise that if I make it, I will never do anything stupid like this again."

It was a rainy autumn around the early 2000s. A regular weekday evening when, a little bored by the routine of student life, I needed a bit of a break and some quality time with just myself. Living in Trento, a north-eastern region of Italy, is a blessing for anyone who is interested in the outdoors, no matter what time of year.

The choice fell on an interesting cave system not far from home. Certainly not the best idea on a rainy day like that, but anyway, "I will evaluate the conditions once I get there!"

In any case, my small cylinder was more than enough for the short sump that I knew the cave contained. I had never known it to be fully-flooded, nor was it that night.

A quick drive and a ten minute walk got me to the cave.

An easy climb through the canal of easy rocks that lead to the entrance, just enough to slide through the siphon, get a bit 'dirty' and get back home wet, chilled and covered in mud. The plan was quick but tempting—perfect to turn around a mundane city day.

I have spent my entire life participating in outdoor sports of all kinds. There is a pattern in these activities. Every time we accomplish something 'more', we tend to lower our guard. You could be a very experienced diver using a rebreather, a caver that slides fast in great depths or an alpinist who challenges extreme ice and rock.

The song is always the same. It goes beyond any logical approach to action. Great experience and skill growth bring an inevitable rise in what we consider acceptable risk. We all do it, and we all do it with all things we do in life. That same road we drive to work each day, the myriad other small and seemingly unimportant actions we all do, even if they seem trivial, any of those things can hide life-threatening risks.

Unfortunately we often, as we say in Italy, "put our ass on the kicking foot" when we are not paying proper attention to what we are doing. The pitfall often hides in our comfort zone.

With the following paragraphs that describe my 'simple' but still potentially lethal close call, I hope to manage to transfer my experience. I also hope that no one will experience what happened to me and that my story helps bring home the risks of taking dangerous situations too lightly.

Laying on the sofa, I was on my laptop at the end of a slow day at the University. That sort of behaviour really is not me; I am a very active person and long days on a computer screen seem even longer to me. The urge to 'move' can be so overwhelming that it can make me do things a bit out of the ordinary, at any time, just to not stay still.

It's 20:30, it's dark and I can hear the gentle sound of rain on my roof. What to do, what to do, what to do? The caving helmet that proudly decorates my living room gives me the answer; I am going to the cave.

A quick bit of packing covers the basics: helmet, caving suit, 0.5L cylinder, a regulator. Add a change of clothes and I am already in the car. Less than forty minutes later I am already walking towards the cavern. A few hundred metres in the middle of the countryside and a pathway that climbs through a rock channel are all that stand between me and it.

Meanwhile the rain keeps on. Slow but also inexorable. The wet rocks, covered with leaves and dirt spots, feel like they are covered with soapy water. Every step needs special care and respect in order to avoid a very painful fall many metres below. Each step gets me closer to the cave's entrance. I sit just in the entrance, listening to the rain while I suit up and prepare my minimal gear.

I leave my change of clothes in a bag and start to enter the cave's tight siphon with my mini pvc backpack. As predicted, the sump that often I have seen partially flooded, today was full. No trouble. A quick dip will get me beyond it. When the sump is only partially full, it's enough to slide through it holding my head out of the water. But today a different strategy is needed. No wetsuit, no mask. Just a trusty cylinder with an old Poseidon Triton regulator attached to it. All very minimal, on the regulator there is not even an SPG (what is not there, cannot break). I had checked the pressure back at home.

I remove my backpack, kneel in front of the sump, get the cylinder, and put the regulator in my mouth. As I close my eyes and slide through the small sump, the chill from its cold water makes me smile. A few arm strokes through the sand and without needing to breathe, I am already past it. The dry room is a bit more flooded than I am used to seeing it, but not too bad. As I follow the cave's path, I realise that the water is flooding in much more aggressively than usual, and after just a few minutes of exploration I decide to call it a day.

I reach the sump a few minutes later and I can clearly see that the water level is higher than when I passed through on my way in. I put the regulator in my mouth and slide back into the water. I am not sure of the reason, but at some point through the sump, I exhale.

And, as the natural need to breathe kicks in, the regulator gives me nothing. I can't breathe! My hand goes instinctively to the cylinder valve, but as I turn it, my fears are realised: it was already on! I am in 30 cm/1 ft of cold water, with no wetsuit or mask, no guideline, and I have no available gas!

I have already lost precious seconds, trying to open the cylinder, moving as little as possible and trying not to lose the way out.

As luck and instinct help my body eventually find the way to the exit, my mind keeps fixating on the thought of, "How is it possible to be such an idiot to risk dying in thirty centimetres of water, in such a short and easy sump?!?" Definitely not a very remarkable or heroic way to die.

I feel water leaving my face, allowing air into my lungs! I am out! My deep breath sends an eerie, loud noise all through the cave. I am out! I am out! Fuck! What an idiot. Fully wet, I feel no cold, even though the temperature is not more than 10C/50F. I walk until I get to my bag of clothes. I sit down and look at my cylinder, almost as if it was my adventure buddy. In my mind I feel like it's raising its 'shoulders', apologising somehow. I got lucky. Truly lucky.

When Stratis asked me if I had a story to contribute to this book, it took me some time to find the right one. This is not a major exploration experience, nor the happy ending of a grandiose adventure. It is simply a lucky epilogue to a completely underestimated situation!

Maybe my twenty years of age (at the time of the event) contributed. An age when we often feel invincible. Most certainly though when we get 'used' to exposing ourselves to calculated but also high risk situations, we may underestimate minor challenges that can hide mortal risks. I hope that my humble story will contribute to your archive of experiences.

Simone Villotti *was born in 1978 in Trento, Italy and has always been passionate about exploration and all kinds of outdoor activity. As an adolescent, he was practising all disciplines of alpinism. In 1994, he added diving in his cave exploration. Exploration is a lifestyle for Simone, from mountain climbing around the world to descending more than 1000 m/3280 ft in dry caves and of course diving on a global scale.*

A technical diver since 2000 and a CCR diver since 2006, he has dived to depths of more than 130 m/426 ft, with cave dives of more than three hours runtime. He is also an IANTD instructor for sidemount, Cavern and DPV.

Simone is an outdoor guy. He is a professional Scuba Dive, Kite and Standup (SUP)VDWS instructor and also an active sailing, wakeboard, Apnea, and canoeing athlete. Because of his lifetime involvement with outdoor activities of all kinds, he decided in 2011 to create his company, '4freeworld', which gave life to a series of video productions all around the world and with a mission to help people reach their sport-related dreams in life.

As a professional outdoor developer and team builder, he is helping the development of a series of companies specialised in outdoor activities, from parapende and kitesurfing to scuba diving, focusing on marketing and strategy.

DR. SONIA J. ROWLEY

EVOLUTIONARY MARINE BIOLOGIST
RECIPIENT OF THE SIR DAVID ATTENBOROUGH AWARD
FOR FIELDWORK

LOCATION OF INCIDENT
ANT ATOLL, FEDERATED STATES OF MICRONESIA

This close call is multi-faceted and a clear demonstration of the compromises that I chose to make on dive safety that prompted an evolution of thought with regard to equipment and personnel. Nonetheless, it is my hope that this experience will be in keeping with the overarching aim of this book Close Calls to help others insomuch as to prevent history repeating itself.

In the summer of 2016, I led a research expedition to the Federated States of Micronesia (FSM). This would be my third trip out there and the second as Principle Investigator, where I led a team of 12 researchers representing four institutions.

I operated my expeditions as cost-shares because this type of research is poorly-funded. My motive was to provide an opportunity for dedicated researchers to share expedition costs and achieve their research objectives. My team consisted of three deep divers. We were test pilots for a corporation developing rebreather equipment; therefore, despite being 'in charge,' I had no control over the dive equipment; this was the role of our dive safety officer (DSO).

Expedition Personalities
There was jealousy amongst the group, with my divers extremely jealous of the financial success of one of the other institutions, which had recently been awarded several million dollars for their work. This led to many an unhappy scene behind closed doors. Staying neutral was a challenge that was further exacerbated by three key caveats: poor equipment and safety, unprofessional behaviour, and lack of finances. However, I was driven and determined to pursue the research experiments that I had set up in previous

years and unwilling to permit personalities to interfere with my research objectives. These experiments and expeditions were my profession, so I was resistant to giving them up.

In the small hours of July 22, 2016, I prepared my rebreather ready for an early morning start. We had two boats; one taking the deep rebreather teams and the second taking the shallow SCUBA team, to Ant Atoll, eight nautical miles southwest of Pohnpei. Our research base was in Pohnpei, and it would take approximately 90 minutes to get to the dive site.

The conditions were perfect, yet I was nervous that my rebreather would not make the trip without significant errors. There were always errors, in fact, nearly 80% (79.21% to be precise) of our dives had rebreather errors ranging from alarms, faulty electronics, leaking components, or simply 'crying wolf.' Discernment at significant depths was not an optimal situation to find oneself in; however, it would occur with frequent regularity.

In short: the rig was not built for the job.

However, these units were provided to us via our DSO through a vendor grant, to conduct our research in exchange for providing data and feedback for further unit development. But all our team's rebreathers would have significant problems.

My forebodings would regularly be stilled by our DSO's assurance that we were using and developing the upmost advances in rebreather diving technology and safety, but performance seldom matched these claims. What was more disturbing was that our DSO, although very adept at repair, did not have a keen eye for safety!

Bailout regulators and rebreather components were often faulty and/or out of service. I did not at any point trust the bailout regulators, yet could not afford to purchase my own.

Fortunately, the other team's DSO was very meticulous, for which I was grateful. The previous evening, like any evening after a dive, I broke down the rig, cleaned out essential components and charged others. I also replaced the primary oxygen sensor in my rebreather with a new one due to a variety of issues encountered on previous dives.

As the evening wore on, I processed specimens from the day's dive, boosted cylinders, and patiently waited for everyone else to retire to bed. It's at these times that I grab moments of peace to have clarity of thought for the coming day, what I plan to achieve and the specifics as to how that will all come about whilst ensuring the others fulfill their own research objectives. But there were issues with my divers; one would be consistently intoxicated in the evening, and the other, our DSO, would not leave my side, not even to sleep in his hut. Technically, he was sharing with the lead of the wealthy institution but he insisted on sleeping on the couches in the main hut whilst I worked.

Gasses ready; Trimix 7/66, new sorb packed, errors of the day addressed, loggers programmed, labelled and packed for easy and sequential access and deployment at depth. Additional sampling bags were secured for the inevitable encounter with a novel specimen to collect. I grabbed a few short hours of sleep and set back to work before the others emerged. I seldom slept a full night on those expeditions; it was simply not possible to juggle all the work, the repairs and often the drama! Notably, the rebreathers would often have pre-dive errors that needed to be resolved before departure.

All my gear was checked. The external computer, which managed the rebreather, would be charging enroute to the site. Unfortunately, it would lose its charge very fast, therefore I would charge it up on the way to the site and take the risk of addressing more errors on the rebreather before leaping in. I had developed a habit of taking as many tools and spares on the boat as possible; I've

bought my ticket on the Titanic so I'm taking my boat ride! This was my mental state of play, and the internal politics of our group fuelled my commitment to succeed.

As we loaded all the equipment onto the boats, I observed the antics and interactions of each team member. The biggest distraction, however, was managing the incessant sexual harassment from my DSO. I had been trying to 'manage' it on my own; hoping(?) nobody knew. Where once there was respect there was now contempt; every time something went amiss with my rig, it reminded me of how I was allowing myself to be treated, and it would hit deep. I needed to get into the ocean to escape; it was my solace.

We dropped off the shallow team.

The other researchers were thoroughly enjoying the scenery; it was stunning, but I couldn't relax. I felt stuck in my head, there was no peace, we needed to get to the dive site before the rebreathers malfunctioned, we needed to get in!

All I could see was the fear and the two missions at hand, one of research and one of my search for peace, to get away from the insanity both inside and out.

The Dive
For me, the dive at Ant Atoll would be instrument deployment: temperature loggers secured every 10 m/33 ft depth from 10-140 m/33-459 ft.

Starting at depth, I would secure each logger, photograph it in place, photograph the rebreather computer as confirmation and a safety check, move up to the next depth increment, and repeat. This data was powerful, providing tremendous insights into the local and regional physical oceanographic conditions, permitting me to ask questions of physiological resilience and mechanisms of evolutionary divergence over ecological and geological time. I was compelled to determine why these gorgonian corals were so biologically successful at depth, and I had the necessary skills to do so.

Photo by Dr. SJ. Rowley

We get to the site and tie in. The equipment worked, pre-dives with pre-breathes accomplished, bailouts primed, instruments secured, we dropped in. Thank God. Nothing can surpass the feeling of joy one gets from being immersed in the crystal-clear waters of an ancient and enchanted atoll, descending into the depths knowing that what you will encounter has never been seen before. We kept an eye on each other, and we descended.

Enroute, we deployed certain bailout cylinders of pre-defined mixes and depths. The other deep team carried their cylinders with them. I took it slow, breathing out through my nose so that the ADV would kick in and the diluent would mitigate the PO_2 spike that invariably occurred at around 30 m/100 ft; a cack-handed dil flush! The electronics on our rebreathers do not use decimals for the diluent gas mix; therefore, at depth, any disparity within integer values (for example 6.4% oxygen) causes an alarm. This time, after 100 m/328 ft depth, the alarm went off. I ignored it because it always goes off!

Not a good move. At 140 m/459 ft depth, I deployed my first temperature logger, attached to a beautiful specimen and one I know that I will find the following year.

The alarm cacophony continued; that's normal. In fact, it was such a common occurrence, that the team rarely, if ever, bailed out for these types of events. As I photographed the logger, I looked at the external dive computer that was driving my rebreather, the screen had imploded and none of my oxygen sensors were reading the same value! I had four sensors—two in the unit, one solid-state connected to the aforementioned dive computer and lastly my own independent dive computer, which was plumbed into an independent oxygen sensor on the rebreather's exhalant.

I didn't like it there; however, the others had that configuration, so I let short-sighted self-doubt and fear of criticism influence my decisions (inwardly, I was painfully self-conscious at that time, something that this experience served to change). The rebreather electronics took over the unit, yet followed the secondary sensor, which was reading low.

This meant that oxygen was being pumped into my loop in excessive amounts. This was not new. However, at that depth with a broken screen, lights flashing, alarms galore, four oxygen sensors, none of which agreed, coupled with absolutely no trust in the functionality of my OC regulators, which were poorly-serviced, or those of my team, I looked at the situation and slowly ascended. As the sensors fluctuated greatly, my personal backup computer that plumbed into my exhalant displayed a PO_2 2.5—it was unable to display greater values, but I knew it was higher. "Just calmly get yourself shallower, you'll be alright," were my thoughts.

Through experience, I knew that at a certain depth the readings would 'settle out' and the rebreather would 'settle down' to some slightly more-manageable degree! I needed to keep calm and make it to 50 m/154 ft to get out of PO_2 2.0, then 30 m/100 ft to get down to a PO_2 of 1.3.

"Through experience?" Why would I persist in using equipment that was so consistently faulty that I had gained a good idea of the depths at which it would 'settle out' when it wouldn't work properly, which was very often? Clearly, my thinking was just as questionable.

I felt trapped—that I withstood inappropriate behaviour and used faulty equipment to get my work done and follow my passion in science as a scientist and as a woman. I thought that my work was so unusual that this was the only way,that I had no money, that this was what you did until you got to the 'other side'—to the calm shore of happy research.

I slowly ascended amidst a cacophony of alarms, lights, and the alarming and informative tingling feeling around the edge of my tongue. My buddies, of course, expressed concern but soon returned to their respective interests with one even requesting a photograph of their 'catch of the dive' for social media. I obliged. I did not bailout.

As was common practice with the DSO and team, I decided to manage the problem. Whilst the others played and impressed each other, I kept a slow and steady ascent. A further five hours were spent accompanied by the din, the PO_2 eventually restored and managed manually. For the last 40 minutes of the dive, I plumbed in external oxygen, as mine had run empty due to the unit running off the secondary and erroneous sensor.

The Aftermath

Why this dive, and others prior to and thereafter, did not take my life, I do not know. My independent backup placed on the exhalant revealed that at 65.1 m/213 ft depth (8:40 minutes into the dive) my PO_2 was 1.6, it hit 2.4 at 80 m/262 ft, and displayed as 2.5 at 135.9 m/446 ft where it remained for 5:50 minutes. One can only guess as to the gas I was actually breathing. For 50:10 minutes my PO_2 exceeded 1.6 until I made it back to 34.6 m/113.5 ft depth.

There was no debriefing from my DSO; one would have to sit and grill them for feedback. They did not always know! I changed my secondary sensor and continued the research, leading the team, and addressing the seemingly constant stream of caveats that would arise. I had become so accustomed to the errors and drama that I could see no alternative.

Within two days, my eyesight deteriorated dramatically. I could not see my laptop without glasses. My original prescription was -1.25. I returned with -3.5. I was informed that I had hyperoxia myopia and that it was reversible. In under two months my sight had returned, but the story does not end here. For some time, I had noted that the unit was displaying a PO_2 lower than the independent backup computer, something also observed by others.

This issue was never addressed. As I persisted in using faulty equipment, I did get my independent computer tested; it was not at fault. However, on the final expedition that I used this equipment, I had my eyes tested prior to and directly after my return. Where I had left with -1.25, I returned with -4.5 and -5 in the left and right eye respectively.

Today, I have cataracts with a current vision of -3.25. After the near-fatal dive in July 2016, I resolved to make a change.

Over the following year, I would quietly purchase another piece of dive equipment with each monthly stipend cheque to the point where I now have my own fully independent expedition research dive setup. Moreover, I was generously funded to purchase a different brand of rebreather.

With the support of my institution, I also finally gathered the courage to walk away from this whole messy scene, report the data, unprofessional behaviour (i.e. misogyny: sexual, verbal, and occasionally physical abuse, in addition to lack of dive safety and financial integrity), and return all the faulty equipment.

It was time to do things differently, and to finally tell my father (who was the head of the British Sub-Aqua Club[(BSAC] Technical and notably unhappy with the rebreather I had been using) what I had been subject to. He was understanding, quick to help and slow to judge. It was time to tell him everything.

I had not wished to concern him before; I was ashamed by my choices, the behaviour that I had permitted others to exhibit towards me, my retaliatory behaviour (whether compliance or anger), the equipment failures and the near-fatal experiences that I had neither communicated to him nor walked away from.

The lessons in this narrative are multiplicative and glaring. Yet, my fear-driven, pride-blindness has left me only with cataracts.

The strength and power of experience have, however, resulted in my unfaltering commitment to provide a clean, well-lit place for upcoming scientists to thrive; where I have failed, they can profit; where I have fallen, they can stand tall; where I have learned, they can grow.

Dr. Sonia J. Rowley's *is a Research Biologist at the University of Hawai'i at Mānoa, USA. She primarily uses the Divesoft Liberty CCR as well as Freediving for her field research.*

Dr. Rowley has over 36-years of diving and commercial ship experience throughout the Indo-Pacific, Europe, Africa, and Australasia. In addition to CCR, she conducts deep-sea research using submersible, ROV, and AUV's on deep-ocean seamount chains such as the Hawaiian Islands, and Louisville Seamount chain (NZ).

Dr. Rowley's primary research focus is on the evolutionary relationships within and between the coral holobiont and it's environment, primarily focusing on gorgonian (sea fan) corals. She seeks to understand the biological success of this group, in particular to its dominance at mesophotic and deeper ocean depths (>50m) of the Indo Pacific. This is achieved through integrating cross-disciplinary approaches from experimental field ecology using CCR, genomics (phylogeography, systematics, and symbiosis), functional morphology, and physiology, in order to further understand phenotypic responses to environmental change over ecological and geological (deep) time.

Over the past decade, her research has shown that mesophotic coral ecosystems (MCEs) within the Indo-Pacific are thermally dynamic environments, and are dominated by diverse assemblages of gorgonian octocorals. Sonia has been awarded the Sir. David Attenborough Award for Fieldwork for her gorgonian research on the mesophotic and shallow reefs of Micronesia.

Dr. Rowley is a Fellow National of the Explorers Club (FN18), A Fellow of the Linnean Society of London (FLS), and the Royal Society of Biology (MRSB), UK. She sees that the most powerful tool for change is to share knowledge and experience gained in the pursuit of scientific understanding and discovery. To this end, Dr. Rowley has conducted numerous presentations around the globe, served as a senior project supervisor and lecturer to graduate and undergraduate-level students, and has led or participated in research projects in over 25 countries.

Photo by Dr. SJ. Rowley

STEFAN PANIS

CCR FULL CAVE DIVER / MINE DIVER / WRECK DIVER
EXPLORERS CLUB FELLOW

LOCATION OF INCIDENT
SECRET SLATE MINE, EAST OF BELGIUM

Each year, between November until the following April, we didn't get a chance to do much diving; we couldn't dive the local wrecks and diving in a quarry got quite boring quite quickly.

That all changed when I got invited to dive an old mining site in east Belgium; a whole new world was opened up for me. After that first mine dive, I quickly realised that I needed the proper training if I was going to continue, so I contacted a cave diving instructor, with whom I did my CCR Full Cave course.

I quickly found out that the Belgian underground looks like Swiss cheese.

During the industrial revolution, there was a very active mining industry (charcoal, limestone, marble, slate). It's estimated that there were up to thirty thousand active mines sprinkled across a country of less than twelve thousand square miles!

Mines always held a special attraction for me. Maybe this is because their environment, with industrial remains and steel 'history', reminds me of a wreck. Soon the search for new, virgin mines developed into an obsession for me, and one that keeps me diving all year round.

One day I got a tip from a friend about the location of a new mine, probably never-before dived. My buddy and I teamed up and, after a few hours of searching, we found the remains of the site and the mine's entrance.

As we always did, we decided to do a "dry" exploration first, to check if there was even water to be found and to judge whether the conditions of the site looked stable enough to proceed with a dive.

Photos by Stefan Panis

This was a slate mine; they often prove to be very unstable and therefore, dangerous.

Inside the mine we found an amazingly beautiful and huge excavation. Eventually, crawling three levels down, we found water. Crystal clear water that looked very inviting, with train rails plunging into the depths and a very old wooden ladder clearly visible.

We chose to dive in sidemount configuration for the first dive, which made logistics a bit less complicated, although it took us about two hours to transport all our diving gear down to the dive site. We knew that the visibility was very likely going to be reduced to zero shortly after entering the water, so the plan was that I would go in first, go under the ladder to take some photos of my buddy near the ladder, and then we would continue our exploration.

We followed our plan and after I took some photos near the ladder, we were surprised to see a main line, which meant that the site had been dived before.

Nevertheless, we continued, and when my buddy made another tie-off with the reel line, close to the main line but not yet connecting, I passed him to proceed in the main shaft, following the main line down a forty five degree slope to take shots as he would come down.

After a few more m/ft, the line went into a narrow side corridor, which would lead to the next big chamber, as we had seen in the pattern above water. I looked up, and could still see my buddy's torches clearly.

After a quick peek into the corridor, I looked up again, and saw no more lights, only big clouds of black silt rolling down. Not that that was a problem, because we are used to this situation, and had been expecting it. Five minutes later my buddy was still not there, so I assumed that he had had an equipment failure and decided to go back for him.

I started ascending the main line, but to my surprise there was no connection of any line to the mainline.

I don't know why, but against all rules I made the worst mistake one could make: I let go of the main line without making a connection with a spool or a reel.

Then and there, in pitch black, my breathing stopped and I felt my heart pounding as the fear kicked in. I knew I had to collect my thoughts. So I did, and I decided to stick to the bottom. Within seconds I found the train rails, my guide to the way out!

When I surfaced, I saw my buddy as white as a sheet of paper! While making the last tie-off with his reel line, he had been so focussed that he hadn't noticed me pass him, so he was not aware that I was already ahead. And, when he didn't see me, as he wanted to proceed, he also assumed that I had had an equipment failure and had returned.

Obviously, he should have left the reel where it was until he was sure I was safe. We both were affected by what happened and decided to call it a day.

For me, the biggest lessons of this close call was to never, never leave a connection to the main line, and never to reel back in until fully aware that everyone has made it back.

Another thing that I could or should have done is given my buddy a signal to let him know that I had passed him.

I hope that my humble story will contribute to your archive of experiences.

Stefan Panis *started diving at the age of six through his father. In 1992, he took his first diving course. Since then he has taken nitrox and trimix courses, and he started diving an Inspiration Rebreather in 2009.*

He started photographing in 2013. Meanwhile he developed a great interest in diving wrecks and researching their history in archives. He did many dives on wrecks in the North sea, the English channel, Sardinia, Portugal and Lithuania just to name a few.

He was involved in different successful expeditions searching for new wrecks, like the identification of the 1852 Josephine Willis.

In 2014, he also obtained his full cave CCR certificate. Stefan also loves to dive, explore and document the (many) old mine sites in Belgium.

He often writes articles for several international tech diving magazines, and has written four books about diving. In 2020, Stefan became a member of the Explorers Club in New York.

STEVE BOGAERTS

OWNER/PARTNER @ GO SIDE MOUNT
FELLOW OF THE EXPLORERS CLUB
RECIPIENT OF THE ABE DAVIS SAFE CAVE DIVING AWARD

LOCATION OF INCIDENT
YUCATAN PENINSULA, MEXICO

Anyone who ever tells you that they have never made a mistake cave diving is either not a cave diver or a liar. Even the 'gurus' of cave diving have made mistakes, in fact lots of them; that's how they got to be the 'experts' in the first place.

We all make mistakes. I have probably made more than most other cave divers, as I do a lot of cave diving, and have therefore had plenty of opportunities to screw up over the many years and thousands of cave dives that I have completed.

While I am never happy to make mistakes, I also try to turn whatever mistakes I do make into valuable learning experiences both for myself and for my future students. I try not to repeat my mistakes, but I do still make new ones from time-to-time, and I am still learning from them.

Here, I want to relate an interesting incident that happened a couple of years ago, in a Cave System I was exploring called Sistema Pandora.

Pandora is located near Xcalak in southern Quintana Roo, Mexico, close to the border with Belize.

My first exploration dives in Pandora took place in 2015, and I was immediately impressed by its very idiosyncratic environment: a brackish water cave system mostly under mangrove that has a huge amount of very loose unstable organic sediment and bacterial silt covering every surface; many passages are full of hanging 'snotites' which resemble stalactites but are actually made up of large hanging bacterial colonies held together with a mucus-like gel covering.

Photos by HP Hartmann

I conducted early exploration dives in Pandora using an open-circuit sidemount configuration; I soon realised that percolation from my exhaust bubbles was knocking down bacteria from the ceiling and walls, often reducing visibility to zero. It felt as if I was swimming in a thick bacterial soup made worse by a seasoning of tannic acid and toxic hydrogen sulphide.

On the floor, silt and organic sediment is meters deep in many areas and is very easily disturbed by a careless fin kick or the misdirected propeller wash from a diver propulsion vehicle (DPV). This silt and sediment also gets moved around by tidal currents and can bury guidelines that run close to the floor even during the course of a dive. For this reason, in many areas, the guideline is laid higher up in the passageways than normal to stop it getting buried in all the silt and mung. In low passages, this means the line is often run across the ceiling of the cave.

The limestone rock and speleothems in this cave are very fragile and brittle due to dissolution caused by the corrosive combination of brackish water, tannic acid, hydrogen sulphide and bacterial action. Attempting to make tie-offs with the guideline, on seemingly secure formations, oftentimes results in breaking the rock or speleothem as soon as the line is tensioned. I was forced in many cases to select relatively large tie-off points on quite substantial formations to reduce the chances of this happening. At a penetration of ~600 m/1970 ft from the entrance, the cave passageway descends to a lowish bedding plane at a depth of 16.6 m/55 ft with a deep silt floor.

I had run the guideline across the ceiling while exploring this section in 2015, and on the other side where the passage opens back up, I tied off on a very large stalactite approximately 2.1 m/7 ft long from base to tip with a circumference of at least 60 cm/2 ft where it was attached to the ceiling. The guideline was tied off about two thirds of the

way down the stalactite where it still had a sizable circumference of ~20 cm/0.6 ft, and the tip of it hung ~1.83 m/6 ft above the silt on the floor.

The bedding plane was not really a restriction but with up to four tanks and two DPVs for some of the longer dives I was making, I had to take care not to plough through the deep bacterial silt and destroy the visibility in this area as I travelled past it on my way further into the cave. Any silt or organic sediments which got disturbed tended to remain suspended in the water column for long periods, and I had no desire to be exiting in zero visibility on my return! During a subsequent exploration project in 2016, I had passed this area several times both on the way in and out of the cave with no incident, although I always had to stop the DPV and negotiate the area carefully.

However, on this particular day things were going to be a little different!

Following a very successful dive during which I had emptied all my exploration reels and gathered lots of survey data, I was feeling pretty good about life as I scootered back towards the exit.

On my return journey, I ran into an area of almost zero visibility close to the bedding plane, which was a surprise, as I felt I had passed it cleanly on the way in. Slightly puzzled, I moved to touch contact on the line, pushing my scooter in front of me.

It quickly became apparent why the visibility was so bad as the line disappeared into the sediment, indicating that a tie-off point had broken while I had been diving and buried both itself and the line attached to it deep in the silt.

Not the first time had this happened in this particular cave and, whilst it is annoying having to fix the line and tie offs, usually it is not a big deal. This, however, was obviously a more serious collapse and in a relatively bad location.

As I moved forward, the line ran at a steep angle down into the silt, and within a few meters, my left arm was fully extended holding onto the line, and I was buried up to my left shoulder in the silt with my head turned all the way to the right to keep my face and the second stage I was breathing from out of it to prevent it becoming clogged. I physically could not go any further along the line unless I buried myself completely in the silt, and I still could not reach the tie off point!

By pulling on the line, I could feel the weight of the stalactite it was attached to, but it was much too heavy to pull up, and I was concerned about breaking the line, which was as taut as a piano wire.

I realised at that point exactly which tie off had broken off and buried itself like a spear deep into the sediment; furthermore, all this activity was definitely not making the already-terrible visibility any better!

Giving up trying to follow the line or unbury the tie-off, I decided to back up, deploy my safety spool, and search for the exit side of the guideline on the other side of the collapsed tie-off.

I marked the guideline with a line arrow just before the point at which it was buried in the silt and then reached back to the reels clipped-off behind me to retrieve my safety spool. My safety spool is the only spool or reel that I carry that is filled with unknotted line just so I am not tempted to use it when I empty all my other exploration reels and the cave is still going.

As I hunted through a gaggle of empty exploration reels, the dawning realisation hit me that my safety spool was gone, and you can be certain that I checked all my reels several times to be sure of this!

The penny dropped. Murphy's Law had decided to bite me for a decision I'd made more than three hours ago while kitting up at the start of the dive. I had known that I was probably going to lay a lot of line on this dive and would need to do a lot of survey, so I'd decided to take three survey slates with me, all of which I put in my pouch.

Normally I always carry my safety spool in my pouch, along with other emergency and backup items, but on this day I took it out and clipped it off to my buoyancy compensator (BC) together with the exploration reels to make room for all the survey slates.

That was a bad choice, and one I was now paying for.

Obviously at some point during the dive, my safety spool had detached itself, either when going through various restrictions, or when removing and replacing my exploration reels, and I had not noticed. Now I was in zero visibility, on a guideline I could not follow, and without a single foot of line on any of my reels with which to do a lost-line search.

I did briefly consider going back further into the cave to look for my missing safety spool but as I had no idea where I had lost it, or even whether it was on the side of the buried guideline or possibly closer to the exit, I quickly dismissed the thought. Since I had a pretty good idea of where I was and a reasonable mental picture of the cave passage, I decided I would swim carefully forward while searching blindly for the other side of the line. Swimming away from a guideline in zero visibility in the hope of finding the other end of it is not something to be undertaken lightly, but at that point I did not see an alternative course of action. I was confident of my ability to swim in a straight line even with no visual references, as I have practiced that skill extensively.

Before I began, I clipped my scooters off to the guideline, one on each side of the line arrow I had just placed, partly to act like giant personal markers and partly because I did not want to be swimming blind in zero visibility looking for a line while pushing one scooter in front and—even worse—towing one behind me. I moved forward slowly sweeping my hand back and forth over the surface of the silt trying not to disturb it even more while searching for the line.

My first attempt was unsuccessful, and I ran into a wall without finding the exit side of the guideline. Then I had to turn 180 degrees and very carefully backtrack to my starting point and my scooters so that I could try again.

After a little while, I ran into another wall which I was definitely not expecting and which indicated that I was off course and going the wrong way back.

My adrenaline spiked at this point, so I took a deep calming breath and tracked to my right slightly. Just at the point where I was starting to think I had gone too far, and would not even be able to find my way back to the line I had swum away from, I bumped into one of my scooters. Hallelujah!

Now that I was back at the starting point, I was able to reorientate myself and adjust my search angle to try again. This time after a very tense, slow, blind swim of ~9 m/30 ft, I found the other end of the guideline where it reappeared from the silt. Fan-bloody-tantastic!

I swam forward a bit further on the line until the visibility cleared a little and marked it with another line arrow. I sat there for a minute checking how much gas I had left and wondering how I was going to get my scooters back. Happily, I had plenty of reserve gas, so swimming out from that point would be no issue.

The swim out was uneventful, but I put thought of the incident behind me until I was at the entrance of the cave completing my deco as I did not want to get distracted and make another mistake on this dive. The obvious lesson from this dive was one that I already knew and had ignored at my peril. Keep your safety spool in a pouch or pocket where you are less likely to lose it.

During deco I realised that I had overlooked another potential solution to my problem. I had several empty exploration reels with me.

I could have swum back into the cave a little distance past several tie offs, then cut the guideline and reeled a section of line back up, as I headed back out to the exit and the buried line. That way I could have performed my missing guideline search with a reel and line.

That would have been far safer than swimming away from the guideline in zero visibility with no line and with the risk of not being able to find my way back to my original starting point if unsuccessful in my search.

Having found the exit side of the guideline, I would then have had a continuous guideline back to my scooters, I could have retrieved them easily, which may have been critical if this incident had happened further back in the cave where I may not have had sufficient reserve gas to swim out.

In hindsight, this solution seemed obvious, and I was kicking myself for not thinking of it even though I had considered the idea of swimming back into the cave to look for my missing safety spool. Now that I have the benefit of experience, this is exactly what I would do in the very unlikely event that I once again have to search for a missing guideline having lost my safety spool.

Hindsight is 20/20, but possible solutions are not always obvious in the heat of the moment, especially when dealing with a stressful situation and a scenario I had never considered or game-planned previously.

Another take-home lesson for me from this was to spend a bit more time considering potential solutions to problems rather than just trusting in my abilities and going straight into 'action mode'.

The following day I dived again and put in a new section of line to bridge the buried section, tying the line off between the two arrows and also on top of the broken stalactite which I named "The Sword of Damocles".

The stalactite is still buried in the silt with line attached, but the lesson from this day continues to hover over me like the fabled sword of legend, and it is not a mistake I will repeat again, although I am sure I will make other new ones to learn from.

Steve Bogaerts *is an enormously versatile and experienced diver and has dived all over the world using the latest in cutting-edge technology including Mixed Gas Closed Circuit Rebreathers and extended duration deep-rated Diver Propulsion Vehicles in an effort to push back the boundaries of the underwater realm.*

He has been involved in many exploration projects that have taken him to places as diverse as the coastal waters of the UK, Scapa Flow, the Maldives, the Egyptian Red Sea, the Yemen, the Mediterranean, the Patagonian coast of Argentina, the Mexican Caribbean, and island of Cozumel, plus of course the jungles of the Yucatan Peninsula.

Steve holds the highest attainable instructor ratings in Recreational, Technical and Cave diving. He is an International Fellow of the Explorers Club of New York and is a recipient of the Abe Davis Safe Cave Diving Award.

He is the National Speleological Society Cave Diving Sections Safety Officer for Quintana Roo. Steve has given presentations on Cave and Technical Diving around the world and has had articles published in various international magazines and newspapers. He has also been involved in Film and TV documentary projects.

Why? What contributed to me taking that route and then, why was I entangled? I thought long and hard about the experience and discussed the events and my actions with a few trusted peers.

What follows are some likely factors and lessons learned.

Firstly, narcosis. The lower plates of the Boiler Room are at about 35 m/115 ft, and we had been at depths greater than 30 m/100 ft for a significant portion of the dive. I have never personally felt I had issues with narcosis on dives as deep as 45 m/147 ft, but that is not to say I have not been affected. The effects can be insidious, and I am quite certain that my decision to enter the upper plates at the back of the boiler was influenced by this factor.

Next: overconfidence. Let's call it complacency. My detailed knowledge of the wreck may have contributed to my error. I was relaxed in my knowledge of the wreck and the route, possibly too much so. Every waypoint, every change of deck or direction should be checked and verified with your team especially if entering any space that narrows or is confined.

Thirdly: on this dive, I carried my deco cylinder with me inside the wreck. Opinion is divided on whether this is a good idea. The potential for entanglement or entrapment with multiple cylinders outweighs the benefit of carrying them during the penetration phase of the dive. After reaching the boat, I noticed that my surface marker buoy (SMB) was missing. It was obvious it was somehow involved in my entanglement along with my light canister. I found it the next day in the bilge under the Starboard Boiler near where I was entangled. I now avoid having items attached to my butt D-ring on penetration dives, preferring to stow them in pockets or a pouch.

Lastly, the buddy system broke down in this instance. I failed to wait for my buddy before turning at the back of the Starboard Boiler.

Had I done this, he would have seen my path and I hope would have at least helped me to remove the entanglement. I have also traded in my 1,000 Lumen light for an 18,000 Lumen canister light. Never again will my light signal go unnoticed!

As a final thought, I believe this highlights that all overhead environments, including purpose-sunk wrecks, need to be taken seriously. *Canterbury* can be a deceptively-easy penetration dive. It is upright and has numerous openings providing natural light. Despite this, it is still a genuine overhead environment, especially on the lower decks and compartments, and it must be treated as such.

Steve Davis *is the host of the acclaimed podcast, "Speaking Sidemount", author of "The Canterbury Wreck - A Diver's Guide" and the eBook, "Sidemount Fundamentals". He is a specialist sidemount diver/ instructor, dives exclusively in sidemount, and is the founder of Sidemount Pros. Steve's philosophy has always been, "To be world-class, you need to learn from the best". To this end, Steve has trained, dived and worked with many of the world's very best sidemount, wreck, cave divers, and explorers, including Tom Steiner, Audrey Cudel, John Chatterton, John Dalla-Zuanna, and Edd Sorenson.*

Steve travels the world diving sidemount in caves, wrecks, and open water. Through "Speaking Sidemount" his mission is to share his passion for sidemount diving and provide a medium for the world's top sidemount divers, instructors, and explorers to share their experiences and thoughts on sidemount diving.

Photo by Steve Davis

STEVE LEWIS

AUTHOR / COACH / GENERALIST
FELLOW ROYAL CANADIAN GEOGRAPHICAL SOCIETY
RECIPIENT OF SHECK EXLEY INTERNATIONAL SAFETY
AWARD / RAID'S WORLDWIDE DIRECTOR DIVER TRAINING

LOCATION OF INCIDENT
GEORGIAN BAY, LAKE HURON, CANADA

My father was a surprisingly simple man; fair-minded but no pushover. Above all else, a true cockney born and bred in London's East End. He was born the year after the First World War ended, 1919.

Back then, London's East End was a no-frills, gritty, uber-working-class area where survival beyond childhood wasn't guaranteed. His community was a mongrel cross of indeterminate ethnicity dressed in ill-fitting, hand-me-down clothing.

In family photographs my dad, his brothers and sisters, his aunts and uncles, and his parents all looked like thugs. Everything was covered in soot. Everyone was poor. Oh, yeah. This was Artful Dodger and Fagin territory, generations before Guy Richie movies made the East End cool and charmingly comic, and before the arrival of the middle-class tapas-nibblers hanging out in gentrified pubs and coffee shops. That's to say, my old man was a tough bastard, a survivor, with an interesting history. He was taciturn but extraordinarily polite, a gifted mechanic and very fast, confident driver. In later life – when this story took place – he spent his time hybridising chrysanthemums and tending roses far, far away from a past of urbanity, street violence and greyness.

I loved him deeply.

One Sunday afternoon during a semi-annual trip to visit him, we were sitting in a British Legion club. Outside the window were the sand and cobbles of Dymchurch Beach. Across the English Channel a faint mirage of the French coast was disappearing and reforming in weak sunlight. He put down his glass of brown ale and quietly looked directly at me without saying a word. It felt like a few minutes but was probably less than 20 seconds.

"When you're scuba diving," he asked, picking up his beer glass again but now staring over its rim at me. "Have you ever thought to yourself, well, this is it. I'm buggered now... I'm gonna die?"

A direct and unambiguous question. No warning. No preamble. He sipped his drink and put his glass back down, adjusting it slightly so it aligned perfectly with the wet circle on the tabletop. He looked back at me and smiled. Big white teeth and a slight indent in the left front from years of pipe smoking.

More beats passed.

Conversations with my father (to this point and thereafter) were always ordinary. Well, I had no control group to refer to and nothing else to compare our relationship and our conversations to, so I had to guess whether or not they were ordinary, and my guess was yes. Ordinary. Questions about death and its proximity were not one of our usual topics. Normally, especially in this part of our lives, him about the age I am today, me visiting from my chosen home across an ocean and half a continent, our conversations were uncomplicated. No references to religion (he was Jewish, I was not), or philosophy (he'd tried to read an Aldous Huxley book once but stopped around page 34), or politics (he was a royalist and I'm a republican). We talked instead about motorbikes, Grand Prix, gardening, the outrageous price of petrol, where we'd stop to buy fish and chips, and occasionally his memories of all the people in those old photographs.

In all those previous conversations, my father had never asked me about death. Or at least, he had never asked if I'd come close to death. If I had experienced a "Come-to-Jesus" moment. If at any time while diving I'd accepted whatever fate had lined up for me,

meekly, angrily, bravely, with humility, or with no thoughts at all, just frozen like a rabbit.

I remember my instinct was to wonder why. Why was he asking that of all things? It certainly wasn't just small talk; something to pass the time. "Nice weather today, a bit windy. Ever look into the eyes of the Grim Reaper and figure you're done for?"

Had my behaviour been different that day? Had I said something that told him, that very, very recently, I'd come very, very close?

Maybe just coincidence?

I'd asked him a similar question once. However, that was a long time before. I was about ten years old, and our relationship was different then. I'd thought to ask him when I realised that the handful of toy soldiers I was playing with were 'British desert rats', same as he once was. I'd seen the photos, I'd played with his medals.

Sitting in the Legion, I thought about giving him the same bullshit response he'd given me back then: "No, not even close." But that was him answering to a child. We were both adults now. Him long retired and starting to lose a little fire, me his grownup son being asked a serious question totally out of left field. A Sunday afternoon shocker, with the bitter taste of fear still in my mouth.

"Dad, do you mean have I had a close call; when I thought seriously that I was going to die?"

He nodded and started the ritual of filling his pipe. We'd be walking outside in a minute or two so he could smoke sitting in the wind and sunlight and not piss-off any of the other people in the bar. And to conform with the half-dozen 'Sorry, No Smoking' signs dotted around the room. There were regulars smoking cigarettes and nobody seemed to mind, but he knew pipe smoke would get the barmaid's attention, and it wasn't worth the

Photo by Jill Heinerth

effort to argue against the newly-minted ban. I told him: "Only one time that I can remember, dad. It was on a shipwreck."

"Not in a cave then," he said.
"Nope."

Looking at his fingers taming long strands of Erinmore pipe tobacco, I thought this was the best possible answer. There was also the time my dive partner got herself stuck getting out of a small, wiggly cave. That became stressful when she started mindlessly banging her manifold against the rock. Then there was the bulkhead that fell on me. I was alone, it was freezing cold, and the debris was heavy. Moving it tore a hole in my dry glove, and I was more focussed on that than thinking how close I'd been to getting squished flat and made immobile. And there was a trimix student who pulled me to the surface from 60

m/196 ft. He was a total dweeb, but I spent our ride to the surface trying to keep him alive and had no time to think about myself.

Nope, none of those counted. I did not see Jesus. Not once.

The one time I was admitting to had happened deep inside a wreck with someone I did not know climbing all over me trying to get to my regulator and possibly drown me in the pursuit of it. I had seen Jesus, a burning bush, the Wailing Wall, Buddha, my pet dog, and a mess of arms, legs, and terrified eyes. And it had happened about two weeks prior.

My father nodded. He was ready to light his pipe now. I motioned at the door and we carried our drinks onto the patio – really just a few metal chairs and a couple of round tables perched on the sea wall. We sat.

He took a puff from his pipe, and a sip of beer. He looked over his shoulder, squinted at the sun, and turned back to me. "Tell me all about it," he said. He was not letting go.

I gave him the shortened version. I told him I was with three friends. We often dived together. One of them had trained with me.

I didn't bother explaining that we'd made the long drive from the city to get to a little wooden resort—more like a hunt camp than a hotel—or that the owner wore a long ponytail and a brand-new cowboy hat. I skipped over the meal waiting for us that night and our cabin, basic but warm and friendly with an original Norval Morrisseau painting hung above the mantle. I left out the bit about needing to shoot video for a TV pilot, and that the wreck was pretty and dangerous, just like they all are.

I simply explained that we had laid lines into the stern castle from the starboard rail, round a few corners and into the meat locker in the ship's galley. We were about thirty five metres deep. I was checking out places to fix our second video light when someone started clawing at my face.

My first thought was that one of my buddies was playing silly buggers. But within a second it was obviously not that. A diver with a single tank had followed our line and had run out of gas. He'd come at me first because I was outside the meat locker. I was fighting him, trying to push him away and stuff the long-hose regulator into his mouth, get to my necklace, and keep track of where my mask was going. One of my buddies had seen a cloud of silt, realised what was happening, and had come to help.

"So, if my buddies hadn't helped get him off me, and help me get the guy back outside the wreck," I told my father, "things would have turned out nasty."

My father nodded, blew more smoke and said: "Well, they were there and they did help."

He smiled again and a seagull landed on the chair beside him.

"When was this?" He asked.
I said: "A fortnight ago!"
He nodded again, waved an arm at the seagull and said: "So, what did you learn?"
I blinked, took a drink from my glass, thought for another moment and said: "That it's good to have friends you can trust, and that my father is ****ing clairvoyant!"

He laughed. I laughed.
We had another drink.

Steve Lewis *began teaching "technical diving" in the 1990s but is still waiting for someone to explain exactly where ordinary diving ends and technical diving begins.*

Teaching scuba diving in all its forms, like so much else, has changed, developed, evolved over time, and he feels lucky to have witnessed those changes. "They were, they are," he explains, "very welcome."

An avid cave diver, he is most at home inspecting soda straws, flowstones and stalagmites to make sure their colours tell the truth about what happened in the jungle overhead 15,000 to 20,000 years ago. He lives in a converted one-room schoolhouse on a dirt road somewhere in Canada with coyotes and wild turkeys and the occasional moose for company.

When he isn't diving, he writes, paints or picks up a hammer and builds.

TOMASZ "MICHUR" MICHURA

TECHNICAL SIDEMOUNT INSTRUCTOR
OWNER OF SIDEMOUNT SILESIA

LOCATION OF INCIDENT
QUARRY, POLAND

So many factors drive our choice of hobbies and interests; ambition, desire to explore uncharted territories; desire to increase confidence, self-esteem and experience, or simply challenging ourselves.

I could add at least two that were on my personal list when I took up diving, namely independence from weather conditions and independence from people. Previously, I had somehow imagined myself as a chopper rider; a romantic vision of Michur, travelling the length and breadth of the country with flies in-between his teeth and wind through his non-existent hair! But gosh! The nights preceding a journey were spent analysing weather forecasts, as it would be highly inappropriate to get on a chromium-plated, shining piece of machinery on a rainy day.

As for 'People'…during my musician days I was a total workaholic; I inherited this feature from my father in fact. I needed rehearsals, I needed to practice, I needed the full band to coordinate. This, unfortunately, was disastrously unachievable, like trying to herd cats. All of a sudden, diving materialised. An activity that could take place regardless of the weather (mostly) and requiring no more than one buddy before plunging into the water!

What a relief!

I dumped my drumset in a corner of my garage, to be later sold on eBay or exchanged for diving gear. I had a new hobby now. A safe and convenient one. Little did I know that my overenthusiastic attitude was to be challenged sooner than I expected.

Photos by Barbara Glenc

A few years passed. I did my homework.

Having fallen for sidemount, and in love with practicing my diving skills, I became a technical diver, then an instructor, and finally I completed my full cave course in Mexico. I felt safe. What could possibly go wrong in my local quarry where I went almost every day either running courses or customising some complex or less-advanced side mount skills?

The limestone quarry I tended to use is not too deep, perfect for conducting any kind of scuba training, excluding overhead or deep diving. There is no sloping entry, as there are walls on all sides. Nowadays they have added platforms and a suspended pool for beginners, but a few years back we still had to perform a giant stride entry. The quarry itself has a very good safety record and infrastructure. Non-divers are not admitted unless they have paid, and there is a gate with a caretaker/ticket-collector to chase out any trespassers.

"Hi Michur! What are you up to?" – asked a hoarse voice from my phone on a mid-January Wednesday night a couple of years back.

"Nothing. Miss diving. Not been in the water for 4 days. Freezing cold outside," I responded calmly.

It was a close friend of mine, a diver who had accompanied me on a number of trips before, and whose fine talent for photography still remained to be discovered.

"Why don't we go and shoot a few pics? The vis is great. Not many people on the site tomorrow as it's a Thursday," he said.

The idea felt promising. I had been longing for a dive. I could also practice some reeling and line laying techniques. Killing a few birds with one stone.

Why not? I immediately agreed and set up our meeting time for around midday the next day.

There were a couple of things I would have to take care of that evening; I knew the water would be very cold, around 2C/35.6F degrees with a thick layer of ice covering the surface of the whole quarry. I knew that I needed to charge my heating and primary light batteries, but it was already late at night, so I just plugged in the chargers and packed the gear: regs, drysuit, hoods, heated gloves, and a heating system cable splitter so that I could heat up both my jacket and gloves.

The following morning as I looked out the window I could see frost on the panels. The thermometer showed -17 C/1.4 F degrees. I sighed. "Life is hard," I mumbled and carried on packing. Hot tea, a sandwich and a fully charged smartphone. Ok. Off I went.

On the way to the quarry, I collected an axe for the blowhole, if needed. When I arrived, it was just the caretaker and me.

He looked at me suspiciously and shook his head in disbelief as if to let me know he found it hard to comprehend people could be so stupid to dive on a day like this. I asked him for the location of any existent blowholes but he only pointed at some spots claiming I would have to use the axe to clear them myself, as the water kept on freezing in such low temperatures.

As soon as my buddy arrived, we started drilling and chopping. It took us a while. We then installed the ice screws. We would use cave navigation techniques in order to get to one of the giant excavators. No big deal. Done it before.

We planned our dive, checked gases and breathing gear, prepared the reel and spools, and agreed to spend around an hour at one of the excavators while taking pictures. There was one more thing to do: inform the caretaker that we were about to jump in. I called him and explained the details of our plan; we wanted him to check the blowhole every ten minutes and clear it with the axe if necessary.

We could see how fast the water was freezing; we had to give the ice layer forming in our blowhole an occasional kick whilst we prepared.

The caretaker nodded.

After a twenty-minute-long dressing ritual we were both in the water, our heating systems ready to use, our cables connected, still feeling warm. The idea was that we would switch our heaters on the moment we started to feel cold, so for now we kept them off.

The blowhole could easily fit two divers, so

we did our buddy check, submerged and started laying the line. I knew every inch of the quarry, so it only took us ten minutes to reach the excavator.

The photographer took over. I was the model. Everything took place in close vicinity to the line. After about twenty minutes into the dive, I started getting chilly; I put my finger under the bladder that covered the heating battery switch and turned it on.

Thirty seconds passed but I was not getting warmer. Strange. I fiddled with the switch for a few seconds.

Nothing.

I realised that staying longer would put us at risk, so I called the dive. My buddy did not question the decision and we started our return. I was rolling up the line and thanking God the exit was not too far, as I was getting increasingly cold. Once we reached our ascent spot we began going up.

The dive was within NDL limits, but I made the effort to stay an extra two minutes at the safety stop. We were at the end of our dive; in a few minutes I would be drinking my hot tea.

"Let's get out of here."
We exchanged Ok signals.

But...instead of surfacing, I banged my head against a layer of ice in the blowhole. My heart started pounding.

"Why is there ice above my head? Where the hell is the caretaker," I thought. I saw my buddy's widened eyes and took a few deep breaths, trying to calm down. It worked. I unclipped my right sidemount cylinder and using the bottom of it, I hit the ice. It cracked. A few more strokes and the opening was wide enough to stick my head out. We were safe!

Getting out was not easy. We doffed our gear first. Upon surfacing, we did not utter a single word. There was silence only.

No sign of the caretaker.

Had my heating system not malfunctioned, we would have arrived at the blowhole 40 minutes late, and I doubt we would have been able to batter our way through the thick ice.

Honestly speaking, we did not have the desire to pay an angry visit to the caretaker in his small booth. We were fully conscious that it was our own fault. He had the right to forget about us. Or maybe he had misunderstood. We should have had surface support and not relied on a person who had other, non-diving, duties at the same time.

I realised that, when I did my packing the night before, I had mistakenly grabbed a cable splitter that was put aside for maintenance, rather than the spare one I had just received from a dealer.

This mistake saved our lives.

Since that day, I have never again gone ice diving without adequate surface support and a proper cable check.

Tomasz Michura *is a Tec instructor, chiefly associated with sidemount. He has devoted most of his time and efforts to developing sidemount skills and procedures as well as promoting this configuration around the world.*

He is best known for his multi-cylinder skills. He is a 'new kid on the block', but already established in the sidemount community.

Although he is a high school teacher by profession, he tries to hit the water every day and is a great advocate of constant underwater practice paying attention to every detail.

His motto is: "As sidemount is a craft of tricks, I need to master them all". Tom continues his sidemount adventure getting educated himself as well as teaching beginner and advanced courses.

THORSTEN WÄLDE

CAVE EXPLORER / ADVENTURER
CCR CAVE INSTRUCTOR TRAINER / INVENTOR
OWNER OF PROTEC SARDINIA

LOCATION OF INCIDENT
CAVE UTOPIA, SARDINIA, ITALY

In 1989, a Canadian army soldier introduced me to the world of diving in quite a challenging way: he told me, "Put this harness on," (without a wing) "put this regulator in your mouth," (no alternative air source) and said, "…just survive."

So I did. I had no idea what buoyancy was and I struggled (alone) on the floor of a small, dirty lake. Somehow I survived and went back to the surface where he was waiting on the shore. I took out the regulator and yelled "Yes!" That was my first dive and my first survival.

Others would follow.

After many dives in Sardinia's Utopia Cave, I asked my good friend and fellow cave explorer Rick Stanton if he wanted to join me pushing the unknown territory at the end of the line. Only one diver had been there before us, Markus Schafhäutle.

From his records, I realized that there was a shaft which started at 12 m/40 ft, dropped straight to 100 m/328 ft, and then a tunnel which just continued with only a question mark drawn on the map.

Cave Utopia starts at 12 m/40 ft at the sea and drops down to 35 m/114 ft. The tunnel continues for about 1 km at this depth, then it ascends to 10 m/33 ft, drops to 45 m/147 ft, then deeper to 70 m/229 ft, up again to 15 m/50 ft, then down again to 60 m/196 ft and so on. The constant up-and-down profile of this cave is rough; a dive in this cave can easily be six to eight hours long, with many hours of deco. At least 3.5 km/2.17 miles of penetration without any sign of an end to it.

Rick agreed to come to Sardinia and help me extend the cave. We would be dealing with depths of 120 m/393 ft after several km/miles of scootering and extreme multilevel profiles.

Photos by Irena Stangierska

We wanted to push beyond what Markus Schafhäutle did. We agreed to use Dual CCR systems. Each of us had 15 years experience with rebreathers at this point.

For this project, I wanted to use two sidemount CCRs, so I started to work on the configuration. I wanted it to be as light as possible, easy to handle, and streamlined. At that time, I was very busy, teaching and guiding in the caves every day. My confidence was super-high. I was feeling like I could do anything in cave diving. I just felt really good. But had I practiced with this new system? No. I did one dive with the configuration: it worked excellently and felt good, so I told myself, "Hey it works, it has a great balance, and I handle all CCRs well. What could go wrong!!!!".

The day came, and Rick and I met to prepare for our exploration dive. All went well, we had fun, sorted out our gear, and made the final plan. Early morning, we packed our gear, loaded the boat, and headed out. In the water a last check to confirm that all was good, and we began our dive. The dive started without any problems; all the gear was perfectly trimmed.

For non-cave divers it is very hard to understand the feeling of flying through a cave labyrinth; it is just unreal. It gives you goosebumps from head to toe. After a smooth ride of almost an hour, the deep passage started at 80 m/262 ft. The cave is very complex and can lead to areas where one would struggle to find the way back so we had to mark the several intersections carefully.

After around two hours, we found the shaft, but about ten minutes before we got to it, I had a weird feeling that something was up, something was happening. I said to myself: "All is good, the machines are working fine, we have enough gas, we have the way back clearly marked." When you are far away from the entrance in a deep cave, you realize that you are very fragile and that you are in one of the most unforgiving environments on the planet.

For a while we were repairing lines that were broken, but finally we came to the top of the shaft. The dive profile at this point was uncompromising, and as we were going to rack up a lot of deco time, it would be a very long journey back to the surface. We looked down the dark shaft; the walls in that part of the cave are almost white - it's incredible to see what water can do and how it shapes a cave's morphology.

We checked our gear once more. Everything was good. I gave Rick the "OK" and he responded. We went down the shaft. What an awesome feeling. Almost 3.5 km/2.17 miles into a cave and falling like a base jumper. It didn't stop. We kept going deeper and deeper. I am sure Rick was as impressed as I was. I never saw a cave like that before. At 100 m/328 ft, we found a tangle of line and realized that was the end of Markus Schafhäutle's line.

We cut a bit of the line, attached ours to it and kept going into the unknown. At 120 m/393 ft we reached the bottom of the shaft, where the cave continued further horizontally.

Such an amazing feeling, being somewhere no human has been before. Hearts pumping, we looked at each other, and smiled. It was just great. Rick went to check a smaller hole while I went further with the line to where I saw the cave could continue.

Our deco was building to what we thought was the limit, so after I fixed the new end of the line to a rock and took a last look around, we started heading back. The way up the shaft to 12 m/40 ft took us around two hours. It was going to be a long dive. My calculations came to around 9-10 h of total dive time, even though our computers showed more. Calm thoughts like, "We could reduce our deco by swimming closer to the cave's ceiling," went through my mind.

Everything was good. I felt perfect, calm with no stress. We reached the bottom of the massive vertical shaft at 80 m/262 ft.

The diameter there is around 15-18 m/50-60 ft, and as I looked up to its ceiling through the crystal clear water, the view was mind-blowing. I was first and started to ascend.

When I reached 70 m/229 ft, I realized that no gas was coming out from my DSV. I immediately checked the valve from my diluent supply. It was open! I switched straight to the regulator but nothing happened. No gas was coming out! I started to worry and switched back to the DSV again. But again, no gas was coming out. I told myself: "Okay, Toddy, calm down, and fix this thing. It's easy. You've done it many times before."

As I went up another couple of meters, the gas expanded and I was able to take a deep breath again. I felt better for a while, but soon I had no gas again, so I switched to my second CCR unit.

At that point, I was still calm and didn't have any stress. But when I switched to my second CCR and again no gas was coming out, I began to seriously worry! What was happening? Why were both my CCRs not working? My reaction was: "fuck!, move to shallow water as fast as you can to get more gas to your CCRs".

I went up and started to breathe from one unit, then I switched to one of my Open Circuit regulators. Nothing. I switched to the other regulator, nothing. I started to get very stressed at that point. I switched back to one of my CCRs from which I got a very-needed breath and calmed down for a second. Not for long though, as with many hours between me and the surface with no gas available, I would die. I skipped a few of the deeper deco stops. I said to myself: "I need to come to the top of this shaft. On the plateau, I can be on my knees and figure out what the problem is".

So I did.

Both of my diluent tanks, which were attached on the back of my sidemount system, were empty! I checked my pressure gauges. "Fuck, this is serious, I am in a very dangerous situation!" I started to think of my next step. Many will say, "Easy, take one of the stage tanks, plug in and all is done!" The only problem was that I didn't have one with me. All the diluent I carried supplied my CCRs, OC gas, and my dry suit.

That was my strategy: slim and minimalistic, but in this case disastrous. I thought, "Concentrate, try to be as calm as possible".

Not easy when you know you have more than five hours to travel back, no diluent in your tanks, no dry suit inflation available anymore, and passages at more than 60 m/196 ft that you need to go through on the way back!

"How the hell do I do this?"

The only option was waiting for Rick, who I saw 20 m/65 ft below me doing his deco. Of course he didn't know what had happened to me, so he looked calm and relaxed. I was breathing very slowly and didn't move at all to save as much gas as I could. After 20 minutes, Rick arrived at my level and looked at me. He saw me kneeling on the ground as I told him, speaking through my loop, "Rick! Shit happened! I don't have any diluent anymore!"

He looked at me with wide open eyes, and I just heard one word: "Oopssss…" We sat there for another minute or so, which felt like a half hour. I checked his bail-out CCR and realized his fittings would not match my system. My next option was to use one of his bail-out tanks, but again the same problem: the fittings did not match.

The last option was that he could hand me his 10 litre steel tank with 32% Nitrox inside. "Better than nothing," I said to myself. "This will be a dangerous gas for the depths which lie ahead, but I need to try." I remember trying to understand my problem: I had two functional CCRs with me but without any gas connected to them. The only way to survive was to breathe in from the OC regulator of Rick's steel 32% cylinder and breathe out into my CCR to supply it with fresh gas. I had to do this at regular intervals or face a catastrophic carbon dioxide hit, which would be the end of my life.

"There is no other way, and I have to do it for the next five hours to stay alive!" I thought. I would have to rely on my experience, my skills, my mindset and techniques to make it work. I said to myself: "You will do it, you will come out of this situation. This cave will not kill you! I want to go back to my friends, my family, my girlfriend, and I will make it. I will not quit. I'll fight to the end." That was my thinking on the way back. I concentrated on my rhythm, changing from the OC regulator to the CCR.

So began my long journey of survival. Rick stayed close. It was mind-blowing. I didn't have any gas in my drysuit anymore. It was squeezing me so much in the deeper passages. To move forward I was crawling on the floor. Even with the scooter, I was too heavy. I was worried about my gas, but I kept breathing slowly.

"Don't increase the gas consumption too much. Maybe it will work." At the -60 m range, I held my breath to reduce the risk of oxygen toxicity. As I went up again, I could breathe again. I held on to the ceiling, trying to relax a bit. One hand on a rock and the other on the OC regulator. Take a breath, switch to the CCR, exhale the gas into it. It was a nightmare that lasted for many hours.

Rick was in front. We had to find the correct way back. The line was not easy to follow.

Haloclines caused low visibility. I had to rely on my instinctive survival techniques. Then, as we passed an intersection, I saw my cookie.

I tried to tell Rick that we were going the wrong way, but he was moving fast and it was hard for me to keep up. We were going the wrong way! I knew we would lose time and I would lose precious gas. I felt so desperate in that moment, but I kept fighting. Finally, after a short time, the line ended. Good. As Rick turned around I said "we need to go back, we missed an intersection."

That was a tricky moment. He knew that my gas was coming to an end. When that happened, there would be nothing he could do for me. I started leading the return again. When I realized where we were, I knew we were around one hour from the exit. My confidence grew. "Toddy, you have a chance to survive. Just be focused. Just keep going!" I stopped watching my pressure gauge. "When it is enough it is enough; when it's not, well, that's it."

I remember the feeling when I saw the light. The light of the exit. My heart was jumping and I realized that I could do it!

I knew my gas was almost finished. I also knew after so many hours of changing from the regulator to the DSV one of my CCR units was flooded. I felt its weight on my side. It was hard to breathe, but I had no other option. I needed to use both units, because of the long decompression that was ahead of me. The danger was still there and the 'real' exit out of the water was still very far.

Rick was behind me, but I could not see his light anymore. I was so close to the exit but I had to go back to see where he was! I turned around, went back into the cave and after around 10 minutes of scootering I saw him swimming towards me. His scooter had failed. I towed him to the exit.

We began our decompression.

When I got to my oxygen cylinder I was so happy, I cannot describe it. I went up to 10 m/33 ft and took some deep breaths just to fill my lungs with oxygen and get back the feeling of breathing a proper amount of gas. In the cave, for all those hours, I was afraid to use too much gas. I then went back to my hybrid method with the CCRs.

My oxygen cylinder would not be enough in Open Circuit for my deco. As I was exhaling the oxygen into my CCRs, I realised that both units were partially filled with water.

I decided to stay on the open circuit for as long as I could. I could maybe share some gas with Rick.

Deco was endless.

It felt like time stood still. I was lying on the ground, looking at the surface, so close to the exit, praying. I can't describe the feeling of that moment.

When the gas ran dry I went up to the surface and swam to the beach. I took off my gear really slowly, sat down and looked at the sky. The sun was shining, but it was all unreal. The sea was calm, boats passed by like nothing had happened, like nothing was wrong. It was not—for them. A boat came by. They looked at me like I was an astronaut who landed back on earth. I was smiling. I was so happy to be alive.

Rick came out of the water, took off his gear and sat close to me. We didn't speak for a while. I turned my head and told him "Rick, you saved my life, you know that. You are my hero."

What went wrong? Overconfidence.

Even after thousands of cave dives, no one is immortal. Caves have no mercy. Don't dive a dangerously-minimalistic configuration, it's not worth it. Plan well and be safe. Get ready and train before you do any kind of exploration dive. Or any dive in general.

Did I go back and explore that passage further? Yes. I went back in 2019, finished that passage and found new ones. I did it with a full team, proper equipment, lots of training, and medical support. It was outstanding. Learn from your mistakes and you will succeed.

Own words from Rick Stanton:
"I regularly travel to Sardinia for its world-class dry caves and cave diving, and from my first visit in 2007, I had gotten to know Toddy and made many fun & interesting dives with him.

These experiences led to a high level of trust and communication between us and were a key factor in assisting our dramatic exit. The furthest reaches of Utopia had been on my wish list for a while, as it was a cave I'd heard much about from the original exploration group, centered around Markus Schafhäutle.

Toddy was keen to join me, and although I was vocally sceptical of his hastily-configured and unconventional dual sidemount rebreather rig, especially his taking smaller cylinders, I trusted his diving experience.

You can imagine my shock when, over 2.5k m/1.5 miles from the entrance, I was confronted with Toddy's out-of-gas situation. I usually dive alone, so there had been no thought applied to compatibility between our equipment in terms of hose fittings and gas transfer. The only option was for me to hand over a cylinder. I had two choices: Nitrox or Trimix, so I passed across

the Nitrox, it being the more suitable gas to exit with from that point.

Toddy describes the exit well, but I would add that as we started this outward journey, I trusted in Toddy to have the experience to continually add gas by repeatedly swapping between mouthpieces during the variable-profile exit dive. I also realized that this would have been too extreme for many divers to manage for such a long period, under extreme pressure. Even here it proved a close call, but with my cylinder, Toddy pulled it off."

Thorsten "Toddy" Wälde *is an expert cave diver and explorer. He explored caves mainly in Mexico and Sardinia but also Australia, Spain, France and the Philippines.*

He is an expert in multiple sump diving, spending countless days in cave systems. He has a deep knowledge in the Dual CCR techniques, which are used on his Exploration Projects.

Together with Dr. Frank Hartig, he built a unique team for the "Utopia" project. They developed completely new techniques in medicine to prove that with some specific gear and medical support you can do exploration in a modern, much safer way. At the moment they are working on new techniques, with the full support from the Uni-Clinik Innsbrug (Tirol-Austria). An article about these techniques will be presented at the prestigious medical journal, The New England Journal of Medicine.

Toddy holds the highest instructor trainer level in Recreational, Technical, CCR, and Cave diving. Toddy developed a unique sidemount system called the "TS-System" and many other pieces of diving equipment used worldwide. He has written many articles in technical and diving magazines and has given presentations in technical conferences worldwide.

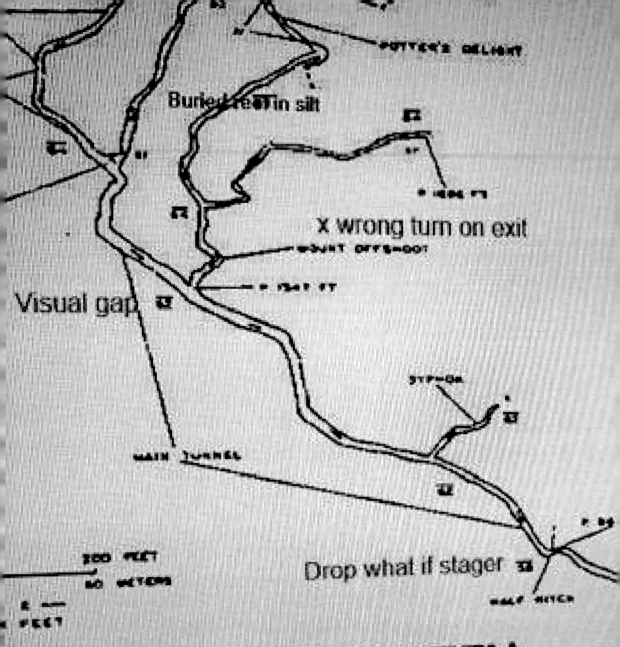

POTTER'S DELIGHT

Buried tree in silt

X wrong turn on exit

Visual gap

Drop what if stager

SPRINGS CAVE SYSTEM

FLORIDA

CAVE DIVING SECTION

DIVING SECTION OF THE NATIONAL SPELEOLOGICAL SOCIETY

TOM MOUNT

IANTD CEO

LOCATION OF INCIDENT
MADISON BLUE SPRINGS, FLORIDA, USA

Cave exploration in the 60s was still new, and techniques such as line management, gas management, and communication were constantly being developed and refined during exploration projects; it was during this phase of development that many of the current cave diving practices emerged. This account is based on a dive that involved Dick Williams M.D. and me, although in those days I was also exploring Madison with other divers, including Frank Martz and Jim Lockwood.

Back then, explorer groups experimented with their own gas management practices, which were generally chosen according to the strength of any flow and syphons. Other factors considered were cave size, visibility, silt outs etc.

Madison is a high outflow cave, so exiting the system is much quicker than going in.

As a result of this, we had discovered that if we planned our exit gas to be half as much as the gas in, it would still leave adequate reserve gas with which to end the dive.

On those earlier dives in the system, when we had been putting line in, we started our dives with 200 bar/3000 psi in the tanks and tried turn points on gas of 124 bar/1800 psi, then 110 bar/1600 psi, then 100 bar/1500 psi. Each time we ended the dive with adequate reserve gas. We also always carried a full 10 L/72 cf 'What-If' stage cylinder for emergency use only.

Next, we laid line in a new passage we called the 'Mount Offshoot'. Based on previous dives, we felt a dive turn pressure of 96.5 bar/1400 psi was safe, allowing 110 bar/1600 psi to be used on the way in. As it turned out, the exit on this dive only used 41 bar/600 psi, so we

ended with a comfortable 55 bar/800 psi, plus the What-If stage cylinder.

On our next dive, we planned to add more line into the Mount offshoot. We had decided not to run a gap line from the main line to the Mount offshoot, as there was a good possibility that Randy Hilton and John Harper might be in the cave prior to our exit, and we did not want to make this new passage visible to them. What we did do was to place an outrigger clip with some reflector tape on it onto the line, and do a visual gap.

On this dive, we were using our doubles and carrying a 10 L/72 cf bailout stage for safety plus, of course, the What-If stage.

We planned to turn around at a pressure of 83 bar/1200 psi, allowing 124 bar/1800 psi gas to be used entering the system. We also placed a 10 L/72 cf cylinder of oxygen at 9 m/30 ft. As on previous dives, we left the What-If stage at the half-hitch restriction. Up until the time of the visual gap, the dive was perfect.

When we entered the Mount Offshoot, I tied the reel into the line we had started on the last dive and began to run it out. Eventually, we reached the end of that reel but could not find a good tie-off point; I jammed the line into the clay with the intention of bringing a spike on the next dive to use as a tie off. This of course produced a total silt-out.

We turned the dive, and when we arrived at what we thought was the main line, we turned onto it.

As we swam, the visibility got a little better, and we belatedly realised that 1) we were not in the main tunnel and 2) there was no line. With no other option, we doubled back and began to skip breathe excessively. Eventually, we saw our outrigger clip and the line, but as we travelled towards the half hitch, I realised I was running out of air and let Dick know.

He signalled back that he was out of air! Luckily, at that time both Dick and I had been free diving more than 30 m/100 ft, so we held our breath up to and through the half hitch, and recovered the What-If cylinders. Then we spent a few minutes just tasting and rejoicing in the sweet breath of life. I assure you the taste of air and the act of breathing has never felt so good and has never been so-so-so-appreciated!

We recovered our oxygen cylinders and decompressed out on oxygen. Once out of the water with throbbing headaches, I told Dick that from this point on I would divide my gas into half plus 14 bar/200 psi and turn the dive at that point. I would do this regardless of whether it was a high or low flow cave.

The half plus 14 bar/200 psi gained acceptance for cave dives. Most wreck divers also adopted it at that time. It then became an accepted gas management practice through NACD, the only USA cave diving agency in those days.

This gas management tool then evolved into a rule for stage diving, and we actually converted our What-If cylinder to use as a stage cylinder since, with this half plus 14 bar/200 psi rule, we felt there was enough safety to not require the additional gas.

In the 70s, the Rule of Thirds proposed by Rory Dickens, Bob Wolf and Sam Depernia, and heavily promoted by Sheck Exley, evolved. Today most divers follow the Rule of Thirds exclusively. For rebreathers, bailout cylinders and bailout duration are factored in, plus the use of redundant rebreathers in exploration is becoming more popular.

In the 1973, NACD text book, in Chapter 10: 'Planning Air Duration For Cave Dives', Rory Dickens wrote, "'The One Third Rule' or in the case of high outflow caves the 'One Half plus 14 bar/200 psi Rule', is a simple method of ensuring that a total air failure for one diver will still allow a three-diver team to exit under the worst conditions, which is the experiencing of one total air failure at the maximum penetration."

This dive will always remain in my memory, as it taught me just how sweet breath can taste when you have been 'breathless' for a while. It is also typical of evolving exploration techniques and practices.

Warren T. Mount (Tom) Ph.D. Th. D, *begin physical training at the age of nine, starting with a Charles Atlas training program combined with boxing. From that beginning, he moved into various styles of martial arts and different conditioning systems. At the age of 81, Tom continues to work out in martial arts and resistance training. When Tom was 12, he saw the movie 'Navy Frogman', starring Richard Winmark, and vowed he would be a diver.*

Upon discharge from the USN in 1963, Tom went to work at Cape Canaveral (Now Cape Kennedy) on the space program and also opened a dive business: Aquamarine Services.

Tom is a pioneer in cave and mixed gas diving, in both OC and Rebreathers.

Tom is an Aquanaut; he was one of the founding members of the USA's first Cave diver training agency: NACD. He has been the training director of the YMCA SCUBA program and Diving Officer at the University of Miami Rosenstiel School of Marine and Atmospheric Sciences, where he introduced the first graduate school use of mixed gas in 1971, as well as CCR diving (GEMK10 and CCR 1000. While at UMRSMAS, Tom made and supervised saturation diving projects.

Currently, Tom is the CEO of IANTD.

Tom is an accomplished martial artist. His pursuits have included both the martial aspects and the healing aspects based on energy and meridians (pressure points etc.). Tom is a three-time inductee to the United States Martial Arts Association Hall of Fame.

He has a 100-ton Captains license, instrument and multi-engine pilot, and has been a driver in offshore powerboat racing. He has worked with film crews such as Benjamin, Stoneman, Cousteau's, Valletti, and others on both TV series and documentaries.

WITOLD HOFFMANN

CAVE EXPLORER / DIVING INSTRUCTOR

LOCATION OF INCIDENT
KOWARY, POLAND

There is a small hole in the ground – it looks like an old, dug-up grave lurking in the forest, somewhere in the vicinity of a small city in southwestern Poland. The city is Kowary; the building complex visible through the treeline from the hole in the ground is 'R-1', a uranium ore processing plant.

Historical sources say that, in 1945, after conquering Berlin, the Soviets found containers of uranium oxide indicating the presence of an old iron mine called 'Freedom', beneath Kowary. The Soviets started local searches and soon realized that these iron sources were also rich in uranium; massive, predatory exploitation swiftly followed.

I have always been drawn to underground spaces; these days that means two to three full months a year, participating in caving and cave diving expeditions. However, back in 2012, when this story happened, I was just starting to get into technical diving, and there were not exactly a lot of overhead diving spots in Poland.

I had dived in a few caves in the Tatra Mountains with some grim and remote sumps and a couple of flooded small mines and industrial objects. After diving most of the man-made spaces, I started to look for potential other flooded objects with Filip, my diving partner in most of these poor places.

We had a little bit of "sump style" training, a lot of motivation, and a passion for rotten wood and debris piles. This was around the time when the first ever dives were done in another uranium mine – Podgórze, also in Kowary. There, clearing the main shaft of debris resulted in access to a vast and continuous network of amazing passages at various depths. When we realised that the 'Freedom' mine was nearby, with the potential for over 90 km/56 miles of passages, we immediately started to look for possible ways to access its flooded corridors.

Our first reconnaissance dive down the main shaft was disappointing, with zero visibility and water polluted with chemicals. Our second option was another shaft: 'Vulcan'; this too turned out to be non-viable, with probably 80 m/262 ft of debris thrown into it.

Fortunately, there was a last option: 'Marta', which was most likely an evacuation or ventilation shaft. Our exploratory dives revealed a short, horizontal section leading to a small room at 12 m/40 ft, where another ladder down a circular shaft beckoned us deeper inside.

My first dive down that narrow shaft, head first to 'overtake falling sediments', showed that progress was likely to be possible, but we would have to remove some wooden logs and planks.

We embarked on a whole series of diving trips to the mine. I would load dive gear and tanks onto a train, travel two hours to my friend's city, and then, once we had met, we would board another train heading to the city in which he grew up. Once there, we would borrow his mother's car to—finally—drive to Kowary. We were only able to transport enough resources and equipment for two or three dives at a time, as there was a lot of zero visibility woodcutting, compressed air metal cutting, and other unconventional diving operations to do.

These were usually no-mount dives with no fins, one 'safety' 4L cylinder mounted on the body and a 10L aluminium cylinder dragged above as the main gas source, the idea being to leave us unencumbered enough to carry out deconstruction work at around 20 metres. After a couple of trips, we had cleared the shaft enough for us to at least attempt to proceed. As the depth was 28 m/90 ft, time limitations and precise planning for working in this area became crucial.

I made it my habit to spend the train journeys going through worst-case scenario calculations. This resulted in a pile of notes with different plans, based on various possibilities.

For the current push, I decided to use a very minimalistic setup: two 4L cylinders, plus one dropped at 22 m/72 ft depth. As my main concern was that falling pieces of wood might block the way out, I was also carrying a foldable wood saw as one of my 'emergency cutting devices'.

While planning the push dive, I added a simple calculation: how many minutes would I potentially need if I had to cut through an unexpected blockage? I allowed five minutes, considering that it could happen during the return, with elevated stress.

The push dive went exactly as planned, to begin with.

I went into the final shaft, dropped off the 4L emergency cylinder, and turned head first, as this was the only position that really allowed me to see where I was going. After passing through the first restricted area, I reached the end of the ladder. I looked around, still head down, into the space below.

There was a possible continuation!

Excited, I was tying-off to the ladder when I felt a stone hit me. Then, another one. I heard a rumble, increasing steadily. All went black and I could not move! The rumble was now coming from above my legs. Worse, some small stones got into my exhale membrane, resulting in my regulator giving me an air/water mix.

Realising what was happening, I felt the beginning of a panic attack. And suddenly all I could think was: "What kills divers? Panic does!"

This helped me focus on deep breathing and calming down as much as possible. I remembered that I had calculated an additional five minutes for eventual cutting through a wood obstacle. It was not the case, but somehow as it was in the plan I could count on this extra time.

I tried to reach my second regulator, but it was not possible.

On the plus side, despite occasional water swallowing, I was somehow breathing and still alive.

Eventually the rumbling stopped and I took a moment to consider my situation—not great. I was head down in a tight shaft, with rock blocking almost all my movements.

Panic started to reappear, and I realised that I had no idea what to do. My efforts to move, to push, to go forward, did not work. Then I had a strange thought; I was climbing a lot these days, especially bouldering, and solving situations where there was not an

361

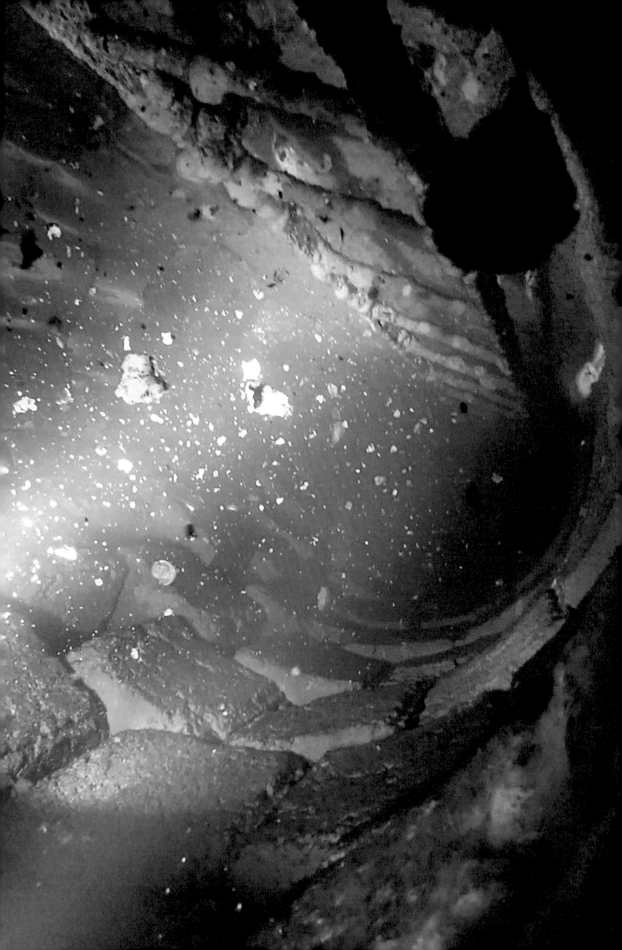

obvious sequence of moves to be followed. I was wearing no fins and I knew there was a solid steel ladder close by; one of my legs must surely be almost on it. I hooked my foot onto something.

I thought maybe it could be the ladder! I started to pull with all my available strength and simultaneously made worm-like body movements. It was working!

The small rocks and stones blocking the passage, which were the majority of the collapse, started to shake off on the sides of my body, allowing me to gradually move up.

A few moves later I was free, but my primary light head was stuck in the debris below me. I reached for my cutting tool, ready to sacrifice it. After a quick thought about its cost and the fact that it was borrowed, I went back for it and dug it out.

At this point, due to a prolonged upside-down position and a possible building up of CO_2, I was not thinking clearly. I started ascending legs up, missed my 4L cylinder and found myself briefly wedged in the doors securing the access to the pit, at 12 m/39 ft of depth.

Exiting the water, I exchanged glances with Filip.

"What happened?"
"I got buried alive," I replied.
"No way!"

As I was taking off my helmet, a kilogram of gravel must have fallen out, leaving no room for further questions.

What had happened?

Probably the bubbles of my exhaled gas had started to flow into a deposit of small rocks and gravel; these were often left behind by the original miners. The air bubbles disturbed the small stones at first, which later started to create the momentum for the bigger ones, until the entire pocket was emptied down on

top of me. It does not matter what kind of situation you find yourself in. Even if there are no visible solutions, do not panic. Breathe, think and just never give up - there could be unexpected options.

Do not underestimate the importance of factoring-in catastrophe scenarios during gas planning. It is not possible to plan and prepare for everything, but I believe that knowing that I had contingency gas available for an emergency scenario prevented me from falling into pure panic, and gave me the time I needed to somehow get out.

Always know how much time and gas you have left. Numbers help us to remain calm, giving us reliable, unbiased, information.

Witold Hoffmann *is a technical diver and a cave diving instructor. He started his professional diving career by moving to Sardinia in 2013 to work full time as a cave guide and instructor.*

His passion is pushing the last true exploration frontiers in our century: caves, regardless of whether they are underwater or require hours of crawling in the mud to discover unknown new places.

He has participated in various exploration projects, ranging from fast solo actions, passing seven sumps in the longest polish underwater cave, and the three-month-long USDCT expedition into potentially the deepest cave in the world, Sistema Cheve in Mexico, camping for fourteen days after Sump 1 to push its limits.

A very-special thanks to Nata Kas and to my family who supported my crazy dream into cave diving, from CCR diver to Cave Instructor, since day one.

I am eternally grateful for your support and motivation.

Stratis Kas, December 2020.